PRIDE AND SHAME IN CHILD AND FAMILY SOCIAL WORK

Emotions
and the search for humane practice

Matthew Gibson

P

First published in Great Britain in 2019 by

Policy Press
University of Bristol
1-9 Old Park Hill
Bristol
BS2 8BB
UK
t: +44 (0)117 954 5940
pp-info@bristol.ac.uk
www.policypress.co.uk

North America office:
Policy Press
c/o The University of Chicago Press
1427 East 60th Street
Chicago, IL 60637, USA
t: +1 773 702 7700
f: +1 773-702-9756
sales@press.uchicago.edu
www.press.uchicago.edu

© Policy Press 2019

British Library Cataloguing in Publication Data
A catalogue record for this book is available from the British Library

Library of Congress Cataloging-in-Publication Data
A catalog record for this book has been requested

978-1-4473-4479-7 hardback
978-1-4473-4481-0 paperback
978-1-4473-4480-3 ePdf
978-1-4473-4482-7 ePub
978-1-4473-4483-4 Mobi

Cover design by Robin Hawes
Front cover image: iStock

Contents

List of figures   vii
Acknowledgements   ix

one   Introduction   1
   The relevance of pride and shame to professional practice   3
   The study of pride and shame in professional practice   7
   An outline of the research   10
     How the data were collected   12
     How the data were analysed   15
     Limitations of the study   17
   Chapter summaries   18

two   Conceptualising pride, shame, guilt, humiliation and embarrassment   23
   Foundations of emotion concepts   23
     Basic emotions as a foundation for theories of pride and shame   24
     Appraisals as a foundation for theories of pride and shame   26
     Constructions as a foundation for theories of pride and shame   27
   Defining pride, shame, guilt, humiliation and embarrassment as constructions   30
     Interoception   30
     Sociocultural context   31
     Self-concept   32
     Social representations of self-conscious emotions   33
     Embodied experiences of self-conscious emotions   37
   A framework for a constructionist conception of the self-conscious emotions   38
     Content   39
     Speech acts   39
     Episode   39
     Relationship   40
   Experiencing self-conscious emotions   41
   Summary   48

three   Pride and shame in the creation of child and family social work   49
   Theorising pride and shame in the professionalisation of child and family social work   49

Pride and shame in the construction of professional
representations of practice   53
   Social administration   54
   Social policing   56
   Activism   58
   Therapy   59
   Practical helper   61
   Creating and maintaining child and family social work within
   the bureaucratic field   62
Contemporary child and family social work   64
   Re-evaluating the welfare state through the discourse of
   neoliberalism   64
   Reconstructing the boundaries of shame and pride through
   the discourse of derision   66
   Resisting the neoliberal re-conceptualisation of child and
   family social work   73
Summary   74

four   **Pride and shame in the creation of the 'appropriate'**
      organisation   **77**
      Part one: theorising pride and shame in the creation,
      maintenance and disruption of child and family social
      work services   78
      Part two: a case example   83
         Creating and maintaining an organisational identity   83
         Disrupting and creating new professional identity claims   85
         Disrupting and creating new public administration identity claims   86
         Recreating the new service   87
         Creating organisational emotional safety   89
         The new child and family social work service   99
      Summary   100

five   **Pride and shame in the creation of the 'appropriate'**
      professional   **103**
      Part one: theorising pride and shame as mechanisms of
      organisational control   104
      Part two: a case example   107
         Refashioning the organisational representation of the social
         work role   108
         Refashioning the characteristics of the organisational
         representation   116

	Policing and deterring deviation from the organisational representation	123
	The organisational representation of a social worker	125
	Summary	127
six	**Theorising social workers' experiences of self-conscious emotions**	**129**
	Compliance and resistance in social work	131
	Pride and shame in social workers' situated conceptualisations	133
	The level of conflict between identity meanings and the organisational representation	135
	The level of empathy for the people they work with	136
	The level of emotional safety in a situation	137
	Experiencing self-conscious emotions in practice	138
	A framework for understanding social workers' responses to organisational attempts at control	139
	Summary	140
seven	**Forms of identification: a case example**	**143**
	Enacting	144
	Accepting the organisational interpretive framework	144
	Responsibilising parents	147
	Creating emotional safety	150
	Complying	152
	Feeling unsure	152
	Prioritising shame avoidance	154
	Feeling shame and guilt	156
	Alleviating feelings of shame and guilt	159
	Parental experience in the context of identification	161
	Othering	163
	Shaming and humiliating practice	165
	Shaming as part of organisational risk management	168
	Summary	169
eight	**Forms of resistance: a case example**	**173**
	Compromising organisational expectations	174
	Concealing acts of resistance	176
	Influencing institutional sources and processes	180
	Parental experiences in the context of resistance	183
	Summary	186

nine   Conclusions   187
        Towards a theory of pride and shame in professional practice 188
        A case illustration of the theory of pride and shame
        in professional practice   190
        Towards conditions for authenticity and pride in practice   196
        Summary and future directions for pride and shame research 201

Appendix 1: Theoretical foundations of the study   205
Appendix 2: Theoretical codes   209

References   211

Index   245

List of figures

2.1   Core affect   31

2.2   A framework for conceptualising the process of experiencing self-conscious emotions   42

4.1   The organisational identity management project   80

6.1   Conceptual framework for social workers' responses to organisational attempts at control   141

9.1   Emotion regulation, emotion work and professional practice   190

Acknowledgements

This book developed out of my doctoral research and so I would like to thank my supervisors, Professor Sue White and Professor Jerry Tew, for their advice and support in undertaking this research and in developing and writing up the ideas. The discussions, challenges and encouragement have helped immensely. I would also like to extend my gratitude to Sue for her suggestion and motivation for turning this research into a book and for her continued support in my developing ideas and attempts at writing these up.

I would like to thank the local authority involved in this study for their courage and openness in being involved in this research. The senior managers and, particularly, the principal social worker were always supportive and eager to learn and improve practice within the service, and this research could not have been undertaken without their help, support and determination. I am grateful to the team managers for volunteering their teams, and I am eternally grateful to the team managers and social workers for taking the time to be part of this study, for being open about their experience and for sharing their successes and struggles. Furthermore, I am grateful to the children and families who allowed me into their lives for a short time, allowing me to hear their stories and observe their pride and shame.

There are a number of people who have been significant in the practical, intellectual and emotional aspects of completing this book to whom I am exceptionally grateful. Mark Chesterman has been my biggest supporter and sounding board, and he has been eternally encouraging and supportive throughout the process; without him, it simply would not have been achievable. Jean Bond and Tim Jennings opened my eyes to a new way of seeing the world a good number of years ago, and without them, I would not be here thinking or researching about these topics. Indeed, in many ways, this book began in 2001 when I met them and I started to learn about shame. I am privileged to have had the opportunity to learn from them.

I would like to thank those who have meaningfully engaged with my draft papers and book manuscript to provide constructive feedback as this has helped my ideas and writing. I hope what I have produced is an improved end result. I do not know who these people are, but I know it takes a lot to really try to understand what a writer is trying to convey and find ways of helping them develop their arguments for the benefit of the community that these have been written for.

I would particularly like to thank my daughter, Eva, who was born as I was writing this book. I have learnt more about child and family social work from my relationship with her than I think I did in 10 years of practice. The relationship between a parent and their child is not only profound but ineffable, and I hope that this book goes someway to helping us as a community work with humility to honour these relationships. Most importantly, I would like to thank Louise Overton, who, as my partner, has provided practical, emotional and intellectual help and support in writing this book. Our relationship has explored the issues of pride and shame in so many ways and I owe her for listening, even when she did not want to, and teaching me, even when she did not mean to.

ONE

Introduction

We can, perhaps, all remember a time when we felt proud, ashamed, guilty or embarrassed. We are likely to recall how pleasant or distressing such experiences were or how they altered our perception of ourselves at the time. We can also, perhaps, all think of a time when we were praised, shamed, humiliated or embarrassed by someone else, and we can probably link such experiences to how we act in similar situations now. Such experiences have generally come to be referred to as 'self-conscious emotions' (Tracy et al, 2007) as the focus of one's consciousness in such emotional experiences is the 'self', even when this is in relation to 'others' (Goffman, 1959; Lewis, 1971). Indeed, we, perhaps, all have a desire to present ourselves in a way that makes us feel good and encourages us to be included and accepted as a friend, a lover or a team member. At the same time, we, perhaps, all have a desire to present ourselves in a way that avoids feeling bad about ourselves and prevents rejection and isolation. To these ends, theory and research suggest that self-conscious emotional experiences play a significant role in what people do and how they do it (eg Cooley, 1902; Lynd, 1958; Goffman, 1959; Lewis, 1971; Scheff, 1988; Tangney and Dearing, 2002).

This book is about the role that these emotions play in child and family social work practice. Social work is hard and mistakes and tragedies happen, and it is only natural that people worry about not being good enough, blame themselves when things go wrong or be concerned about what other people think of them. Such painfully personal feelings have been identified in a number of research studies. Weuste (2005: 106), for example, identified social workers who felt 'incompetent', Nelson and Merighi (2002: 70) identified social workers who felt 'inadequate', while Stanford (2010: 1073) spoke to social workers who felt 'not skilled enough to do this'. Smith et al (2009: 88), furthermore, highlighted the difficulty that social workers have in deciding what to do and how to do it, with one social worker asking 'am I doing the right thing by this person?', and Elks and Kirkhart (1993: 556) finding another asking 'how much what you're doing in your office is really helping?'. While such self-conscious experiences may be considered inevitable, and fairly minor, in everyday practice, on the more extreme end of the challenges faced by social workers, Ting et al (2006: 334) identified social workers feeling shame after a suicide, reporting one practitioner as saying 'I was ashamed. I felt talking about it would be admitting weakness ... so I never talked to anybody about it'. Furthermore, Van Heugten's (2010: 645) qualitative study identifies social workers feeling 'ashamed at having stood by and taken no action' when they witnessed violence against a service user. Self-consciousness, it seems, is not only an aspect of everyday practice, but a component of every aspect of practice. Conversely, then, while social work may be hard, it is also rewarding and self-consciousness plays a role in the more positive experiences of practice. Indeed, the qualitative study by Branta et al (2017) concluded that satisfaction in social work was achieved through a process of balancing, establishing and recreating professional pride. Social work takes a great deal of skill and practitioners can utilise a wide knowledge base to provide a service that other people find helpful and supportive, and such achievements can make us feel very proud.

Clearly, self-conscious emotions play a role in practice, but what role, and how big a role? In an attempt to address this question, I undertook a systematic review of the literature to identify the nature and extent of the research evidence into experiences of shame in social workers (Gibson, 2016). While this found that many studies presented data that were consistent with experiences of shame, humiliation and embarrassment, what none of these studies did was focus on the experience of shame as the subject of the research. Consequently, the role, impact and significance of such emotions in practice remain unacknowledged and underappreciated. This book, therefore, fills this large and significant gap in the evidence base by reporting on the first empirical investigation into these experiences in practice. It outlines, for the first time, a general theory of pride and shame in professional practice and a more specific framework for understanding social workers' experiences of self-conscious emotions. As will be discussed in more detail later, all the theoretical ideas that I present in this book are grounded in empirical data. However, these ideas and evidence will not just be important to social work students, researchers and academics interested in social work with children and families; they are also relevant to practitioners, practice leaders, managers and policymakers of social work with adults and professional practice of any focus.

Furthermore, while this book argues that pride, shame and other self-conscious emotions are the most significant emotions for analysing, and understanding the experiences within, practice, caution needs to be taken in applying concepts from pure disciplines to applied ones. As Russell and Barrett (1999: 805) state, 'the experts do not agree on what is an emotion and what is not'. Consequently, there are many different views on what counts as an experience of a specific emotion and how to research them. This book begins, in Chapter Two, with a critical review of the field and identifies the limitations of the established theories relating to self-conscious emotions. By building on recent developments in emotion theory, this book outlines a new, constructionist, theory for self-conscious emotions that is able to account for the complexity and diversity of lived emotional experience, and that addresses the limitations in the established theories, enabling it to be used as an analytical tool in researching professional practice. This book, therefore, provides not only new insights for social work practice, but also new ways to analyse self-conscious emotions in any form of professional practice.

The relevance of pride and shame to professional practice

This book links pride and shame to the most pertinent issues relating to professional practice, that is: who decides what good practice is; how organisations are shaped in accordance with such definitions; how leaders and managers seek to control what social workers do; how practitioners come to decide whether to comply or resist such attempts; and how social workers engage with family members, and their experience as a consequence. Consequently, this book moves the theory and research of pride and shame beyond seeing them as by-products of practice – simply experienced as a result of other, more important, elements – to argue that we cannot understand the creation of professional services, and what practitioners do, without understanding the role that pride and shame play in their construction.

Pride is often characterised as 'good' and shame as 'bad'. Indeed, it can feel good when we are proud of what we have done or who we are. Equally, it can feel very bad when we are ashamed of what we have done or something about who we are. It is not that pride is necessarily 'good' and shame 'bad', however. Rather, as Burkitt (2014) argues, they are simply indicators of the relationship between the 'self' and the environment. Indeed, the proverb *'pride comes before a fall'* suggests the negative aspects of feeling proud of oneself, while shame ensures that we feel bad about things that we believe are morally wrong. Most people would argue that we should feel ashamed of certain actions, such as murder or abuse, and failure to feel ashamed of such actions would result in them being labelled as 'shameless'; a derogatory term. Ferguson et al (2007), therefore, argue that shame is a morally warranted experience, while Gausel and Leach (2011) outline research which shows that feeling shame can lead to pro-social behaviours and self-improvement.

While the experience of emotions such as pride and shame is very personal, at their heart are notions of power and influence. We are not born with an inherent idea of what is considered praiseworthy or shameful. We learn these things through our relationships and interactions, and someone has to decide that one way of thinking, doing or being is desirable and admirable, and, conversely, that other ways of thinking, doing or being are undesirable and even reprehensible. It is, however, those with more power and influence that are able to define a certain set of boundaries that other people come to accept and uphold themselves. It was not that long ago, for example, that parents, school teachers and other people in roles of authority hit children with their hands, canes or belts. In response to such accepted social and cultural norms, the ideas of a few with influence were able to promote an alternative perspective on how to treat children, and the collective action of many has rendered such action today as shameful and, in the main, illegal (Zelizer, 1985). We can see, therefore, that why people feel pride and shame is determined by wider structures and processes. People can now feel ashamed of hitting children in ways that they may not have previously. Pride and shame can, thus, be seen as social, cultural and political resources that change, shape and direct what people do and how they do it so that they are in line with what is considered 'acceptable' or 'appropriate'.

The same process can be seen in contemporary professional practice, which, as detailed in Chapter Three, has certain boundaries for praiseworthy and shameful actions imposed upon it by those with power and influence. Indeed, what professional services should do and how they should do it has long been debated, with different people promoting different ideas about this. By influencing those in power to accept one set of standards and expectations over others, such ideas form the basis for discussions and plans to improve services. When social work practice is reported on in the media, for example, it is usually negative (Lombard, 2009), such as the headline in *The Guardian* on 6 September 2017 that read: 'Social workers missed signs to save toddler stamped to death by mother' (Halliday, 2017). Such evoking of shock, shame and disgust in the wider public leads politicians to 'do something about it' (Warner, 2015), with an example from the, then, UK Prime Minister, David Cameron (2016), saying:

we must have zero tolerance of state failure … we will set new, demanding standards that we will expect every single child and family social worker to meet by 2020. And a new regulator will be brought in to oversee this new system.

Social workers, and social work organisations, are therefore provided with a set of standards and expectations from those with power and influence, together with new systems and processes created to ensure that such standards are adhered to. Indeed, the Office for Standards in Education (Ofsted), which has been set up to inspect and judge child and family social work services in England against standards that they set themselves, provides a source of very public pride and shame for social work services following their judgements, with one newspaper headline stating 'Ofsted praises council's children's services' (Cotogni, 2018) and another 'Five years of shame: how Wirral Council failed its most vulnerable' (Thomas, 2017). Such messages are amplified by politicians (Warner, 2015), which can result, in extreme cases, in directors, managers and individual practitioners being removed from their posts. We need only look to what happened in the cases of Victoria Climbié and Peter Connelly to see such examples. Victoria Climbié's social worker, Lisa Arthurworrey, for example, who was identified and heavily criticised in the media following Victoria's death, explained the personal impact of such public shaming by stating 'I hated myself so much' and that she frequently considered suicide (Fairweather, 2008). By making such stories available to the public and within the profession, the possibility of being shamed and humiliated remains a distinct possibility in the minds of practitioners, which shapes what they do and how they do it. Indeed, these national issues are felt very personally by practitioners, as one social worker demonstrated to me when I asked her what her biggest fear was:

> SOCIAL WORKER: "Ok [starts crying]. Flipping heck, missing something and a child getting hurt."
> INTERVIEWER: "What would happen to you if that happened?"
> SOCIAL WORKER: "What would happen? We'd be sacked wouldn't we, we'd be on the front page of the *Daily Mail*, you know, your whole career's gone." (Interview data)

This book illustrates how the wider influences and pressures provide the boundaries for what people feel pride and shame for, and how individual people are treated when they meet, or fail to meet, expectations, which provides the context for how and why social workers feel pride and shame in practice. These very personal experiences are, therefore, central to practice, management and policy development. Indeed, this book demonstrates how they can be seen as the primary driver in organisations, systems and leadership that seek to get practitioners to do certain things in certain ways. It may not be that pride is necessarily good and shame necessarily bad, but, as this book will demonstrate, they can be used as social resources to meet political agendas by creating specific boundaries for praiseworthy and shameful actions for practitioners. The result can feel like a web of competing and conflicting demands and expectations that are impossible to live up to (see Brown, 2006), leaving practitioners feeling personally inadequate, as one social worker explained to me when I interviewed her: "I start beating myself up, thinking 'What have I missed?', 'Should I have seen that or why didn't I ask that?', and then that's when my mind starts, you know, and that's when I think how crap I am" (interview data).

Of course, the construction and imposition of certain boundaries for practice has implications for what practitioners and managers do in response to the promise of being praised and the threat of being shamed. Many managers and practitioners decide to adhere to the new rules, regulations and social norms, either because they believe this to be the right thing to do or because they fear the consequence of not doing as expected. I conceptualise such action by developing Catherall's (2007) notion of emotional safety and apply this to an institutional context as they can still do what is expected even when they do not agree with it, providing safety from being shamed. Some managers and practitioners, however, decide that they have little interest in being praised for doing things in the way that they are told to and are prepared to risk being shamed by doing what they believe is right. Such acts of resistance can even result in feeling pride. It is not, therefore, a simple process of offering pride and threatening shame in certain ways to get individuals to do what is organisationally and politically desirable. Indeed, such purposive actions can result in practitioners resisting managerial aims and objectives, and even questioning whether they want to remain in the organisation, or even the profession, at all, as one social worker explained to me:

> "I'm quite disillusioned by it all.... I think I've just come
> to accept it now, there's not a lot I can do about it, I can't
> change it.... I'm looking around to see what other kind of

work I can do with this qualification; I don't think it will be local authority forever." (Interview data)

In response to such resistance, those who are seeking to impose a certain set of ideals and cultural norms on professional practice can attempt to eclipse undesirable emotions (see Moisander et al, 2016) by intentionally seeking to evoke other feelings, and/or directing them to feel and act in certain ways. A social worker may resist the administrative expectations of the work to feel proud of spending a lot of time with a family at the expense of their paperwork, for example. In attempts to get the social worker to do what is expected, their manager may seek to regulate their emotions by eclipsing their feelings of pride in direct work by evoking shame and guilt in failing to do their administrative tasks. Meanwhile, the leaders and managers of the organisation can create and promote specific stories that remind practitioners of the consequences of failing to adhere to the standards and expectations. Such action not only guides what individual practitioners do and how they do it, but shapes their emotional experience.

The main argument of this book, therefore, rests on how professional practice is shaped, manipulated and controlled through the interrelationship between the strategic action of one group of people intended to regulate the emotions of pride and shame in others, and the work that individuals undertake in response to feeling pride and shame. This process can be seen at any level of analysis; at one level, we can see how the media and political spheres purposively seek to evoke, eclipse or divert experiences of pride and shame in the wider public, specific organisations and individuals in attempts to shape, manipulate and control policy, procedure and practice; at another level, we can see how organisational leaders and managers strategically organise systems, processes and interactions to evoke, eclipse or divert experiences of pride and shame in practitioners; and at another level, we can see how individual professionals seek to evoke, eclipse or divert pride and shame in family members in attempts to change their behaviour. This book outlines this argument and concludes with a model that summarises this theory of pride and shame in professional practice.

The study of pride and shame in professional practice

Since the publication of *The expression of the emotions in man and animals* by Charles Darwin in 1872 (Darwin, 1872), there have been growing debates about what emotions are and what practical effects they have (eg James, 1884; Arnold, 1960; Freud, 1962 [1905]; Schachter and

Singer, 1962; Tomkins, 1962). While pride and shame have received much less attention than other emotions, such as happiness, anger, sadness and fear, in recent years, there has been a growing interest in them and other self-conscious emotions. There is now a range of books applying different ideas and conceptions of shame to a wide array of topics within philosophy (eg Williams, 2008; Nussbaum, 2009; Deonna et al, 2012; Dolezal, 2015), psychology (eg Miller, 2013; Gilbert and Miles, 2014), psychotherapy (eg Lee and Wheeler, 2003; Dearing and Tangney, 2011; Morrison, 2014; Pajaczkowska and Ward, 2014), sociology (eg Scheff and Retzinger, 2001; Gubrium et al, 2013; Chase and Bantebya-Kyomuhendo, 2014; Walker, 2014), history and culture (eg Munt, 2008; Bewes, 2010; Farrell, 2011), and theology (eg Pattison, 2014). Also, while much fewer, there is a growing body of literature on pride (eg Sullivan, 2014; Tracy, 2016), guilt (eg Hughes, 2007; Berger, 2012), humiliation (eg Kaufmann et al, 2010) and embarrassment (eg Newkirk, 2017).

Given the rise of pride, shame and other self-conscious emotions as research topics in themselves, their role in practice within the professions has begun to be considered. Indeed, shame, in particular, has been theorised and researched in relation to clients being treated by therapists (eg Goldberg, 1991; Lansky and Morrison, 1997), health-care service recipients (eg Jones and Crossley, 2008; Dolezal and Lyons, 2017), therapists and psychologists (eg Hahn, 2000, 2001; Klinger et al, 2012), physicians (eg Davidoff, 2002; Bancroft, 2007; Cunningham and Wilson, 2011), nurses (eg Felblinger, 2008; Bond, 2009; Sanders et al, 2011; Kaya et al, 2012), and teachers (eg Troman and Woods, 2001; Kelchtermans, 2005; Chang, 2009).

There is a long history of recognising, theorising and researching emotions in social work practice (eg Reynolds, 1934; Miller, 1969; Kahn, 1979; Fraser et al, 1999; Ferguson, 2005; Morrison, 2007; Ruch et al, 2010; Ingram, 2013), yet pride and shame have hardly made an appearance within such literature. With the rise of the recognition of shame as an experience and a concept, however, it has begun to be considered in social work. For example, Walker (2011) argued that shame was relevant to child protection social work, Golding and Hughes (2012) considered shame's role in looking after children in care, and Longhofer (2013) considered shame in working with lesbian, gay, bisexual, trans and queer (LGBTQ) people. Furthermore, I sought to develop the notion of shame and guilt as important experiences for parents involved in child and family social work (Gibson, 2013), Gupta (2015) elaborated on this further to consider the role that shame plays in parental experiences of poverty (see also Gupta and

Blumhardt, 2016; Gupta et al, 2018), and Houston (2016) outlined processes for dealing with shame experienced by users of social work services through the lens of Honneth's (1995) recognition theory. Moreover, I sought to develop the idea of shame as experienced by social workers (Gibson, 2014) and Frost (2016) further explored the ideas of recognition and shame in social work practice.

Of course, the idea of shame and other self-conscious emotions being experienced in practice by social workers and family members is not new. The experience of shame has long been linked to the themes and issues that social work relates to and engages with, such as poverty (eg Sen, 1984), class (eg Sennett and Cobb, 1973; Sayer, 2005), mental health (eg Breuer and Freud, 1895; Lewis, 1971) and other stigmatised attributes (eg Goffman, 1963; Elias, 1978), all of which identifies the experience of power in social groups as the central element of such experiences (eg Foucault, 1977; Scheff, 2000). Consequently, threaded throughout the research on family members' experiences of child and family social work are feelings of shame and humiliation (see Dale, 2004; Dumbrill, 2006; Buckley et al, 2011; Sykes, 2011; Ghaffar et al, 2012; Harris, 2012; Thrana and Fauske, 2014; Gupta, 2015; Gupta and Blumhardt, 2016; Smithson and Gibson, 2017; Gupta et al, 2018).

What we know from the theory and research on self-conscious emotions in social work practice, therefore, is that they are important and significant experiences. What has not been undertaken, however, is an empirical study where these emotions are the focus of the research to more clearly identify their role and influence. While Branta et al (2017) studied pride in social workers, their interview sample of three social workers still leaves much to be learnt about the role of this emotion in practice. This book, therefore, complements and extends the theoretical work already undertaken within the field, and addresses the empirical gap by reporting on original research into a range of self-conscious emotions in professional practice. While there has been much theoretical work written about shame in social work practice, this book takes a wider perspective to include pride, shame, guilt, humiliation and embarrassment. Indeed, while the focus on shame provides important insights for the profession, it limits our understanding of self-consciousness, emotional experience and the interactions that practitioners engage in. As will be illustrated throughout this book, shame can be a powerful driver for practice in terms of what to avoid, but pride tells us a lot more about the drivers in practice of what to aspire to. Together, these emotions provide an analytical frame to understand how meanings, standards and characteristics for professionals are created, maintained and disrupted, which sets them apart from the more often identified, discussed and theorised emotions of fear, anger, sadness and happiness.

An outline of the research

The research that this book is based on sought to answer the following question: what role do self-conscious emotions play in child and family social work? All studies have some theoretical foundations to start with and these are outlined in Appendix 1. To answer the research question, a case-study approach was used (Thomas, 2016). This is an approach to social research that Flyvbjerg (2006) argues is commonly misunderstood. He states that rather than being too specific to be able to generalise and develop theories from single case studies, as is commonly argued, it was the study of single case examples that facilitated the development of theory for Newton, Einstein, Darwin, Marx, Freud and many others. As case studies provide an in-depth look at a particular issue within real-world contexts (Stake, 1995), they are perfectly placed to generate and develop theoretical and conceptual ideas about pride and shame in professional practice. Indeed, as an approach to research, case studies are flexible in terms of what methods can be used and how to analyse the data (Stake, 1995; Flyvbjerg, 2001; Thomas, 2016).

Given the inspectorial arrangements, as described earlier and in more detail in Chapter Three, the judgement provided by Ofsted says something about the perceived quality of the institutional arrangements of a particular organisation. To keep a focus on the role of self-conscious emotions in what was considered legitimate and socially acceptable child and family social work practice, any organisation with an 'inadequate' inspection grading was excluded as a possible site, and a number of child and family social work services local to me were contacted. One that had a 'good' rating by Ofsted agreed to take part in the research and the organisation will be referred to as 'the Council' throughout this book.

To get close to the experience of the social workers and understand their feelings and actions in context, I needed to collect data on the real-world, real-time, lived experiences of these emotions as they practised social work. Methods to collect data in this way are rare in social work and emotion research, and unique to studies on self-conscious emotions. Indeed, given that social interaction is the cornerstone of social work practice, Ferguson (2016) argues that it is surprising that there has been such little research undertaken into what social workers actually do on a daily basis. Furthermore, Parkinson and Manstead (2015) argue that emotion research is dominated by methodologies that ask people to self-report following some controlled intervention in a laboratory. They argue that given that emotions are complex and inherently social, scientific knowledge and understanding of emotions can only be progressed by collecting data on real-time interpersonal and group processes. Further still, despite emotions such as pride and shame being explicitly acknowledged as inherently social phenomena (eg Cooley, 1902; Lynd, 1958; Goffman, 1959; Lewis, 1971; Scheff, 2000; Tangney and Dearing, 2002), the majority of research into these emotions has tended to rely on some sort of retrospective self-reporting or occasionally the sorting of vignettes (Crozier, 2014). There has been very little research into the real-world, real-time, context-specific experiences of these emotions. This leaves a gap in our understanding of the experience of these emotions from a real-world perspective on the one hand, and their role in professional practice on the other.

Given these aims of the research, I principally used ethnographic methods. I wanted, however, to move beyond description of the setting to provide an insight into the internal states and experiences of the social workers, both through the data collection methods and my interpretation of these data. Charmaz (2006: 23) argues that constructivist grounded theory provides the methods to 'move ethnographic research toward theoretical development by raising description to abstract categories and theoretical interpretation'. Grounded theory ethnography, therefore, provided the means to construct a framework of ideas to answer the research question.

The teams were selected on the basis of which team agreed to participate. I sent information about the research to the principal social worker, who passed it on to the child and family teams. Two teams invited me to discuss it further at their team meetings. All those in both teams agreed to participate following these meetings and signed consent forms agreeing for me to collect data on them and their practice. They were also, however, told that they could withdraw their consent for specific incidents, or even entirely, from the research at any point during the time I was collecting data, and some social workers did, indeed, request that some incidents or discussions were not included. A team consisted of one team manager, two senior practitioners, five social workers and two newly qualified social workers (NQSWs). Overall, there were 19 social workers and two team managers involved in the study. Experience ranged from less than one year to 24 years; ages ranged from 24 years to 63 years; there was one male social worker and the rest were female; and there was one Black–Caribbean social worker and the rest were White–British.

Data were collected for each team separately, stored separately and analysed separately. While there were differences between the teams, these were not significant when analysing these data for the purposes of answering the research question. Indeed, comparing the data for each team presented a very similar picture and all data were amalgamated so that the individuals were treated as nested within the wider case irrespective of which team they worked in. To ensure anonymity, the organisation, teams and individuals involved in the research are reported using pseudonyms and any identifying details relating to the individual or the team have been removed in the reporting of the findings.

How the data were collected

Data were collected on the child and family social work service within the Council to gain a historical perspective of the service and to understand the current arrangements. All publicly available Council documents dated from 2005 to 2014 that related to the service were collected. These included policy documents, minutes of meetings, reports from committee meetings, reports from the lead councillor, chief executive of the Council and head of the service, briefings for internal and external audiences, and current policies and procedures, employee structures, and intended service aims and outcomes. Audit/ inspection reports that related to the service in the Council were also collected from 2005 to 2014. These data were available on publicly available databases related to the Council or the inspectorate, while some were collected during field visits. Together, these documents totalled 329 pages.

Principally, however, data were collected from me shadowing the social workers and observing what they did, how they did it and their facial expressions, body language and general presentation. I observed the environment and the social situations in which they were engaged for one to two days per week over a six-month period in 2014. I asked them what they were doing and both why they were doing it and why they were doing it in the way that they did. I asked them about how they were feeling while they were doing it, as well as asking about how they perceived themselves or how they thought that they were being perceived in these moments. I listened to their conversations and their use of language, gestures and tone. I enquired about the background to their conversations and how they perceived themselves or how they thought they were being perceived in the situation they were referring to. I would go with the social workers when they went to talk to their manager, to meetings, on home visits, to schools or to the court. This was either on an ad hoc basis, with me being invited by a social worker as they were leaving, or through me organising to attend with them at the start of the day. Such organisation ensured that I was able to collect data that related to all components of the work they had to undertake. Fieldnotes were taken throughout the day in a notebook that I carried around with me according to advice provided by Emerson et al (2011). These notes were then typed up when I got home that same night. In total, I conducted 246.5 hours of observation across the two teams.

Observations including parents, carers or children were only undertaken following a discussion with the social worker as to the capacity of the parent/carer to consent to me observing the session. The social worker then spoke to them about the research before the session and provided them with an information sheet. If they agreed to me observing, I then spoke to them immediately prior to the session on their own to explain the research further, answer any questions and confirm that they were in agreement that they were happy for me to observe. I then talked them through a consent form, which they signed, and then discussed what they felt about the situation and anything else they wanted to talk to me about. I recorded all information in my fieldnotes. Some parents declined to be involved and I did not observe or record any information that related to them. Children were only seen in the presence of their legal parent/carer who had agreed that I could observe the session. Occasionally, I went with the social worker to observe them working with the child(ren) on their own in the family home if the parent/carer and the child(ren) agreed to this. In all of these sessions, I sat or stood back from the situation so that I could observe everyone and make notes if I thought it would not interfere with the interactions.

While there were direct participants, that is, those who had signed consent forms to be involved, there were indirect participants, such as other employees of the Council in the building where the teams were based. I gained consent from these indirect participants through prior approval at the start of the research by explaining what I was doing and would do with the data I collected as I toured the buildings introducing myself. Where an observed situation involved people other than this, such as other professionals in meetings or visits, the social worker spoke to them first before I provided more information and they signed a consent form. If anyone objected to my presence, I did not observe the situation. Ethical approval was granted through the University of Birmingham's ethical review panel and the research was approved by the Council's research governance process.

To gain a more specific focus on the participants' internal self-conscious emotional experiences, I designed a diary sheet that was given to each member of the team at the end of the day to complete and give back to me before they left the office. Not everyone was in the office at the end of the day, so the number of diary entries I received each day varied. Furthermore, some participants were more willing than others to complete the logs. Participants were provided with two logs, one for positive self-conscious experiences (asking participants to 'describe any situation which made you feel good about yourself today') and one for negative experiences (asking them to 'describe any situation which made you feel bad about yourself today'). From these situations, the participants were asked to describe what they were thinking at the time, along with any bodily sensations that they felt. Following Scherer's (2005) methodology on collecting data on emotions, participants were then asked to write down what word or words they would use to describe how they felt in that situation and then to choose which word or words most closely corresponded to their experience from pride, shame, guilt, humiliation and embarrassment. Finally, the diary sheet asked participants how these thoughts and feelings influenced what they said or did at the time and how this may have changed things for them in the future. Each diary entry was typed up on a computer that same night. In total, I collected 99 diary entries. Together, these logs provided data with greater detail on the internal experiences of specific situations, which I could combine with my observations and discussions with the social workers to build a more comprehensive picture of the role of self-conscious emotions in their practice.

I collected and analysed the data as the research progressed (see later), enabling me to interview the social workers about topics and issues that arose from the developing analysis. I developed a semi-structured interview schedule that looked at the three areas that had become most pertinent in answering the research question, namely: (1) how they perceived themselves and their practice within the context of the Council; (2) their experience and perception of the context in which they practised; and (3) specific examples of practice where self-conscious emotions were salient. Seventeen social workers[1] and two team managers were interviewed and a further consent form was provided for these interviews. Each interview was conducted in a room within a Council building. Interviews lasted between 55 and 100 minutes and were recorded on a digital recording device, transferred to a computer and transcribed verbatim. Finally, I wanted to compare my observations, discussions and diary entries with how specific cases were formally presented by the practitioners and so I asked each participant to provide me with two pieces of their written work. As I had no knowledge of the content of this work, I asked them to decide which documents they wanted to supply and I was provided with 33 documents in total, consisting of a range of different types of reports.

How the data were analysed

Constructivist grounded theory (Charmaz, 2006) was used to organise the collection and analysis of data. The aim of this process was to start with what Blumer (1969) calls sensitising concepts, that is, theoretical ideas about the research topic, and to move on from these to construct an analysis grounded in the data. By visiting the teams on one or two days a week, I had time between visits to study the data, write memos and read relevant literature to inform my understanding of the data. The data were initially coded line by line in a Word[2] document using a gerund that best represented the action within that line (Charmaz, 2006). This initial coding guided what data to collect in subsequent observations and discussions, allowing me to identify patterns and significant processes, to compare experiences within and between individuals, and to find similarities and differences (Charmaz, 2006) – what Glaser and Strauss (1967) refer to as the constant comparative method. As the analysis/data collection progressed, more data could be compared to more data and the most significant codes; that is, those that made the most analytical sense to understand the actions of the social workers could then be used to categorise the data – a process that Charmaz (2006) calls focused coding. Data could then be compared to these codes, enabling further refining. As I learnt more about the emotional experiences of the social workers in their specific context, I found it useful to categorise the data using a further set of codes so that I had an overall category, subcategories and initial codes.

Memos were written throughout the data collection and analysis process (Charmaz, 2006) and helped consider the possible theoretical explanations for the data, develop hypotheses, test these hypotheses in the field and come to the most plausible explanation – a process that Peirce (1903) termed abduction. I wrote memos to help me formulate ideas about the data, and used them to make comparisons between data, codes, subcategories, categories and concepts. I wrote memos in the back of my notebook when I had a spare moment while with the teams, on my phone when an idea came to me and I was not near my notebook or my computer, and while I was studying the data, coding or reading the wider literature. At first, I wrote memos to consider the codes and guide my observations and discussions. They also helped keep a focus on the role of self-conscious emotional experiences in practice by enabling me to continually ask the data questions about these experiences in this context.

As I began to construct the categories, the memos aided my collection of relevant data through, what Glaser and Strauss (1967) refer to as, theoretical sampling, that is, seeking data to develop the emerging theory. As Dey (2013) argues, categories are constructions with fuzzy boundaries and it is not always easy to categorise data. Theoretical sampling enabled me to define the categories, outline the properties of the categories, specify the conditions under which the categories arose, were maintained and changed, and describe their consequences (Charmaz, 2006). The memo writing was able to bring the fieldnotes, diary entries, documents and interviews into an integrated analysis. All memos were typed up and stored on a computer for later retrieval and sorting. I did not aim for theoretical saturation, however, as is the aim in classical grounded theory (Glaser and Strauss, 1967); rather, I aimed for what Dey (1999: 257) terms 'theoretical sufficiency'. Following Charmaz's (2006) advice on gaining sufficiently rich data for constructing a theory grounded in the data, I stopped collecting data when: I believed that I had enough background data about persons, processes and settings to understand and portray the contexts of the study; I had gained detailed descriptions of a range of all of the participants' views and actions; I had confidence in my interpretation of what lay beneath the surface of these views and actions; and I was able to develop analytical categories and make comparisons between them to generate and inform my ideas in answering the research question.

The final stage of the process was to sort, compare and integrate the memos through theoretical sorting (Glaser, 1998; Charmaz, 2006). The memos were considered in relation to a range of theoretical codes that had become pertinent either through the data collection and analysis phase or in the sorting of the memos. The theoretical codes were identified from my own background knowledge and the reading I undertook throughout the data collection/analysis, and these can be seen in detail in Appendix 2. The memos were sorted (and re-sorted) by using tables and diagrams according to different theoretical codes in order to create the best possible balance between the studied experience, the categories I had constructed and my theoretical ideas about them (Charmaz, 2006). Sorting the memos enabled the integration of these categories into a conceptual framework. While the core of this study has always been about self-conscious emotional experiences, these codes have helped to construct a coherent analytical story, grounded in the data, about their role in child and family social work practice within the Council.

Limitations of the study

As a new male figure within predominantly all-female teams, and one with experience of practising and teaching child and family social work, I acknowledge that my presence altered the dynamics within the teams. Observing and asking questions about their work while they undertook it, and asking participants to construct textual data, inevitably altered some of what they did and how they did it. The data can, therefore, be considered to have been contextually co-constructed (Charmaz, 2006). In order to minimise the effect I had on their practice, I sought to develop positive relationships with each team member to allay any anxieties about the research process and outcomes, and to make myself a familiar figure within the teams. I therefore spent two to three days a week, over a number of weeks, exclusively in one team at the start of the data collection period to normalise my presence and activities, and then repeated this in the other team. The majority of those in the teams told me that they wanted to tell me about what it was like to do their work and a number of the social workers commented to me early on that they had accepted me as a social member of their team, albeit temporarily. I also acknowledge that asking questions about how they were feeling could change how they perceived the current, or even future, situation. Indeed, I was told by a number of the social workers that over the time I was with the teams, they had started to think more deeply about how they felt and that they found it therapeutic talking to me. Rather than seeing this as a limitation, however, I considered this to be a benefit to the study as the participants provided a richer, more reflexive, account of the role of their self-conscious experiences in their practice.

While all efforts went into gaining as holistic a picture as possible of the role of self-conscious emotions in the practice of those within the teams, the resulting picture has been limited by the amount of time I spent in the field and the types of situations I observed. Not only were the situations I was able to observe limited by the amount of time I could spend with the teams, but they were also limited by the social workers themselves, who invited/agreed to my observations of certain situations and not others. Clearly, the more time I spent in the field, the more diverse situations I could have observed and the more corroborating data I could have collected for the evolving and ongoing analysis. Furthermore, being an observer-as-participant (Gold, 1958), with no formal role in the situations I was observing, made some situations inappropriate for me to be present within, which a complete participant role (Gold, 1958) would have gained legitimate and appropriate access to. Such limitations are acknowledged. Furthermore, while I have sought to collect data that provide as close a representation of the emotional experiences of the participants as possible, given practical considerations, the resulting data and analysis can only be understood within the context of my interactions and interpretations within the teams, within the Council, at that specific time (Thomas, 2010). Indeed, it is an ontological commitment within this study that the resulting theory is interpretive, contingent and tentative (James, 1907; Dewey, 1929; Mead, 1934; Rorty, 1979).

Chapter summaries

This book is aimed at anyone interested in pride and shame generally, and pride and shame in professional practice more specifically. While I do not believe that there is a meaningful distinction between the academic and practice worlds, different readers' contexts may direct them to different components of the content and analysis within this book. This book can, therefore, be seen to be aimed at both an 'academic' audience, in terms of demonstrating how the research was undertaken and how the analysis of the data generated new theoretical ideas about pride and shame in professional practice, and a 'practice' audience, in terms of illustrating what, and how, people feel in the context of current cultural, organisational and political arrangements, and how these feelings influence what practitioners do and how they do it. The two, of course, are interrelated and interdependent.

Chapter Two is a theoretical chapter, grounded in a critical review of the field of emotion theory and what we mean by the terms 'pride', 'shame', 'guilt', 'humiliation' and 'embarrassment'. This chapter is necessarily technical from an academic perspective so as to be able to define these emotions and begin to explore what role they play in practice. In this chapter, I argue that while pride, shame and other self-conscious emotions have been studied, theorised and conceptualised from a range of philosophical positions, there has been a lack of attention to these emotions from a constructionist perspective. I argue, however, that a constructionist account of emotions offers the most useful way of conceptualising self-conscious emotions and this chapter synthesises a range of constructionist ideas to develop a new framework to understand and analyse the experience of these emotions in professional practice.

Chapter Three applies the ideas detailed in Chapter Two to the field of child and family social work, providing an analysis of the role that pride and shame played in the development of the profession. This chapter, therefore, details the evolving standards and expectations that have provided the boundaries for praiseworthy and shameful behaviour for social workers and social work organisations that have shaped practice and service structures. It further outlines the competing and conflicting perspectives on what child and family social workers should do, which provide different ideas about what are praiseworthy and shameful actions for social work practitioners, managers and leaders. In beginning to outline a theory of pride and shame in professional practice, this chapter identifies and defines the current political struggle over the profession, which has seen new standards and expectations imposed on social workers through new government agendas designed along neoliberal principles. This chapter demonstrates how pride and shame can be seen as at the heart of these struggles and developments.

The book then turns to detailing the analysis and theory developed out of the original research outlined earlier. The focus of Chapter Four is the influence that pride and shame have on how social work organisations are designed and shaped. Social work services have competing and conflicting pressures, demands and expectations placed upon them from the public, the profession and government institutions. In attempts to get these services to address the government's agenda, politicians and governmental bodies seek to regulate organisational leaders' and managers' feelings of pride and shame by evoking, eclipsing and diverting how they feel so that their focus is on doing what is considered politically 'acceptable' and 'appropriate'. In attempts to avoid being shamed and attract praise, organisational leaders and managers seek to shape the organisation and the practice of individual social workers so that it is in line with these boundaries. This chapter illustrates this process through the case example of the child and family social work service. This service was shamed through a poor inspection grading and faced ongoing threats to its identity as a high-performing, well-respected service. By seeking to avoid being shamed and to attract praise from external sources, the leaders and managers were able to create emotional safety by refashioning what the service did and how it operated. These changes can be seen in light of the wider agenda of the government to embed the expectations for neoliberal ideals, goals and practices into public services.

Following the analysis of the influence of pride and shame on those who create, lead and manage social work services, Chapter Five considers the role that pride and shame play inside organisations to realise the aims and objectives of the organisation. This chapter first develops the theory of pride and shame in professional practice further by considering how these emotions are evoked, eclipsed and directed according to organisationally prescribed standards and expectations. It argues that not only can social workers' emotions be regulated, influencing and altering what they do and how they do it, but that this influences and shapes how social workers come to understand what it means to be a social worker in their organisational context. Pride, shame and other self-conscious emotions are, therefore, central to the development, maintenance and disruption of professional identities, which provides a mechanism by which organisations can create and enforce the control of its employees. This argument is illustrated in the second part of the chapter by detailing how it played out within the case example being used throughout this book. It demonstrates how an ideal-type of social worker was constructed and embedded into the social workers through regulating their self-conscious emotions, on the one hand, and policing transgressions through evoking humiliation, on the other. Consequently, the social workers developed experience and knowledge of what it means to be a social worker within the organisation.

While Chapter Four and Five focus on how self-conscious emotions are regulated in order to influence and direct organisational and individual behaviour, social workers, and indeed managers, do not necessarily end up feeling or acting as expected. Chapter Six outlines out a conceptual framework to detail how social workers come to identify with, or resist, the ideal-typical form of practice within their organisation. In some situations, some social workers willingly identify with it, enacting an 'organisational representation' of social work and evoking feelings of pride and acceptance for adhering it. Some, however, only reluctantly comply with the organisational expectations to avoid being shamed, resulting in feelings of shame and guilt for their actions. While different, both are a form of identification with the organisational representation as both provide what the organisation requires. In contrast, a social worker may not feel able to comply and will seek ways to resist what they are being asked to do through compromising the organisational expectations by working only to the minimum standard, ensuring that they avoid being shamed. This frees up some of the social workers' time, enabling them to spend it on tasks that they feel proud of. Furthermore, a social worker can exert greater levels of resistance to defy the organisational expectations to practise in a manner that they feel proud of, yet, due to the anxiety of being shamed or humiliated as a consequence, conceal such acts. Further still, social workers can exert even greater levels of resistance, seeking to influence, control or defy those who sought to exert the pressures, expectations and demands. While they risk the possibility of being shamed or humiliated, they at least avoid doing something that they feel they could not live with. Together, these forms of action constitute resistance to organisational attempts at control. The theory of pride and shame in professional practice as developed in Chapter Six is then illustrated through the case example in the following two chapters. Chapter Seven demonstrates the forms of identification with the organisational representation, while Chapter Eight details the forms of resistance.

Given the theoretical arguments and empirical data provided throughout this book, Chapter Nine synthesises and summarises these ideas to provide a concise overview of the general theory and its application to the specific case-study site. By outlining a model of the overarching processes involved in pride and shame in professional practice, the final chapter is able to consider these within child and family social work, and makes the case for the consideration of such a perspective across the spectrum of professional disciplines. It considers the influence of the political agendas and neoliberal ideals that have used pride and shame to influence, shape and manipulate the professions and professional practice, and how these have, at times, moved the practice of social work away from the humane ideals envisaged by many who have helped to create the profession. Given these developments, this chapter considers the new opportunities provided by the analysis in this book that can help move social work systems, policies and practices towards a more humane approach to working with people in need. It is through such action that an authentic form of pride can be felt within the professional community and by the general public.

Notes

[1.] Two social workers stated that they could not find the time to be interviewed due to their workload.

[2.] All analysis was undertaken in Microsoft Word documents.

TWO

Conceptualising pride, shame, guilt, humiliation and embarrassment

To be able to provide an analysis of professional practice from the perspective of pride and shame, we have to be clear on what we mean by the terms. While we all hold common-sense knowledge about these emotions, and therefore have little problem in understanding what someone means when they say 'I feel ashamed', for example, such 'folk theories', as D'Andrade (1987) refers to them, fail to provide an adequate definition for the purposes of research. Yet, despite over a hundred years of theorising and researching (eg Darwin, 1872; Cooley, 1902; Lynd, 1958; Goffman, 1959; Freud, 1962 [1905]; Lewis, 1971; Scheff, 2000), there remains a healthy academic debate regarding the nature of these emotional experiences, with no agreed-upon construct that can be applied unproblematically to research and practice.

This chapter critically reviews the field of emotion theory and locates the different ideas relating to pride, shame and other self-conscious emotions within this. As will be discussed, however, not all theories and ideas about these emotions are able to account for the biological, physiological, psychological, social and cultural components of the experience, or adequately explain the findings derived from research studies. I argue that a constructionist approach to emotions offers the most useful way of conceptualising emotions generally, and the self-conscious emotions more specifically, yet I also identify that there is no agreement within the broad field of constructionism on what these self-conscious emotions are and how to research them. This chapter, therefore, synthesises a range of constructionist ideas to outline a new framework for theorising and researching the self-conscious emotions in professional practice.

Foundations of emotion concepts

Thoits's (1989: 318) review of emotion theory states that 'there are almost as many definitions of emotions as there are authors'. Yet, despite the complexity of the field, Gendron and Barrett (2009) broadly categorise conceptions of emotions into three differing foundations: emotions as basic entities, as appraisals or as constructions. Each provides a different way of perceiving what an emotion is and, therefore, provides different ways of explaining and predicting emotional experience. While Gendron and Barrett's (2009) categorisation of models of emotion is a useful starting point to explore emotion theory, not all theories, or theorists, will fit neatly into such categories. This framing does, however, demonstrate the pertinent issues that emotion theorists have been grappling with for over a century. Proponents of each camp can be seen to make claims to support their own way of thinking and cast doubt on the others (see, eg, Barrett et al, 2007; Panksepp, 2007). Research into emotions is often undertaken within specific camps, sometimes without the acknowledgement of other positions, and sometimes with the aim of supporting and developing ideas within one way of thinking. While it is not always clear what the theoretical foundation for pride and shame is in some writing, and there are some authors who ignore this issue, it fundamentally matters which theory is used as to what counts as an experience of the emotion, what data need to be collected and what claims can be made from any findings.

Basic emotions as a foundation for theories of pride and shame

The basic emotion argument conceives emotions as a preformed entity that exists within the human mind and that can be 'triggered' by external events or circumstances. These entities are considered to be genetically transmitted mechanisms that are hard-wired within every human's brain. From this perspective, therefore, some emotions are considered distinct and irreducible. Being biologically based, it is argued that when a basic emotion is triggered, this produces a universal pattern of sensations and behaviours. Secondary emotions are thought to be produced from combinations of triggered basic emotions.

Conceiving emotions as basic entities has a long history, starting from McDougall (1908), popularised by Tomkins (1962, 1963) and embedded as the dominant perspective of emotions within psychology by Ekman and Friesen (1971) and Izard (1971). Research interest in emotions within the discipline of sociology began much later than within the field of psychology (Turner, 2009). While sociologists concern themselves more with the influence of social and cultural processes in the experience and functions of emotions, Turner and Stets (2005) demonstrate the dominance of the idea of basic emotions, which provide the foundation for many sociological theories (see Kemper, 1987; Turner, 2000; Scheff, 2003). Indeed, Burkitt's (2014) analysis of Hochschild's (1983) work argues that she assumed some form of basic biological entity at the heart of experiences of emotion. Even Solms and Zellner's (2012) analysis of Freud's (1962 [1905]) psychoanalytic model of emotion, which assumes that emotions occur when instinctual drives are blocked from expression, demonstrates that his theory assumed biological entities at the core of the experience. The basic emotion model, therefore, is firmly established within Western cultural ideas of what emotions are (Barrett, 2006a).

Despite the dominance of this conception of emotion, however, there remains no agreement on which emotions are basic, innate and natural (see Ortony and Turner, 1990). Indeed, Tomkins (1963) proposed that there are nine basic 'affects', of which shame and humiliation are one, arguing that they were the same affective state albeit at different intensities. He believed that this was 'triggered' from the impediment of enjoyment-joy or interest-excitement. Nathanson (1994) develops Tomkins's theory but retains the idea of shame and pride as basic entities. Scheff (2003), meanwhile, inspired by Tomkins, argues that shame is a 'primary' emotion relating to an internal 'bond affect', where threats to a social bond result in shame and secure social bonds result in pride (Scheff, 1997, 2014). Similarly to Tomkins and Nathanson, Scheff (2003) argues that guilt, embarrassment and humiliation are simply terms for different intensities of shame. Lewis's (1992) psychological theory is predicated on the idea of primary and secondary emotions, while the psychologist Gilbert (2003) accepts that there are some primary emotions but argues that these blend with self-representations to result in feelings of shame and guilt. Kemper's (1987) sociological theory, meanwhile, argues that shame is a socialised response to the arousal of the physiological conditions of the primary emotion of anger, with guilt a socialised response from fear, and pride a socialised response from satisfaction. Turner (2000), meanwhile, argues that shame and guilt are principally socially constructed from the primary emotion of sadness, with differing amounts of fear and anger producing shame or guilt. Such theories generally argue that the behavioural response of shame is one of hiding or avoiding, and guilt of reparations of the perceived mistake.

The basic emotion model has also been challenged by linguists, such as Wierzbicka (1992), who argues that terms in the English language, such as fear and anger, cannot represent universal experiences. Indeed, the anthropologist Lutz (1988) identified that the Ifaluk language, spoken by a small population on a Micronesian atoll that had had no contact with Western culture, does not have a corresponding concept to the English word 'anger'. Russell and Mehrabian's (1977) psychometric analyses of self-reported experiences of emotion, meanwhile, failed to find an agreed-on set of discrete emotional experiences. While doubts about the existence of 'basic' emotions have existed for decades (eg Schachter and Singer, 1962), Barrett's (2006a) comprehensive review of the empirical evidence concluded that there is little evidence to support the claim that they exist.

Appraisals as a foundation for theories of pride and shame

Rather than emotions being habitually or reflexively triggered by objects, as in basic emotion models, appraisal models consider emotions to arise from the meaning attributed to events (Arnold, 1960; Frijda, 1986; Ellsworth, 2013). Some appraisal theories assume there to be literal cognitive processes that produce the emotional response (eg Lazarus, 1991; Roseman, 1991; Scherer, 1984), while other appraisal theories do not. Appraisal theories are founded in the notion that 'emotions' stem from the situational meaning provided by the person (Frijda, 1986). In simple terms, appraisal models can be considered to have antecedents (the input) that the perceiver interprets using a range of evaluations, resulting in an emotional response (the output). The appraisal is considered to be the process that detects and assesses the significance of the environment for the person's well-being (Frijda, 1986), which is assumed to be automatic and, therefore, need not be available to conscious awareness. Appraisal theories place this component as the central element in experiences of emotion as the appraisal is considered to trigger and differentiate emotional episodes (Moors et al, 2013). Gendron and Barrett (2009) argue that appraisals rival basic emotions as the dominant foundation for emotion theory and research.

Appraisal theories are similar to basic emotion models in that they tend to presume that once an emotion is triggered, an automated set of responses follows that identifies the experience as an instance of a specific emotion. Tangney and Dearing's (2002) widely cited appraisal theory, for example, follows the work of Lewis (1971) to propose that shame and guilt are evoked as a result of moral transgressions. Shame is considered to be experienced when a person believes the 'self' is the reason for their moral failure or lapse, which results in a desire to hide, escape or strike back, while guilt is experienced when the person believes that their behaviour is the reason for their moral failure, which results in a desire to confess, apologise or repair. Gausel and Leach's (2011) appraisal theory of shame, meanwhile, similarly argues that shame results from a negative self-evaluation but, in contrast to Tangney, argues that shame leads to pro-social behaviours. They suggest that a negative evaluation from another, that is, rejection, should be distinguished from shame. Tracy and Robins's (2004) appraisal theory argues that embarrassment results from becoming aware of a discrepancy between the public aspects of the 'self', such as one's appearance, and others' evaluations, while they argue that pride stems from a person believing that they have lived up to some actual or ideal self-representation, and shame that they have failed to live up to such self-representations. While humiliation is often overlooked empirically and theoretically, or simply considered as a form of shame, for Klein (1991), humiliation results from the belief that the person has been ridiculed, scorned or experienced contempt or other degrading treatment at the hands of others. Despite the assertions of appraisal and basic emotion theories, however, studies have found only a weak correlation between a particular experience of an emotion and facial expressions, physiological reactions or behaviours (see Ortony and Turner, 1990; Shweder, 1994; Bradley and Lang, 2000; Russell, 2003).

Constructions as a foundation for theories of pride and shame

Constructionist models conceive emotions as a combination of components that combine to create a unified experience emergent within the moment, which can be categorised with an emotion label. Constructionist models deny the existence of basic emotions and consider appraisals to be but one component of the experience of an emotion, rather than the foundation of the emotion. At the heart of constructionist accounts is a relational perspective of human life, where a person is engaged in interactions with their social environment embedded within a particular culture. Over time, a person learns culturally specific ways of perceiving, understanding and communicating about their interactions; emotions are one element of this learning process. Specific dimensions of experience, such as situational cues, social stimuli, the experience of pleasure/displeasure, physiological arousal/relaxation, changes in somatosensory sensations, appraisals and expressive gestures, can be learnt as an 'emotion'. To say that one feels an 'emotion', such as shame, is to communicate that the situation fits a socially agreed-upon set of knowable features, such as specific social situations, personal thoughts and bodily sensations (Averill, 1980; Wierzbicka, 1992).

Similarly to theories based on appraisals or basic emotions, emotion constructionism is not a unified field. While there may be many lines of disagreement between authors, there are some key differences.

There are those who argue that knowledge is constructed through language and social relations, and therefore that reality cannot be understood independently of the knower, that is, strong social constructionists, and those who argue that there is a reality independent of our representations of it that serves as the foundation for social constructions, that is, the weak social constructionists (see Nightingale and Cromby, 2002). Furthermore, there are those who consider power to be located at the micro-level of social interaction and consider it to be an artefact of conversation, that is, the light version of social construction, and those who locate power at the macro-level to consider the effect of social structure, that is, the dark version of social construction (see Danzinger, 1997). Further still, there are those who place the emphasis on how a person's sociocultural context creates the conditions for emotional experience, expression and meaning, that is, social constructionists (eg Averill, 1980; Gordon, 1981; Armon-Jones, 1986; Lutz, 1988; Harré, 1990; Burkitt, 2014), and those who place the emphasis on the psychological determinants of emotional experience, that is, psychological constructionists (eg Russell, 2003; Barrett, 2006a; Mesquita et al, 2016).

Gendron and Barrett (2009) argue that conventional history within psychology has popularised 'basic emotion' and 'appraisal' approaches to emotions at the expense of constructionist accounts. Consequently, many social constructionists have grounded their emotion theories in the idea of basic emotions, as described earlier. Strong constructionists, however, argue that it is most useful to conceive of emotion terms as cultural scripts (Averill, 1980), schemas (Markus and Kitayama, 2001), concepts (Lutz, 1988) or prototypes (Russell, 2003). Such concepts of emotion are thought to be cultural products that constrain, enable, shape and guide individual emotional experience. While an emotional episode may resemble such concepts, they may not neatly fit into such categories, leading individuals to use a range of terms to describe their experience. The stronger version of constructionism has received minimal attention within the main texts on the sociology of emotions (Turner and Stets, 2005; Stets and Turner, 2006, 2014) because it has been considered an 'extreme' position (Turner, 2009: 341) for denying the existence of basic emotions. Indeed, some have criticised (stronger) constructionist accounts as generally failing to take into consideration the biological component of emotional experience adequately (Turner, 2009), ignoring studies that support the existence of common human emotions (Izard, 2007; Panksepp, 2007) or simply not having the capacity within their theoretical abilities to really explain human emotional life (Reddy, 1997). The debates are vigorous and long-standing, and can be read elsewhere (eg Barrett, 2006a; Turner, 2009). Barrett et al (2007), however, argue that (strong) constructionism is the only model of emotion that can explain the variability of emotional life that has been observed within individuals over time and across cultures, as well as within individuals within the same culture.

Scheper-Hughes's (1993) anthropological study of mothers in the shanty towns of Northern Brazil exemplifies this constructionist perspective. In a context where poverty, hunger and malnutrition were rife, with high infant mortality rates, there was no expectation that a newborn baby would survive. Scheper-Hughes documented a belief within the communities that babies and infants had no feelings and were, therefore, not considered to be human yet, were in fact replaceable and even that some babies were born 'wanting' to die. Consequently, the mothers did not cry when their babies died, with Scheper-Hughes concluding that they experienced pity rather than grief. In her 25 years, following three generations, she did not observe negative psychological consequences for the absence of grief, which led her to reject the possibility that this was a defence against their 'real' feelings. Instead, she argued that the most useful way of conceiving of emotions was as a 'symbolic representation' (Scheper-Hughes, 1993: 401) that structures the emotional experience of those who hold such representations. With differing conceptualisations of mother love, the mothers in the shanty towns of Brazil experienced the death of their babies very differently to mothers in Western cultures.

With the dominance of the basic emotion and appraisal paradigms for emotions, less theoretical attention has been provided within the strong constructionist perspective to emotions such as pride and shame, more often seeking to outline a general theory of emotions (eg Barrett, 2006a; Burkitt, 2014) than to provide a detailed analysis of such specific experiences. Within this perspective, however, Gordon (1981) provides a brief overview of shame, pride, guilt and embarrassment as constructions from imagining how other people judge our appearance to them. Harré (1990: 199) relates shame and embarrassment to the virtue of modesty, and defines shame as the feeling 'occasioned by the realization that others have become aware that what one has been doing has been a moral infraction, a judgement with which I, as actor, concur', and embarrassment as 'occasioned by the realization that others have become aware that what one has been doing has been a breach of convention and the code of manners, a judgement with which I, as actor, concur'. Also, Elshout et al (2017) define humiliation as the experience of feeling powerless, small and inferior in a situation where one is brought down in front of an audience, which involves appraisals of the situation as unfair and feelings of disappointment, anger and shame. Such theories do not, however, provide a holistic analysis of the self-conscious emotions that addresses the ontological and epistemic issues necessary for a deep analysis of their role in professional practice.

Defining pride, shame, guilt, humiliation and embarrassment as constructions

From an emotion constructionist perspective, an 'emotion' cannot be considered a thing, but rather a process. This process is both macro, operating within a social group over a long period of time, and micro, operating within a person over a short period of time. To define an emotion such as shame is, therefore, to define the components of the process. First, we need to define what is 'felt' in an emotional experience, followed by how sociocultural context provides meaning and definition to such bodily sensations. For self-conscious emotional experiences, the sociocultural context provides the context in which a person develops their self-concept, providing the foundation for such experiences, together with social representations of specific emotions, which are used to categorise and communicate emotional experience. Together, these provide the means for individual experiences of self-conscious emotions.

Interoception

Interoception is the phenomenological experience of the sensations within the body, whether due to changes within the body itself or as a result of interactions with the environment (Ceunen et al, 2016). In other words, it is the perception of the state of the body. We can conceive of interoception through two dimensions. The first is valence, or how pleasurable or displeasurable we find our current state. Wierzbicka (1992) states that all known human languages have words to communicate pleasure and displeasure, while Russell (1991) states that the pleasure–displeasure dimension is pan-cultural in emotional lexicons. The second dimension is arousal, or how activated or deactivated we experience our physiological state (Russell and Barrett, 1999). This can be low, such as sleep, to increasing levels, such as drowsiness, relaxation, alertness and hyperactivation, to high, such as heightened excitement.

Russell and Barrett (1999) argue that we are in an ever-changing bodily state, with a 'feeling' being the awareness of such a state, while

Barrett's (2006a) comprehensive review of the empirical evidence from the study of emotions concluded that the basis for all emotional life stems from these two dimensions. Russell and Barrett (1999) refer to the interaction of these two dimensions as 'core affect', which is represented in Figure 2.1.

A person's biological bodily changes, interoceptions, appraisals and actions are inherently connected but we can separate them for the purposes of explanation and analysis. What we do, and what we think, can change our bodily state, while our bodily state can change what we do and think (eg Ortony and Turner, 1990; Damasio, 1994; Frijda et al, 2000). Changes in a person's bodily state can be non-cognitive, however, such as via hormones, hunger or pharmacological agents. Barrett (2006a), meanwhile, argues that they are more usually a result of evaluating situations for their personal value and relevance. While it is possible to communicate the experience of our bodily state with words, Russell (2003) argues that we experience this state without the need for words. It is possible, therefore, for us to 'feel' something unconsciously.

Sociocultural context

Through active engagement with the environment, people come to develop experiential knowledge of the world and their relation to it through social interaction (James, 1907; Rorty, 1989). This

Figure 2.1: Core affect

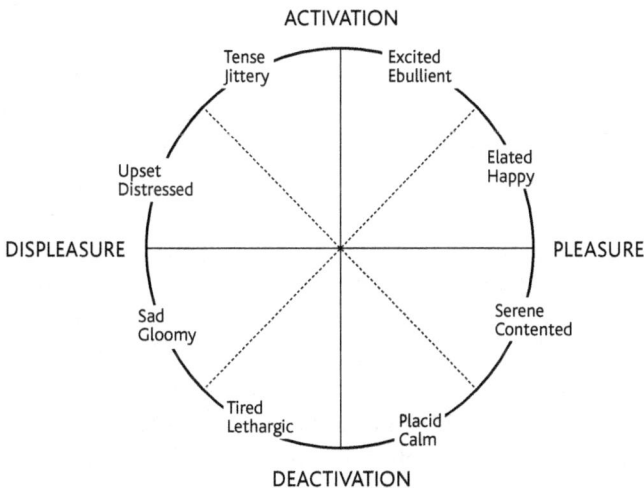

Source: Russell (2003: 148)

develops a set of shared meanings and definitions that include the rules and expectations for behaviour. While such shared definitions are sometimes held as conscious beliefs, they are more commonly held as implicit taken–for–granted understandings (Ridgeway, 2006). These shared meanings create boundaries for what is expected and what is not, what is normal and what is not, and how to act and how not to, which seem objectively correct and natural within that context. Such boundaries are created, and are reinforced, though social interaction, creating a form of power that is relational, distributed and often invisible within the social group (Foucault, 1990). Acting or being outside of these boundaries is, therefore, seen negatively, which Creed et al (2014) term 'systemic shame' and define as an ever-present and all-encompassing form of disciplinary power that produces conformity to established rules within the community. Such boundaries provide the means by which behaviour can be judged within a certain social group as acceptable or not. Those who have a cognitive, emotional and/or moral commitment to such ways of being, which Creed et al (2014) define as institutional guardians, can then police the behaviour of others through criticising, blaming and shaming transgressions. Of course, this argument can be extended to pride in order to consider systemic pride as a relational, distributed and mostly invisible form of power in social groups that makes shared rules of what constitutes praiseworthy behaviour seem objectively correct or natural. Individuals with cognitive, emotional and/or moral commitments to such ways of being can then praise others for adhering to such boundaries.

Self-concept

Cooley (1902), Dewey (1929) and Mead (1934) all argued that we are permanently evaluating ourselves in our social environment from the point of view of others. Within such social interaction, we come to understand who we are in different contexts (Markus and Wurf, 1987), our roles in society and our social status, the groups we belong to, and what is unique about us compared to others (Mead, 1934; Stryker, 1980; Burke and Stets, 2009). Other writers, such as Rosenberg (1979) and Higgins (1987), have proposed that we develop ideas not only of what we are actually like, but also of how we would ideally like to be, and how we ought to be in different situations. Others still, such as Sullivan (1953) and Markus and Wurf (1987), argue that we also develop negative self-conceptions. The multitude of self-representations that a person holds about themselves can be considered as the complete self-concept (Markus and Wurf, 1987). Given that such self-representations develop within particular sociocultural contexts, a person's self-concept can be considered the product of social engagement. The systemic shame in operation within such social environments, with the threat or promise of being shamed or praised, therefore, 'penetrate[s] community members' identity constructions as they strive to meet conditions for ongoing membership through enacting praiseworthy rather than shameful ways of being' (Creed et al, 2014: 282). Systemic shame and pride can, therefore, be considered to provide the foundations for the construction of personal identity standards.

Many theorists of the self, however, argue that all of these self-representations are not accessible to the self at the same time (see Markus and Wurf, 1987; Burke and Stets, 2009). Rather, we have a more limited set of ideas about ourselves in the moment relevant to that context, referred to by some as a working self-concept (Markus and Wurf, 1987; Stets and Burke, 2003). There may be some aspects of the self that are core to a person's idea of who they are, which are available to the self in every moment, but there may be other aspects of the self that change depending on the context and situation. With such standards for the self, it is possible to evaluate the self in the moment against such standards, whether these relate to who one is, who one should be or who one ought to be in that moment (Cooley, 1902; Mead, 1934; Stryker, 1980; Higgins, 1987). Indeed, identity theorists have routinely found that people feel negative emotions if they believe that they have not lived up to standards they believe they should have (Burke and Stets, 2009).

Social representations of self-conscious emotions

From a constructionist perspective, it is necessary to consider human experience through the interrelationship between the individual and the collective, where there is no beginning and no end to the ongoing recursive social system. Individuals' attitudes, beliefs and emotional experiences are constructed by those of the collective, which are, in turn, constructed by the individual. At the collective level, we can consider an emotion as a social representation (Moscovici, 1961), which can be defined as a:

> system of values, ideas and practices with a twofold function; first, to establish an order which will enable individuals to orient themselves in their material and social world and to master it; and secondly to enable communication to take

place among the members of a community by providing them with a code for social exchange and a code for naming and classifying unambiguously the various aspects of their world and their individual and group history. (Moscovici, 1973: xiii)

By collectively elaborating on personal experiences, over time, societies are able to construct a shared, but not consensual, way of understanding and communicating about their emotional lives, which includes categories of experience, such as pride and shame, and the typical content of those categories, such as the causes, beliefs, feelings, physiological changes, desires, actions and expressions. The social representations of emotions, therefore, provide a social structure that specifies the typical ingredients, causal connections and temporal order for each emotion concept. An emotion term simply enables an event to be classified as an instance of that emotion and then communicated (Wierzbicka, 1992). Scherer (1992) argues that aggregated data on experiences of emotions simply reflect the social representations of the emotion, rather than the specific detail of individual emotional experience. The culmination of the research on specific emotions, therefore, provides the typical content of the social representations of the emotion, that is, what we collectively understand it to be. By bringing the findings from English-language studies on self-conscious emotions together, the social representations of each term can be outlined.

Pride

Research has identified that pride is a term used to describe a pleasurable experience (Cooley, 1902; Kovecses, 1990; Mascolo and Fischer, 1995; Tracy and Robins, 2004). Linked to these bodily sensations are a set of attributions that relate to (1) a positive evaluation of the self (2) as a result of the person living up to a standard (3) that the person believes they are responsible for (Mascolo and Fischer, 1995; Lawler, 2001; Tangney and Dearing, 2002; Tracy and Robins, 2004; Turner, 2009; Scheff, 2014). Some scholars link such experiences of pride to living up to identity standards (eg Tracy and Robins, 2004), while others link it more to the improved quality of social relationships (eg Scheff, 2014). Linked to such bodily sensations and cognitive appraisals, experiences of pride have typically been considered to be linked to such behavioural responses as an expanded and upright posture, head tilted slightly upward, a small smile and arms raised above the head or hands on the hips (Tracy and Robins, 2004, 2007). Equally, these experiences have been considered to include telling others of one's achievements (Kovecses, 1990).

Shame

Research on shame links such experiences to an unpleasant, activated bodily state (eg Cooley, 1902; Goffman, 1956; Lynd, 1958; Lewis, 1971; Scheff, 2000; Tangney and Dearing, 2002; Brown, 2006; Turner and Husman, 2008; Chase and Walker, 2012; Leeming and Boyle, 2013). Linked to these bodily sensations are a set of attributions: (1) a negative evaluation of the self (2) as a result of the person failing to live up to a standard (3) that the person believes they are responsible for (eg Lewis, 1971; Tangney and Dearing, 2002; Gilbert, 2003; Ferguson et al, 2007). Indeed, Tangney et al (1998) found that shame was the emotion that people experienced no matter what the type of self-discrepancy. There is debate about whether shame relates to a threat to the status or quality of a person's relationship to the other(s), with Tangney et al (2007) and Gausel and Leach (2011) examples of those who believe that it does not, and Elison (2005) and Scheff (2000) examples of those who believe that it does. Also linked to our social understanding of shame, as highlighted by qualitative studies on shame experiences, are avoidance behaviours, such as withdrawing from social situations, hiding from others and attempting to escape from the experience (Gilbert and Andrews, 1998; Tangney and Dearing, 2002; Brown, 2006; Turner and Husman, 2008; Chase and Walker, 2012; Leeming and Boyle, 2013).

Guilt

Similarly to shame, qualitative studies of experiences of guilt indicate that it is a displeasurable affective state, often with highly activated bodily sensations, such as increased heart rate and feeling hot (eg Lewis, 1971; Silfver, 2007; Karlsson and Sjöberg, 2009; Behrendt and Ben-Ari, 2012). While people often use the terms 'shame' and 'guilt' together or, indeed, to refer to the same emotional experience (Tangney and Dearing, 2002), there is arguably sufficient evidence to suggest that what we mean by these two terms is, indeed, different. While the focus in a typical experience of shame is on the 'self', the focus in an experience of guilt is on (1) one's behaviour (2) that is seen to have transgressed a moral boundary (3) that adversely affects another person. Indeed, experiences of guilt typically involve feeling responsible for disadvantaging another as a person could 'be' guilty, in a socio-legal sense, but not 'feel' guilty if they did not accept their actions had caused the disadvantage (Sabini and Silver, 1997). Consequently, experiences of guilt have been found to relate more to the person taking the perspective of the other than in experiences of shame (eg Leith and Baumeister, 1998). Therefore, typically, (4) the person would feel bad about the impact that their actions have had as a person may not necessarily 'feel' guilty if their intention was to harm or disadvantage another. Linked to these components of an experience of guilt is usually a desire to make amends, repair relations or apologise (eg Lewis, 1971; Baumeister et al, 1995; Silfver, 2007; Karlsson and Sjöberg, 2009; Behrendt and Ben-Ari, 2012).

Embarrassment

Studies on embarrassment suggest that it relates to surprising, trivial accidents, which engender humour, smiles and jokes, with a need for a public audience, whether real or imagined (Goffman, 1959; Miller and Tangney, 1994; Tangney et al, 1996). The experience of embarrassment within these social situations is usually negatively valenced (Miller and Tangney, 1994; Tangney et al, 1996; Tracy and Robins, 2004; Elison, 2005; Lizard and Collett, 2013), although we can feel embarrassed as a result of being the object of someone else's humour or their praise. What links them within the same category of emotion is the focus on (1) how the person's current presentation (2) deviates from a personal or societal standard, and (3) a belief that this discrepancy is, or at least could be, perceptible by another. The typical behaviours considered to be associated with an experience categorised as embarrassment are blushing (Miller, 1996; Buss, 2001), giggling and laughter (Miller and Tangney, 1994; Buss, 2001), smiling (Buss, 1980; Lewis, 1992), looking at the other then looking away, and nervous self-touching (Lewis, 1992; Miller, 1996).

Humiliation

Studies have identified that humiliation is considered a negatively valenced experience, usually with highly activated bodily sensations, such as an increased heart rate and feeling hot (Jackson, 2000; Elison and Harter, 2007; Thomaes et al, 2011). These bodily sensations are associated with (1) a focus on the actions of another person or persons who (2) publicly and (3) intentionally (4) rejects, devalues or invalidates them (Klein, 1991). These bodily sensations and cognitive appraisals are typically associated with the person feeling angry and enraged, with a desire for revenge (Jackson, 2000; Elison and Harter, 2007; Combs et al, 2010; Torres and Bergner, 2010; Thomaes et al, 2011). Humiliation is, therefore, similar to embarrassment in that it relates to how one perceives themselves in relation to others. Unlike embarrassment, however, it is more related to the purposeful actions of the other to devalue them in a social context. It is considered to be like shame, therefore, in that it relates to who one *is* rather than what one *does* (Klein, 1991).

Embodied experiences of self-conscious emotions

As individuals learn and internalise the emotion concepts of their sociocultural context, these social representations provide the blueprint for individuals to develop knowledge that is both embodied, involving the mind and body (Dewey, 1929; Lave and Wenger, 1991; Clark and Chalmers, 1998; Rowlands, 2010), and embedded, within specific social and cultural contexts (Rosaldo, 1984; Csordas, 1994; Barsalou, 1999; Zwaan, 2004; Rowlands, 2010). People do not all feel the same, however, or feel solely in neat categorical experiences (Barrett, 2006a; Burkitt, 2014). Indeed, some argue that experiences of a prototypical emotional episode, that is, one that closely resembles the social representation, are rare (Russell, 1991; Barrett, 2006a). Deviations in individual understanding of what shame is, for example, can occur as a result of inconsistencies in communication within different groups of the same culture and/or because of personal experiences that provide personal meaning to the experience (Moscovici, 1961). Social representation of self-conscious emotions is, therefore, translated into personal emotion concepts, which act as guides for emotional experience. A person may develop a range of concepts of the different self-conscious emotions in different contexts (Barrett, 2006a). In an emotional experience, the more features that are present in the experience that resembles their emotion concept, the more appropriate the emotion term (Russell, 2003). Some emotional events may fit a person's concept of shame in that context well, with the term 'shame' being sufficient to communicate such an experience, while other emotional events may only loosely fit their concept, leading people to use a range of emotion terms to describe their experience. At the individual level, therefore, we can consider an emotion to be an embodied experience of their emotion concept, either through enactment, within the continually evolving interaction between the person and their environment (Dewey, 1929; Gergen, 1994; Burkitt,

2014), or through simulation, in the imagination of the individual (Barsalou, 1999; Barrett and Russell, 2015). Enactment and simulation can be considered to be a result of an effortful process of reflecting on one's interaction with the world, or it can be automated and habitual.

With knowledge of the conditions for feeling pride, shame, guilt, humiliation and embarrassment, people can assess the potential to feel these emotions in a given situation and, therefore, alter their behaviour or the situation in an attempt to avoid feeling, or being, shamed, humiliated and so on. Focusing specifically on shame, Scheff (2000) argues that this creates a 'sense of shame', which can, of course, be extended to a sense of pride, too. While a situation in which a person experiences shame or senses the potential to experience shame is qualitatively different, the social and psychological process remains the same. A person interacts with their social environment and uses their store of conceptual knowledge to make sense of their present situation, consciously or unconsciously (Barrett et al, 2014; Burkitt, 2014). A person experiences shame, or indeed any other self-conscious emotion, when they conceptualise their interoceptions, appraisals and actions in the moment as fitting their concept for that emotion. A person experiences a sense of shame, meanwhile, when their concept of shame plays a role in understanding the social interaction and deciding how to act. While this effect of shame cannot be considered an experience of shame, it has been used to argue that shame plays an important role in the production of social order and social control as people actively attempt to avoid being shamed, thereby complying to social expectations, norms and ideals (Goffman, 1963; Scheff, 2000). The English language, however, does not provide a term for a person's feeling that they are at risk of experiencing shame, only whether they are experiencing shame or not. Scheff (2003), meanwhile, highlights that the French language provides a term for shame, *honte*, and a term for a sense of shame, *pudeur*. French speakers, therefore, are able to discuss the effect of shame and the experience of shame in a manner that the English language does not facilitate.

A framework for a constructionist conception of the self-conscious emotions

Analysing social interactions for experiences of shame requires an understanding of the ways in which a person evaluates the self in the moment. From the constructionist perspective being outlined here, this can be understood through the hierarchy of sociocultural meanings, from the micro- to the macro-levels involved in a social interaction (Cronen et al, 1982; Thoits, 1989). While some of these levels have been defined earlier, Cronen et al (1982) argue that it is the content, speech acts, episode and relationship contained within social interaction that provides the substantive meaning to the experience.

Content

The content of an interaction provides the information of the episode, which may be verbal or non-verbal communication. Certainly, body language can be highly significant in an emotional experience. However, certain body language, behaviour, spoken words or how the words are said do not indicate what kind of message it is; higher-order contexts are required to provide a meaning (Cronen et al, 1982).

Speech acts

The content of a message can then be considered to be situated within speech acts (Austin, 1975). These can be considered to be actions performed by speaking or gestures, such as providing a compliment, an insult, a threat, an assertion or a question. All individuals involved in the episode require knowledge of the intentions of the speech acts to be able to participate in the exchange. The most important speech acts can be considered to be 'illocutionary utterances', which seek to make contact with another individual, and 'perlocutionary utterances', which seek to alter the behaviour of the other person (Austin, 1975). So, while the content provides the basic information necessary for communication, the speech act provide the underlying intention of the speaker.

Episode

Content and speech acts are contextualised within a specific episode (Pearce and Cronen, 1980). Episodes can be considered to be a scenario or situation in which the individual experiences it as a 'whole' or as distinct from other situations. For example, a job interview can be considered to be an episode as it has a beginning, middle and end within a specific time and place. The episode brings together the knowledge of the other person and provides the expectations about how the conversation should progress in terms of speech and non-verbal behaviour (Cronen et al, 1982).

Relationship

Individuals have implicit agreements between each other regarding the nature of the relationship, which provides the relational meaning of the episodes. For example, a couple may consider themselves to be 'equal partners in love' or 'a real man and his obedient wife' (Cronen et al, 1982). Such beliefs about the nature of the relationship contextualise the subsequent episodes, speech acts and content. While it may be easy to see such relationship dynamics as strangers, co-workers, parent–child, teacher–student and employee–employer, appropriate interactions between such individuals will be informed by higher-level contexts, such as one's self-concept and culture.

These analytical levels can be incorporated to provide a framework that outlines the process of experiencing self-conscious emotions. Individual emotions involve the full complement of personal experience, such as interoception (ie the bodily sensations felt in a situation), appraisals (ie the evaluative judgement of a situation) and actions (ie the behaviour, movement, expressions and gestures in a situation). Burkitt (2014) terms this a situated complex as each situation involves a complex of biological, physiological, psychological, social and cultural processes. A person's sociocultural context provides the boundaries for acceptable behaviour and characteristics. With understanding of these boundaries, individuals create and maintain ideas, meanings and standards of who they are and who they are not, on the one hand, while being able to evaluate the content, speech acts and relationships within a specific episode, on the other. The sociocultural context, therefore, structures the self-concept and the social interaction. Who one sees themselves as in the moment, and what one perceives in the episode, influences their situated complex. In turn, their situated complex influences who one sees themselves as in the moment and what one perceives. The sociocultural context, furthermore, provides categories for feeling through terms for emotions and offers ideas, stories, meanings, metaphors, scripts and examples for such labels. Such social representations provide a structure for individuals to understand their situated complex. Over time, individuals develop their own personal concepts for emotions, which enables them to conceptualise their situated complex and categorise their experiences as instances of specific emotions. It is these situated conceptualisations, as Barrett (2006a) refers to them, that we experience as discrete emotions. Shame, for example, is experienced at the point of conceptualising one's experience as shame.

This constructionist model is represented in Figure 2.2, which outlines the process of experiencing self-conscious emotions. It can be considered to take into account the main concerns of constructionist theorists: the knowledge that emotions are socially constructed through relationships and social interaction, as well as through language and discourse, where power is enacted in social interaction and embedded in social structure.

Experiencing self-conscious emotions

The need for a theory as outlined here can be illustrated by analysing the experience of self-conscious emotions and identifying the limitations of established theories, on the one hand, and demonstrating the utility of the presented framework, on the other. As described earlier, the dominant theories of self-conscious emotions rest on the idea of emotions as 'natural kinds', that is, a non-arbitrary grouping of instances that occur in the world, which is given by nature and is, therefore, discovered, not created, by people (Barrett, 2006b). Such theories argue that there is either a cluster of observable properties for each emotion, for example, specific facial movements, autonomic activity or instrumental behaviour, or a causal mechanism underlying each emotion, such as the same neural circuit or biological process. Such conceptualisations reduce the lived experience to a small number of factors, enabling simplified definitions to be created. Scheff's (2000) and Tangney's (Tangney and Dearing, 2002) theories represent the two main theories in this vein, with Scheff representing the basic emotion approach and Tangney the appraisal.

Scheff's (2000) theory of shame, for example, argues that it is a 'primary' emotion triggered by a threat to a social bond. This assumes that shame is triggered by such a situation and the emotion of shame is 'not only embarrassment, shyness, and modesty, but also feelings of rejection or failure, and heightened self-consciousness of any kind' (Scheff, 2000: 97). Not only do such definitions reinterpret lived experience by denying that different terms mean different things and that such nuance is purposeful and necessary to understand their experience, but it also removes an important side of the experience. Shame may be a social emotion but it is also very personal. It is possible, for example, that shame could be experienced as a result of doing something that would, in fact, strengthen the person's social bonds but they could still feel ashamed of what they have done for very personal reasons. Conversely, a person could do something that

Figure 2.2: A framework for conceptualising the process of experiencing self-conscious emotions

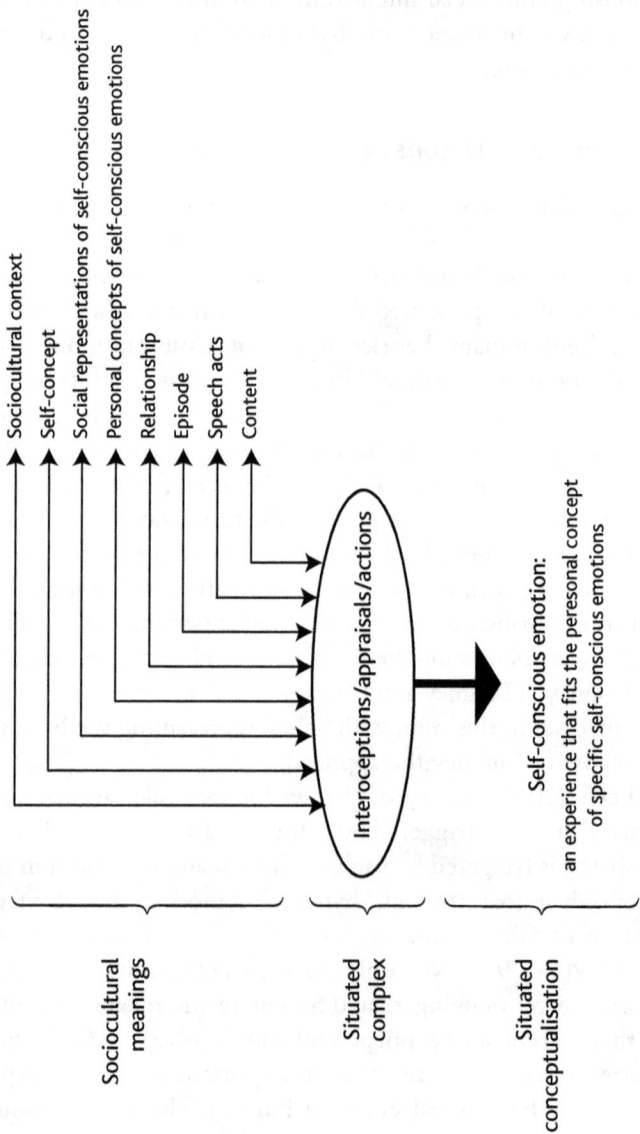

Sociocultural context

Self-concept

Social representations of self-conscious emotions

Personal concepts of self-conscious emotions

Relationship

Episode

Speech acts

Content

Interoceptions/appraisals/actions

Self-conscious emotion:
an experience that fits the peresonal concept
of specific self-conscious emotions

Sociocultural
meanings

Situated
complex

Situated
conceptualisation

threatened their social bonds and yet feel very proud of themselves and their actions.

Tangney's theory (Tangney and Dearing, 2002) of shame, meanwhile – that it is felt as a result of appraising the self negatively due to a moral failure or transgression – reinterprets lived experiences of shame that stem from non-moral issues, such as failing a test or from some personal attribute (see Smith et al, 2002). Furthermore, such a definition has led to research focusing on shame as some property of the individual, seeking to identify the differences between shame-prone and less shame-prone individuals, and thereby stripping analyses of how and why they experience shame (see Leeming and Boyle, 2004).

Further still, such claims of emotions as natural kinds limits the explanatory power of cultural differences. Contrary to Scheff's argument that shame not only threatens social bonds, but, when unacknowledged, tears societies apart, and Tangney's that shame is an anti-social emotion, the experience of shame in Japanese culture is argued to be conducive to self-improvement and perspective taking (Romney et al, 1997; Heine et al, 1999), and instrumental to interpersonal relations (Boiger et al, 2013). Different cultures can provide different social representations of emotions that then have an effect on both the individual experience and the social consequences. Natural kind theories provide a limited ability to account for such differences simply because they claim some non-socially constructed reality behind these experiences. While these are only two theories, the point is that human emotions are complex and complicated, and scientific theories need to be able to account for such complexity without redefining lived experience or limiting our ability to describe and analyse it.

Indeed, for both Tangney et al (2007) and Scheff (2000) to maintain their positions, experience is categorised by the theory, rather than the individual experiencer, resulting in them arguing that people mislabel, or even fail to recognise, self-conscious emotional experiences. The use of a social representation of emotions and individual embodied concepts provides a theory that does not need to relabel or reinterpret lived experience. A person may describe an experience similar to the social representation of an emotion, but use many other terms to describe their experience. Rather than believe that the person has incorrectly defined their experience, the framework allows for a more nuanced individual and social analysis. At a collective level, the framework provides an analytical tool to define and consider the role of the social concepts of the emotions, while not reducing this analysis to personal experience, which may or may not be described in terms of the social representation. At an individual level, too often within the debates on and definitions of self-conscious emotions, there has been a lack of clarity about what is meant by the self, identity or social bonds. By defining the self-concept and its development within social groups through ongoing social engagement, the relationship between the self and society is made explicit. This, therefore, provides the ability to outline the standards by which a person evaluates the self-in-the-moment and how this relates to their social relationships. It is not that an experience of shame, for example, needs to be defined by either, but rather that they need to be defined within the processes through which the emotion is experienced.

Mainly due to the focus on shame in the literature and research, we can see such processes in the social construction of shame. Elias's (1978) seminal book *The civilizing process* provides a good example. He charts the changes in European society from 800 to 1900, where physical violence and feuds gave way to political and social struggles for power and prestige. To achieve their goals, people had to become more socially aware of different groups, social location and how they competed and cooperated with others. This gave rise to rules for 'appropriate' behaviour, particularly around violence, sexual behaviour, bodily functions, table manners and forms of speech. Discourses were constructed to cast adherence to such standards as praiseworthy, and transgression as shameful. Those with more power and influence had greater opportunity and resources to influence and shape those discourses, resulting in praiseworthy and shameful behaviour being defined by the higher classes. As the lower and middle classes learnt the rules of the game and appropriated the behaviours of the higher classes, the higher classes sought to introduce new rules that distinguished them from others, evoking disgust and shame in ever-new behaviours. Thus, over time, a sociocultural context was constructed that heightened self-consciousness and increased the possibility of feeling shame. This process, however, resulted in the lower classes – those with less power and resources to influence the discourse or live up to the new rules – being cast as shameful for failing to live up to 'civilised', 'appropriate' or 'moral' standards.

How the self-consciousness of those with less power and resources has been heightened in different contexts has since been developed and expanded. These ideas stem from the notion of respect and respectability and how people should treat, and be treated by, others (Sayer, 2005). Social groups construct certain differences between people as less worthy of acceptance and respect. These attributes serve to distinguish them from others, which legitimises actions of disrespect and contempt. Goffman's (1963) analysis of the experiences of such stigmatised attributes, such as mental ill-health, disability, minority ethnicities and sexualities, and so on, highlights how such people are shamed by others and feel ashamed for believing that they are personally inadequate or flawed.

Poverty and class provide two areas where this process is particularly well developed. Sen, for example, expanded on Adam Smith's (1776) ideas of shame in 18th-century Britain, which argued that those without commodities considered necessary for the day, such as linen shirts and leather shoes, experienced a heightened self-consciousness in public due to failing to live up to such standards and so felt ashamed to show their face. Sen (1984) argued, therefore, that concepts of poverty should include basic social needs just as much as basic physical needs, and defined the poverty line as not only being able to meet nutritional requirements, but also being free from public shame as a result of failure to meet social conventions. Walker (2014) then demonstrated how such societal standards for adhering to such social conventions are internalised so that people in poverty feel ashamed of being unable to fulfil their aspirations or live up to societal expectations as a consequence of a lack of income and other resources. Sayer (2005) makes a similar argument in relation to class: as there are barriers for the lower classes to access the social bases of respect, which often require social and material resources, they are considered legitimate targets for disrespect and contempt. Consequently, shame becomes endemic to the experience of class and people can start to feel inadequate and lacking in worth.

While the analyses and insights of people such as Goffman, Sen, Sayer and Walker have been important to our understanding of stigma and shame, how emotions have been defined within their work poses problems to the analysis of such experiences. Indeed, despite emotions being central to Goffman's analysis, he did not provide a conception of what emotions are. Furthermore, as Sen, Sayer and Walker all ground their work in dominant theories of emotions as natural kinds, they claim that shame is universal and subsume, minimise or ignore other self-conscious emotions in their analyses. For example, their work highlights the importance of power at a macro-level, which structures the sociocultural context so that certain actions are considered shameful, and at a micro-level, where shame is evoked through social interaction. The general thrust of their arguments, however, is that shame is experienced as a result of being treated unfairly and harshly, and that such treatment is contrary to how they believe they should be treated. First, such experiences are more consistent with the research on humiliation than shame (see Klein, 1991; Jackson, 2000; Brown, 2004; Torres and Bergner, 2010). The focus on shame, therefore, may be limiting our understanding of the role of these different self-conscious emotions in social life, while hiding the nuance and complexity of the lived experience of class, poverty and stigma. Second, while such situations may result in feeling shame, such conceptions hide the complexity of such experiences. Indeed, it is possible for a person to hold a negative concept of themselves in certain contexts and act accordingly. They may feel ashamed of what they have done and who they are but they may not have failed to live up to some personal standard, as many psychological theories contend (eg Lewis, 1992), or be treated with a level of unwarranted disrespect, as many social theories argue (eg Sayer, 2005). Rather, they could be acting in a manner that is consistent with their own personal standards and are being treated as they expect.

Consequently, despite the advances in understanding that their work has provided, such theorisation has limited the analyses of experiences of stigmatised attributes, on the one hand, and shame and other self-conscious emotions, on the other. Indeed, Barrett (2006a) argues that theories founded in emotions as natural kinds rarely allow for the flexibility in emotional experience identified in research findings. From the perspective outlined here, it is not that an experience of pride, shame or other self-conscious emotion is universal, but rather that they are experiences organised and structured within certain contexts. One's sociocultural context leads the possibility of experiencing such emotions, but once they become possibilities, their experience is inescapable. The question becomes how and why a person experiences such emotions in particular contexts. The answer to such questions needs to include both the internal, psychological, components of the experience and the external, social, components. While often treated separately by the disciplines of psychology and sociology, these components are interrelated (Burkitt, 2014). The start of analysing lived experiences of pride and shame are contexts that are constructed to heighten a person's self-consciousness. Not all emotional experiences in such contexts result in shame, or indeed any category provided by a social representation, and the details of why a person may experience shame may be complex and, at times, contradictory, requiring theory to account for social and personal representations of such emotions, and the personal lived experiences of them.

This framework for analysing the process of experiencing self-conscious emotions bridges the gap between constructionist accounts that focus more on individual processes for emotional experience (eg Barrett and Russell, 2015) and constructionist accounts that focus more on social and cultural determinants (eg Averill, 1980). Indeed, Burkitt (2014) criticises constructionists that focus primarily on mental representations of emotion (see Barrett and Russell, 2015). While the social representation is assumed, it is not explicit, and neither is the process of how it influences individual processes outlined or defined. Furthermore, Burkitt argues that the focus on mental representations creates a dualism of mind and body that prioritises mind over body in experiences of emotion, rather than recognising the interrelationship and equivalence of both. Barbalet (2001), meanwhile, critiques constructionist accounts that define emotions as social representations while failing to identify them as such. To some constructionists, he argues, the social representation of an emotion is the emotion and, therefore, needs no further definition. The view of emotions as social representations, therefore, disappears from the discourse. As he points out, however, and as has been argued in this chapter, the experience of an emotion is often not consistent with the social representation. In line with such arguments, Griffiths (1997) criticises the social concept approach to emotions for failing to take into consideration the social situation and role of the individual. By explicitly utilising the concepts of social representations and embodied concepts, the account of self-conscious emotions presented here enables a more holistic constructionist approach. There is a relationship between the two but they are not one and the same thing, while the individual experience of an emotion involves a wide range of components not necessarily contained within the social or personal concept of the emotion.

All of this is, of course, relevant to an analysis of the role of self-conscious emotions in social work practice. How power has been exercised and experienced by those who social workers are seeking to help has long been a preoccupation within the profession (eg Hasenfeld, 1987; Chambon, 1999; Webb, 2000; Stanley et al, 2002; Tew, 2006). Particularly in relation to child and family social work, where social workers are often seeking to address issues of harm to children linked to parental actions or inaction, the complex mix of how parents feel as a consequence of their actions, how the social workers interpret and engage with such issues, and how the parents feel as a result of how they have been treated, is central to an analysis of self-conscious emotions in practice (see Dumbrill, 2006;

Sykes, 2011; Gupta and Blumhardt, 2016). Of course, stigma, class, inequality and poverty are central themes in child and family social work (eg Featherstone et al, 2014; Morris et al, 2018). Central to this analysis is the experience of pride and shame by the professionals themselves, who will have pressures and expectations placed on them, which, in turn, will influence how they interpret and feel about the issues and people that they are working with.

Summary

This focused analysis on the process and experience of self-conscious emotions is embedded within the constructionist tradition, which enables a detailed consideration of more general biological, psychological, social and cultural processes in the creation, dissemination and experience of emotions. The framework provided allows for a wider range of components to be analysed as part of a self-conscious emotional experience than many natural kind theories because these are made explicit and considered integral to the experience, and diversity is assumed in individual experience. Such explicit components, and links between components, enable a more comprehensive analysis of professional practice than current theories provide and are, therefore, used in the following chapters to outline a theory of pride and shame in child and family social work.

THREE

Pride and shame in the creation of child and family social work

This chapter begins the theory of pride and shame in professional practice by considering their role in creating, maintaining and disrupting practices that have resulted in what we know today as child and family social work. As people sought to develop ways of addressing social issues related to children and families, different discourses on children, families and social issues provided competing and conflicting messages about what was praiseworthy and shameful behaviour. Different representations of social work practice can, therefore, be seen to have been constructed within these competing discourses. This chapter outlines these representations as social administration, social policing, activism, therapy and practical help, demonstrating how pride and shame were central components in how these practices were institutionalised. Contemporary child and family social work, however, needs to be seen within the context of neoliberalism, which has disrupted and discredited certain institutional arrangements and constructed and consolidated others. This has shifted the systemic boundaries for praiseworthy and shameful behaviour, and has, therefore, influenced, interrupted and adapted established organisational and professional arrangements. This chapter analyses these developments to provide an overview of the current reconfiguration of professional practice and the place of pride and shame within this.

Theorising pride and shame in the professionalisation of child and family social work

There are many ways in which a particular occupational group can organise their work. Throughout the 1800s, however, a new form of organising work emerged that enabled an occupational group to dominate a particular division of labour and control what they did and how they did it (Freidson, 1970; Larson, 1977). This idea of a 'profession' can be considered a social representation (Moscovici, 1961), with core elements being professional knowledge, expertise, autonomy and a commitment to public service (see Friedland and

Alford, 1991). Freidson (1970) argues that the process through which an occupational group is able to fulfil this professional ideal rests, initially, on a privileging by the power of the state. Gaining legitimacy for a particular domain and social acceptance among those with power is, therefore, a necessary first step. Freidson (1970) argues that this is achieved by developing a cognitive basis, made up of a body of knowledge and techniques that professionals apply in their work, and a normative basis, consisting of a service orientation and set of ethics for the occupation. These bases enable a fledging profession to establish the boundaries for both their occupational domain, that is, what they do, and the membership of this domain, that is, who is able to do it. In other words, legitimacy is founded on a system of education and credentialing (Larson, 1977). The emerging profession is then able to gain wider social acceptance for these boundaries, their knowledge base and their expertise, resulting in greater levels of autonomy and social prestige independent of the original sponsors (Macdonald, 1995).

Following Freidson, Larson (1977) argues that a profession attempts to constitute and control a market for their expertise so that the professionals are able to translate one set of resources, that is, knowledge and skills, into another, that is, social and economic rewards – a process she calls the 'professional project' (Larson, 1977: 18). While this project stems from the social representation of organising work as a profession, the process of constructing this representation involves organising and proceduralising a set of standardised interaction sequences that controls the production, dissemination and use of a particular knowledge base and skill set. This is referred to by Jepperson (1991) as 'institutionalisation'. The end result is the more or less stable and enduring structures and practices that guide action by providing templates for acting, thinking and feeling, which Lawrence and Suddaby (2006) define as an institution.

The rise of a profession necessarily involves intentional work to disrupt existing institutional practices and create and maintain new ones. Indeed, the idea that it was possible to improve families' lives, to train a person in the methods of achieving this and for the state to pay them to perform this role required significant changes to established ways of thinking and the relationship between the state and the family. While Lawrence and Suddaby (2006) refer to the process of creating, maintaining and disrupting institutions as 'institutional work', there is an inherent tension between the actions of those intended to shape, enable and constrain, that is, regulate, an institution and the actions of those intended to undermine, refashion and develop existing institutional arrangements and practices. Indeed, establishing a new profession is a complex project. Moisander et al (2016) argue that much institutional work is a form of discursive activity, intended to effect the construction of meaning that supports particular ways of acting, thinking and feeling. Discursive institutional work aims at changing these shared understandings (Maguire and Hardy, 2013), which then open up possibilities for new forms of social action and relations. Emotions, and particularly pride and shame, can be considered at the heart of such processes (Creed et al, 2014; Moisander et al, 2016).

Chapter Two outlined the ideas of systemic shame and pride, that is, the shared rules that constitute shameful behaviour, on the one hand, and praiseworthy behaviour, on the other. It further defined the ideas of a sense of shame and pride, that is, knowledge of shameful and praiseworthy attributes and behaviours within the group, which are used to assess the likelihood of being praised or shamed in the situation (Scheff, 2000; Creed et al, 2014). Systemic shame and pride and a sense of shame and pride work together, providing the boundaries for individual experiences of pride and shame. Such emotional episodes can be considered an indirect product of discursive institutional work. As most people act for much of the time in a way that seeks to avoid feeling shame and attract praise, the effect is to drive people to act within certain limits (Goffman, 1963). As Chapter Two also outlined, however, from a constructionist perspective, emotions do not just happen to a person, they are constructed from a range of components, many of which are open to influence, enabling the limits for thinking, feeling and acting to be altered and revised.

In attempts to avoid shame and attract praise, people engage in what Hochschild (1979: 561) terms 'emotion work', which can be defined as the actions of the person intended 'to change in degree or quality an emotion or feeling'. The idea of emotion work has since been developed by others (eg Thoits, 1990; Rosenberg, 1991; Scheff, 2000; Turner, 2002; Turner and Stets, 2006) to include attempts not just to manage felt emotions, but also to manage the social context in which emotions are experienced. While the former type of emotion work consists of internal activity such as evoking thoughts and ideas, altering bodily sensations, or directing conscious awareness, all of which creates, maintains or changes the emotional experience, the latter type of emotion work involves external activity such as convincing or coercing others into accepting a particular way of perceiving the situation, altering behaviour so as to create specific situational meaning, or withdrawing or selectively engaging in social contexts, all of which promotes, prolongs or avoids particular emotional experiences. A further type of emotion work has also been identified by identity theorists, which relates to changes that a person makes to themselves (eg McCall and Simmons, 1978; Burke, 1991; Stryker, 2004). By changing the standards by which a person defines themselves, they are able to alter how they may feel in future situations. A person may, for example, learn that particular attributes or behaviours are praised or shamed, and in seeking to avoid shame and attract praise, they may change their identity standards accordingly. This identity work is, therefore, a form of emotion work. Together, pride and shame can be seen as at the heart of emotion work, which plays a significant role in people's interactions with themselves and with others, and in changes to a person over time.

Pride and shame can, however, be a more direct component of institutional work. In Moisander et al's (2016) study of the Economic and Monetary Union of the European Union in the 1990s in Finland, they found that institutional actors sought to evoke shame and pride to sanction and reward particular ways of thinking and feeling about the new arrangements. Creed et al (2014) refer to this as episodic shaming, which, as an idea, can be extended to one of episodic praising. Together, these identify the intentional actions of individuals who have cognitive, emotional and/or moral commitments to existing institutional arrangements, that is, institutional guardians, who police the boundaries of acceptable behaviour through attempts to make someone feel shame or pride, thereby coercing compliance. Such attempts to induce, influence or alter the emotional experience of another can be considered as emotion regulation (Gross, 2008). Moisander et al (2016) found, however, that institutional actors not only sought to directly induce pride and shame, but also engaged in strategic attempts to invalidate and redirect the collective fears, anxieties and moral indignation that drove resistance in attempts to gain support for, and achieve, their institutional objectives. Institutional guardians may, therefore, not only use the emotion-regulation strategies of evoking pride and shame in others in attempts to coerce compliance, but also use the strategies of eclipsing and diverting people from feeling shame, guilt or embarrassment from engaging in institutionally prescribed activities, or from experiencing pride as a result of engaging in resistant behaviours.

This process can be summarised as follows: systemic shame and pride provide the boundaries for shameful and praiseworthy behaviour. While this systemic power creates, shapes and guides certain ways of thinking, acting and feeling, it is itself created by the collective actions of those within the social group. Institutional guardians strategically use methods of emotion regulation to police these boundaries, episodically shaming and praising institutional actors, on the one hand, while seeking to prevent pride, shame and other self-conscious emotions, on the other, so that they conform to the established institutional arrangements and relations. This provides a form of emotion regulation that shapes, enables and constrains the institution. With knowledge and experience of pride and shame within their specific context, institutional actors develop a sense of pride and shame and engage in emotion work in attempts to avoid feeling shame and attract praise. While this may involve changing and adapting their identity standards or hiding unacceptable elements of themselves, it may also involve institutional work to change the established rules and standards, thereby gaining social acceptance. The result is a recursive relationship, which can be seen as a creative tension, between established institutions and emerging ones, the regulators and the regulated, the individuals and the collective, and the self and the institution. The result is what Bourdieu (1994) refers to as the 'field', that is, the setting in which people and their social positions are located.

Pride and shame in the construction of professional representations of practice

Rather than conceive the state as a singular entity, Bourdieu (1994) argued that it was better understood as a 'bureaucratic field' in which struggles are played out between different state actors and institutions. Indeed, the state itself is in an ever-changing condition seeking to gain and regain cultural legitimacy. As different communities and constituencies began to address similar social issues and problems, a professional project was created that sought to operationalise the social representation of social work as a profession and move social workers from being low-skilled and often voluntary or low-paid workers to highly skilled and knowledgeable professionals that could command higher wages and better working conditions within the bureaucratic field. Indeed, this new form of work was anchored in the cultural desire to provide support and assistance to those in need; yet the field was constituted by competing discourses providing a range of boundaries for praiseworthy and shameful behaviour for the emerging practice. Consequently, a range of professional representations (see Piaser and Bataille, 2012) were constructed within these different communities and constituencies in their efforts to professionalise social work. These professional representations have different historical processes and resulting content, conceptualising practice and practitioners in different ways, and offering different boundaries for praiseworthy and shameful behaviour. These representations of social work can be identified and outlined as social administration, social policing, activism, therapy and practical help. Such representations enabled the emerging profession to gain cultural legitimacy and social acceptance within the bureaucratic field.

Social administration

While all formal social groups and organisations have required some form of administration to maintain the rules, regulations and relations created to sustain the arrangements, scholars have argued that a discourse of efficiency has promoted and supported administrative practice as an essential component of effective institutions (Miller and O'Leary, 1987; Manzoor, 2014). Tsakalotos (2004) states that this discourse sees efficiency as a very important, if not paramount, social goal and value, which is separate from other social goals or values. Consequently, efficiency, and anything that brings about this objective, is praiseworthy, while inefficiency, or anything that interrupts it, is shameful. Prominent theorists, such as Wilson (1887) and Taylor (1911) in the US, and Weber (1978) in Europe, formalised the ideas of rules, responsibilities, management oversight and supervision of work in public services, together with the need for practice to be based on knowledge, either through experience or research, and performed by trained practitioners. Many concerned with the professionalisation of social work anchored practice within this discourse and appropriated the practices of administration to gain wider social acceptance.

The origins of social administration as a practice can be seen from the 1800s, where there were many charity workers, voluntary organisations and philanthropists who offered help, support and financial assistance to the poor and needy (Young and Ashton, 1967). As the social and economic context changed, the idea that society was made up of individuals, who acted independently of one another, with no intrinsic barriers to individual success (Flax, 1999), became established as the dominant perspective among those with power and influence (Woodroofe, 1962). Consequently, the failure to succeed was considered a result of individual character flaws and helping able-bodied individuals became a shameful activity. This discourse of deservingness (Watkins-Hayes and Kovalsky, 2016) contributed to the reform of the Poor Laws, which were amended to create a new system of the organisation and administration of relief to the poor that sought to efficiently administer the scarce resources available to those who were considered deserving of it (Young and Ashton, 1967). Spicker (1984), however, describes these new administrative practices as shaming, humiliating and degrading those considered 'undeserving' of help and support.

Within this new context, the work of social workers who provided help, support and financial assistance to the poor and needy was criticised and shamed for wasting money and resources on those who did not deserve it, while causing dependency in the poor on charitable giving (Young and Ashton, 1967). To prevent this shaming of these early social workers, the Charity Organisation Society (COS) was established in 1869 as a deliberate attempt to refashion the work of those who sought to help those in poverty. Founded on a guiding philosophy consistent with the ideology of the government at the time, the COS created an administrative system that coordinated and managed the work of the range of organisations involved in charitable giving to ensure that it was only provided to those considered worthy. A social worker visited the home of the person seeking help, interviewed them to investigate their circumstances as to why they needed help, created a confidential document that contained the information and presented their case to a committee that decided on the resources to be provided (Young and Ashton, 1967). The secretary of the COS at the time, Charles Stewart Loch, sought to anchor social work in the more socially accepted practice of medicine by arguing that this provided a scientific method that produced a 'social physician' (Loch, 1895: x). By engaging in emotion work to avoid being shamed, the COS had recreated a form of social administration that evoked pride in its efficiency (Lymbery, 2005).

The rise of sociology as an academic field, which stressed the structural factors involved in individual circumstance and promoted ideas of social justice, human rights and equality, challenged the foundations of individualism and deservingness, and stressed the responsibility of society to ameliorate poverty (Stevenson, 2013). Some, therefore, argued that efficiency in public administration should go beyond the technical relationship between resources and outputs to incorporate outputs in relation to other social goals and values (Manzoor, 2014). These new perspectives provided systemic boundaries that evoked shame in the way in which those in need were treated under the Poor Laws and the COS, and the welfare state began to emerge, which reorganised and developed statutory and voluntary social services, and with them, the roles required to administer these new rules, resources and systems. As social workers had established social administration as a practice of social work, they were employed by different state and voluntary organisations outside of the COS to navigate the range and scope of resources that were being made available to individuals and families within these more complex services and systems (Payne, 2005). These developments turned social administration from a practice into a field of study, moving from a focus on the management and technical planning of social services to encompassing theory, politics, organisation and process (Titmuss, 1951). To Titmuss (1958), social work was a form of social administration that was rooted in the values of social justice and equality.

The administrative representation of social work practice can, therefore, be seen as a means to create efficiency in public services designed to address some social need. The methods of administration have been used, however, as a tool for competing perspectives on the role and value of social work practice. To some, administrative practice has simply sought to meet the needs of individuals while maintaining the social order (Davies, 1994). For others, administrative practice has been an emancipatory and transformative endeavour (Titmuss, 1951). Either way, many have cast social workers as social administrators in some form, seeking to bridge the divide between resources, on the one hand, and people's needs, on the other (Lymbery, 2005).

Social policing

Dodsworth (2008) states that 'police' in 18th-century England was understood as a general system for organising communal life, whose task was to benefit everyone. The boundaries for praiseworthy and shameful behaviour were set by the dominant social norms and values of the day. Dodsworth (2008) argues that a discourse of police developed out of a belief that as some lacked the capacity to adhere to such boundaries, they needed to be governed by others. The established system in the early 1800s, however, was not seen to provide an effective means of social control, particularly given the new temptations within commercial society. An organised police force, with uniformed officers that were paid by the state and undertook surveillance to deter and detect crime, was argued to be a humanitarian move that compensated for the temptation towards corruption and the undermining of the social order. This discourse influenced many outside of those just concerned with public order and safety. Indeed, the creation of the Royal Society for the Prevention of Cruelty to Animals in 1824 can be seen as a response to this discourse as much as the creation of paid police officers.

Some within the COS, such as Loch, sought to anchor social work practice within the discourse of police by arguing that charity should be used to 'help or force' all men to achieve self-dependence by using methods such as a 'fear of destitution, a sense of shame, the influence of relatives, [and] the threat of disenfranchisement on receipt of poor relief' (Woodroofe, 1962: 33). Episodic shaming was seen as a legitimate practice to police moral standards. The experience of such practice led the COS to be given the alternative acronym of 'Cringe Or Starve' by many (Englander, 1998). Social policing in relation to children and families, however, developed out of the changes in sentiment towards children in the 1800s. Reich (2008) argues that the social settlement that existed in the early 1800s protected the home from state interference. While children were an economic asset, starting work at the age of nine (Young and Ashton, 1967), their welfare, particularly for poor children, was not a great concern to wider society. Consequently, Ferguson (2011) identifies that prior to 1870, there were no organised attempts to protect children from cruelty. Parton (2014) argues, however, that the upper and middle classes began to concern themselves with the abuse and neglect of children, mainly among the poor, which provided a foundation for social and political change. Children, and childhood, took on a new symbolic meaning that Zelizer (1985) refers to as 'sacralisation', changing the systemic boundaries for what was considered praiseworthy and shameful behaviour.

Given these new systemic boundaries, the 'child saving' movement developed (Powell, 2001), which sought to evoke shame in the abuse of children and pride in activities that protected them, eclipsing other emotions stemming from old practices relating to children. Societies formed with the express aim of protecting children by deploying uniformed 'inspectors' that policed the slums, inspected homes, removed children they suspected were being abused and took parents to court (Ferguson, 2011). While the National Society for the Prevention of Cruelty to Children (NSPCC) advised their inspectors of the necessity of tact when seeking to help families, Ferguson (2011) argues that parents often felt invaded during inspections, and the inspectors became known as the 'cruelty men' (NSPCC, 1912). Within a shared view that children needed saving from dangerous parents, the ideas of what children needed saving from grew from abuse to incorporate material and moral neglect (Buckley, 2013). Furthermore, there was growing recognition that abuse and neglect were not solely the reserve of the poor, further widening their remit (Flegel, 2016). The inspectors worked closely with the police and some were even situated within police stations (Clapton, 2008). While some have argued that there seems to have been a reduction in the focus on child abuse following the First World War (Ferguson, 2011; Parton, 2014), the need for social workers to perform a policing function was sufficiently established for it to continue. With the expansion of social services and the early development of the welfare state, this representation of social work as social policing was incorporated into the work of state social workers, who were then tasked with protecting children (Ferguson, 2011), with many NSPCC inspectors being employed by state services. Social policing can, therefore, be seen to be concerned with protecting children from 'dangerousness', using methods of surveillance, coercion or forcing people to comply with accepted societal standards (Thomas, 1988; Bell, 1999).

Activism

As social work was developing knowledge and skills in administration and policing, some within the profession began to ask if social work was simply about helping people adjust to their social circumstances or if social workers should seek to change institutions and arrangements to create better social circumstances for those they were working with. Such questions first began to be asked within the COS as some social workers began to question its philosophy and practice (Ferguson, 2009). As people began to challenge the notion of deservingness (eg Booth, 1889; Rowntree, 1901), new constituencies developed around different ideas on the roots of poverty that did not relate solely to individual character. Samuel Barnett, a member of the COS, became influenced by such changing attitudes and the move towards egalitarian ideals and collective responsibility (Young and Ashton, 1967). While Barnett agreed with some aspects of the COS, to him, a person's social environment was a significant factor in the development of a person's character, and, as such, the focus of any action should be on changing this environment (Ferguson, 2009). From this contrasting perspective, the methods used by the COS were considered shameful, and Barnett and others sought to distance themselves from it (Briggs and Macartney, 2011). Instead, Barnett helped develop the settlement movement, which required educated people to live and work in poor areas in order to help improve it, understand the issues that the people faced, educate those living there and tackle the barriers to social change (Young and Ashton, 1967). These new ideas spawned a range of new community action and group work practices that were sponsored and supported by certain institutions, such as Oxford and Cambridge Universities.

These changes provided an alternative anchor for social work practice, with different views within those communities on what were shameful and praiseworthy actions. For social workers who accepted these new ways of understanding, they sought to challenge, discredit and disrupt the established arrangements of the day, and build, change and create new ones (Ferguson, 2009). While some writers argue that such social action has had limited influence on the creation of the social work profession over the longer term (eg Lymbery, 2005), the philosophy and practice can still be seen as an established component of social work. Indeed, even within the 1950s, where Gazeley (2003) argues that many erroneously believed that poverty had been eradicated through welfare reforms, Todd (2014) found that social workers often engaged in some form of activism within their everyday casework. From a wider perspective, the social worker-as-activist can be seen to have much wider influences. Clement Attlee and William Beveridge, for example, worked at the Toynbee Hall settlement in London and maintained their connection with it (Payne, 2005). Within the shared world view provided by the radical and socialist perspectives, Attlee went on to argue that political action and social justice should be a component of social work practice in his book *The social worker* (Attlee, 1920). Beveridge (1942), meanwhile, went on to write *Social insurance and allied services*, which was grounded in the principle of universalism and became the foundation for the creation of the British welfare state, facilitated and implemented by the then Prime Minister Clement Attlee. The social worker-as-activist can, therefore, be seen as a representation of professional practice that seeks to change social conditions, policies and structures for the benefit of specific individuals, groups and communities (see Pray, 1945; Lane and Pritzker, 2018).

Therapy

Therapy, as a general social practice, works to control, resolve or improve specific personal problems (Dreier, 2007). The modern-day roots of therapy developed within the field of psychiatry and psychology, with Freud pioneering the field. While there are many different forms of therapy, Dreier (2007) outlines the core components as a professional expert that works with a client on a problem using particular techniques that cause beneficial outcomes for the client. Traditionally, the work of a therapist has been with the internal psychological state of the individual. The foundation of therapy is the belief that a person is able to develop knowledge and expertise about helping and resolving personal problems and can put these to good use in direct work with them.

Towards the 1900s, social work as an emerging occupation was built on the claim that people could be trained to develop expert knowledge and skills in working with the poor, vulnerable, disabled and those in need (Payne, 2005). It was not a shared view, however, that social workers needed to develop meaningful relationships with the people they served (Young and Ashton, 1967). Indeed, such a relationship was considered problematic by many, potentially getting in the way of the purpose of the work (see Hellenbrand, 1972). The recognition of how social structure created and maintained oppression, disadvantage and poverty, and the development of sociology as a discipline, influenced social work philosophy and practice (Levin et al, 2015). These new discourses influenced the systemic boundaries for what was shameful and praiseworthy behaviour within the communities that accepted them, casting the individualised casework of the COS as questionable and ineffective. Some, therefore, engaged in emotion work to alter what they did so that they felt proud of their work. Mary Richmond, for example, a pioneer of social work practice in the US, advocated for sensitivity in the casework relationship (Hellenbrand, 1972). She moved the focus of the casework method from the individual to the person in their social context (Richmond, 1922), and Montalvo (1982) argues that such innovations laid the foundations for therapy, and particularly family therapy, within social work.

Hellenbrand (1972), however, argues that the treatment component of social casework remained underdeveloped and sociology provided few solutions to this practice deficit. The emerging field of psychotherapy, which was concerned with behavioural change and personal well-being, offered opportunities to achieve better outcomes and feel proud of the work they did. As social work was keen to establish social and occupational status, Leonard (1968) argues that not only did psychotherapy develop social work as a practice, contributing to social work's ability to claim expertise in helping people, but by identifying itself with the more established methods of medicine and psychology, social work also gained greater cultural legitimacy.

Yelloly (1980) outlines how the work of therapists such as Carl Rogers, Clare and Donald Winnicott, and John Bowlby, among others, influenced social work training and practice after the Second World War. While social workers did not consider themselves psychoanalysts, many social workers used psychoanalytic theory to inform their thinking, organise their work and conduct themselves with clients (Turner, 2017). Consequently, there were many, such as Hollis (1964), who argued for social work to become a 'psychosocial therapy'. This new form of practice involved 'intensive casework', a close relationship between the worker and client through regular home visits, attentive listening to the person, and consideration of their emotional state (Todd, 2014). Social workers sought to mobilise strengths, support coping capacities, build self-esteem and change dysfunctional patterns of thinking, feeling and relating to others, while linking to resources and seeking to alleviate environmental stressors (Turner, 2017). The work of such pioneers constructed a representation of the social worker-as-therapist, which has since spawned a range of therapeutic theories and methods (Payne, 2015).

Practical helper

The representation of the social worker-as-practical helper is as one that seeks to provide practical help and pragmatic solutions to the problems that people face on a daily basis. Similarly to the social worker-as-social administrator, this professional representation can be seen to be anchored in the discourse of individual responsibility in the 1800s, and Octavia Hill in London can be considered a pioneer of this perspective. Believing that state support was unnecessary, or even immoral, as it created dependency, she believed that it was a praiseworthy activity to work with individuals to foster self-respect. While her focus was on housing, she believed that the poor should be helped to help themselves and so would seek to help and resolve whatever issues the tenants experienced, such as gaining employment, budgeting or education (Hill, 1877). Despite her involvement in the creation of the COS, Brieland (1990) argues that the main role of the COS social workers was not to provide practical help, but rather to act as a gatekeeper to financial assistance and support. Hill, and her work, therefore, provided an alternative perspective for what social workers should do and how they should do it (Bell, 1943), with different boundaries for what were considered praiseworthy and shameful actions.

This representation has been advocated by a wide range of individuals and communities interested in the specific interactions between people and social workers. Those predisposed to social work practice, such as Titmuss (1958), for example, considered social work as inherently involving practical help in social workers' role as administrators of social policy. Activists, while focusing on wider systemic change, also engaged in practical help, such as by creating meeting places, support groups, communal restaurants, soup kitchens, hostels and businesses for clients, for example (Ferguson, 2009). Even critics of social work practice have considered the social worker-as-practical helper to be a more acceptable form of practice than the alternatives (eg Brewer and Lait, 1980). As a form of practice, therefore, this acceptance within such diverse communities enabled aspects of social work to be seen as a praiseworthy activity.

Creating and maintaining child and family social work within the bureaucratic field

The foundations of child and family social work can be seen to have developed through purposeful actions intended to address some area of need related to children and families. The complex nature of society provided opportunities for different shared beliefs about what needed to be done, and how it should be done, in order to address the identified need. These shared beliefs provided the systemic boundaries for shameful and praiseworthy behaviour within these communities and constituencies (Rorty, 1989; Creed et al, 2014), and certain individuals and groups sought to create and maintain a way of practising within these boundaries that evoked pride in their work and avoided being shamed within their social group.

Once established as a professional representation of social work practice, institutional guardians of these representations sought to maintain and reproduce them through advocacy, promotion and sponsorship. The different views on what was acceptable and unacceptable behaviour provided the means through which social workers, and other advocates for the orientations, sought to evoke, eclipse and divert how people felt to support their cause. For example, Young and Ashton (1967) highlight the pride that workers felt through performing social administration in the COS. Woodroofe (1962), however, outlines how such work was seen as shameful by those advocating for activism through the settlement movement, such as Barnett. While NSPCC inspectors felt proud of their policing work in the early 1900s (NSPCC, 1912), such methods were considered unethical and ineffective from the therapeutic perspective that had begun to dominate social work practice after the 1940s (Yelloly, 1980). The shaming practices of child protection inspections were, therefore, transformed by the more relationship-based, therapeutically informed, partnership approach (Ferguson, 2011). The claims of therapy, however, were criticised by some, such as Wootton (1959), who saw the focus on the relationship and the need to search for deeper meanings of behaviour as deviations from social work's true role of providing practical help to those in need. Such therapeutic practice was further challenged by the global radical political activism of the late 1960s and early 1970s, which opened up new ways of thinking about social work practice (Ferguson, 2009). Bailey and Brake (1975), for example, provided a socialist critique of social work practice that criticised the dominant casework approaches as being overly individualised and pathologising of people, ignoring the structural factors that were contributing to the problems.

The creation and maintenance of child and family social work can be seen as a struggle within the bureaucratic field to gain cultural legitimacy and state sponsorship. As an occupation, different representations of practice, with their respective communities and constituencies, were constructed, contributing to the perception of social work as a necessary, legitimate and socially acceptable form of work with children and families. Pride and shame can be considered to be at the heart of these processes as they provided the boundaries for, and guided the construction of, such representations, facilitating their acceptance within wider communities. These representations can, however, be seen as Weberian ideal-types in that they can be considered abstract, hypothetical concepts, useful for analysing practice. While there were some who advocated for certain ways of practising social work and attacked ideas that posed a challenge, social work as a profession has drawn on the range of ideas contained within such representations. With general appeal and acceptance within a wide range of political constituencies, be they liberal, socialist or conservative, the foundations were laid for the state to provide social and legal support for social work's practices within the emerging welfare state (Payne, 2005), culminating in the formation of social service departments under the Local Authority Social Services Act 1970. While the different professional representations provided a foundation for the profession, as illustrated earlier, they could hold widely varying sets of methodologies, underlying knowledge and philosophies. The professionalisation of social work took these non-contingent and disparate practices and created a non-uniform and diverse way of working with a wide range of social issues. What held these together as a professional practice was a commitment to a core set of values and ethical ways of working, grounded in human rights, social justice and the respect, dignity and worth of every person (Titmuss, 1958; Younghusband, 1981; Reamer, 1998; Stevenson, 2013). Such values and ethical commitments promised to shape social work into a coherent practice (Younghusband, 1981; Stevenson, 2013), and Parton (2014) argues that the creation of national departments where this practice was to be performed marked the high point of optimism, confidence and pride in the profession.

Contemporary child and family social work

The professional bureaucracy that was created with the social service departments in 1970 respected professional expertise and provided social workers with a high degree of discretion. Other than for exercising statutory powers, such as applying for a court order, Munro (2004) states that there was very little paperwork and what records were kept were used to improve professional practice through supervision. Furthermore, the new central government inspectorate was designed to provide a 'promotional, consultative and advisory' function to the new departments (Seebohm Report, 1968: 185). While social work within the UK was an established and legitimised practice, contemporary child and family social work has been disrupted by alternative discourses that have gained prominence within the bureaucratic field, which has led to a re-evaluation of the status, role and purpose of social work.

Re-evaluating the welfare state through the discourse of neoliberalism

Neoliberalism is an idea that many have identified as having no consensus in definition or concepts (eg McCarthy and Prudham, 2004; Springer, 2012), with different theoretical positions taking different viewpoints. Springer's (2012) analysis of the literature, however, identifies a discourse of neoliberalism that incorporates these different viewpoints, which enables us to see how neoliberalism has come to influence and affect social work services and practices. Springer (2012) argues that neoliberalism as a discourse has four different understandings. The first is neoliberalism as an ideological hegemonic project, which defines neoliberalism as an economic conception of market rule. Harvey (2007: 2), for example, defines the founding belief of neoliberal theory as the idea 'that human wellbeing can best be advanced by liberating individual entrepreneurial freedoms and skills within an institutional framework characterized by strong private property rights, free markets, and free trade'.

Such beliefs, however, have consequences for conceptions of the state, organisations, individuals within the state and their roles, rights and responsibilities. In order to enable individuals to engage in the market economy: the state is required to create markets and then limit its role within them once created; organisations need to be transformed to be able to participate in the new economy; and individuals need to be active, autonomous and responsible within this new market-driven system (Woolford and Nelund, 2013). In order to achieve these aims, the second way of understanding neoliberalism is as a set of policies and programmes (Springer, 2012). Henkel (1991) argues that in this new way of evaluating historical and current events, the welfare state was seen within the governing Conservative Party as costly, unsustainable and hampering economic growth. Organising work within hierarchical bureaucracies, such as the new social work service, was further seen as inherently inefficient, which, it was argued, could be made more efficient by using the principles of the market (Power, 1997). This was argued to involve the privatisation of state-run services or, at the very least, the introduction of markets and market principles into such services.

Such policies and programmes, Springer (2012) argues, influence the third understanding of neoliberalism, that of 'governmentality' (Foucault, 1991), or the way in which the state governs. As governments seek to implement these new policies, the failures and successes of the attempts to re-imagine, reinterpret and reassemble services, roles and responsibilities reconstruct what is 'common sense'. Neoliberalism can, therefore, be seen as the internal dynamics of decentring government through the creation of new strategies, technologies and techniques that produce self-regulated and self-correcting individuals. Citizens are provided with freedom through enterprise and autonomy. Providing that individuals abide by society's rules, they have the ability to shape their lives by taking control of what they do. They are, therefore, seen as responsible for their own lives, actions and outcomes, with social risks, such as illness, unemployment and poverty, being the responsibility of the individual's 'self-care' (Lemke, 2001).

Finally, as ideas of what is 'common sense' change, individuals alter their ideas, actions and expectations, changing the nature of the state itself. Springer (2012), therefore, states that the fourth understanding of neoliberalism is as a state form. In order to remain economically competitive within an international marketplace, the state is seen to need to abandon the ideals of social and economic security, and, therefore, to destroy and discredit certain state capacities and apparatus that sustain such ideals, while constructing and consolidating reconfigured institutions, economic management systems and social agendas that create, promote and sustain economic competitiveness.

Threats to the system, such as those who are unemployed, poor or 'irresponsible', are seen to need to be controlled and systems of managing public order, policing and surveillance are implemented (Wacquant, 2010).

Springer (2012) argues that these four components of neoliberalism are interrelated and interdependent, influencing one another in a recursive circulating discourse. From a wider perspective, we can, therefore, see that the systemic boundaries of shame and pride were altered by the creation, promotion and establishment of a neoliberal ideology. This not only serves as a form of institutional regulation, whereby state services are refashioned by neoliberal ideology, but is also achieved in large part through emotion regulation, where pride and shame are strategically used to control and shape the services and individuals within the service.

Reconstructing the boundaries for shame and pride through the discourse of derision

For any organised parties interested in creating new institutional arrangements, it is necessary to discredit and delegitimise the old ones (Lawrence and Suddaby, 2006). Indeed, the anthropologist Bailey (1977: 7) argued that in attempts to promote and preserve one's own views, contrary views are derided through the creation of a myth, that is, 'an oversimplified representation of a more complex reality'. In applying this idea to the changes in the teaching profession brought about by the neoliberal re-evaluation of public services, Wallace (1993) outlined how myths were created around progressive education in the 1990s, which constructed a discourse of derision that framed progressive education as failing children and society, and which argued that a policy of traditional education was needed, along with greater central government control for implementing this policy as local education authorities could not be trusted. As this process stems from the wider neoliberal discourse, it can be seen right across the public services. In relation to child and family social work, this process has four interrelated components: social problems are resolvable; social workers are of poor quality; the system of social work education is inadequate; and social work services are not fit for purpose.

The foundation of the discourse of derision stems from the professional project of social work. As those invested in social work sought to establish a monopoly on working with social problems, claims were made about the effectiveness of social work and its methods. As discussed earlier, there were always questions and debates within the profession as to the best way of achieving the aims of the profession but they, at least, all agreed that they could help and assist with a wide range of personal and social issues. The accumulation of support for, and establishment of, social work practice within the welfare state could be seen as a success of the professional project (Larson, 1977). Once established as a state-sponsored endeavour, however, those invested in the state become more interested in whether the profession was able to live up to its claims.

From 1970 onwards, as neoliberal ideas were embedding within certain constituencies, a number of studies were reported that highlighted the poor experience and effectiveness of social work practice (Mayer and Timms, 1970; Fischer, 1976), leading some to criticise the evidence base of social work and attack the pretensions of its training. Indeed, such criticism was encapsulated in Brewer and Lait's (1980) book *Can social work survive?*. They advocated for social work to be privatised, reducing the involvement of universities in social work education, enabling employers to lead and stopping social workers being taught the therapeutic and activist orientations to practise in order to focus on the practical and administrative aspects of the role as these were considered better suited to modern public services. Through the neoliberal discourse, the established educational practices within social work at that time were derided, refashioning the systemic boundaries for shameful and praiseworthy behaviour in education.

Humphries (1997) outlines the continued criticism throughout the 1980s and 1990s of the Central Council for Education and Training in Social Work (CCETSW), which determined the content and standards of education for the profession from 1970, and states that its very survival as an organisation was placed under threat if it failed, or resisted, change. Consequentially, Webb (1996) argues that the more radical voices were silenced within CCETSW and Humphries (1997) charts CCETSW's adoption of a competence-based curriculum for social work education that was intended to enable social workers to demonstrate competencies in new national standards for practice. She argues, however, that these standards prescribed a highly regulated and narrow role for social work while providing a highly mechanistic approach to education that was 'in line with state intervention in authoritarian ways in the lives of social and probation services' clients' (Humphries, 1997: 647). Furthermore, while probation officers were qualified social workers at that point, Newburn (2003) highlights the derision of social work training within official government papers on the future of the probation service, resulting in the Home Secretary at the time splitting probation from social work by preventing probation officers from being trained by university social work courses.

Despite such changes, in attempts to continue to garner support and credibility within this new regime, social work education continued to be derided by subsequent governments, with Labour disbanding CCETSW and creating the General Social Care Council (GSCC) (see later). The criticisms of social work education in Narey's (2014) government-commissioned independent review are strikingly similar to those made since 1970: the system of social work education is inadequate as social workers are not provided with the necessary knowledge and skills to perform the task as prescribed in statute because social work education is 'dominated by theories of non-oppressive practice, empowerment and partnership' (Narey, 2014: 12). The UK government elected in 2010 has since implemented stronger regulation of courses and introduced a narrowly focused knowledge and skills base that social workers need to demonstrate, while seeking to diversify professional education away from universities (Higgins, 2015).

While the discourse of derision encapsulated real, exaggerated and imagined problems within social work education, the lack of trust in its ability to produce high-quality practitioners was established, supporting the idea that social workers are of poor quality. While such views were in circulation prior to the 1970s, it was the death of Maria Colwell at the hands of her step-father in 1973 after being placed back with her mother and step-father on a supervision order by the local authority that lay the foundations for this to become a deeper belief in the critique of the social work profession. While child deaths prior to Maria Colwell had not resulted in the condemnation of social work practice, the idea that Maria's social worker was individually responsible for the outcome had gained sufficient cultural legitimacy for her to be cross-examined for 25 hours, to be asked by journalists why she had not resigned live on national television and to be subject to threats by members of the public, requiring her to have police protection as she went in and out of the hearing (Greenland, 1986). The perceived failings of Maria's social worker, however, were not considered to be an isolated case (Parton, 1991). Indeed, Warner (2015) outlines how the narrative of incompetent social workers has been supported and promoted by politicians and journalists since the death of Maria Colwell, using it to episodically shame social workers for failing to protect children adequately.

On the one hand, we can see the episodic shaming of social workers for abusing their power. In 1987, for example, 121 children in Cleveland were removed from their homes due to concerns that they had been sexually abused (Parton, 2014). Significant criticism was levelled at the social workers in the press and an inquiry was set up which concluded that most of the medical diagnoses were incorrect and that the children should not have been removed (Butler-Sloss, 1988). Further criticism was made of the social workers in the press and some politicians likened them to the SS (the Nazi's Schutzstaffel, which translates as the 'protection squadron') (Parton, 1991). On the other hand, we can also see episodic shaming of social workers for failing to use their powers adequately. Victoria Climbié, for example, was known to social services at the time of her death in 2000, and under significant criticism within the press, the local authority placed a large proportion of the blame on Victoria's social worker, who was not only sacked, but also placed on the Protection of Children Act (POCA) list, preventing her from working with children ever again (Fairweather, 2008). The social work regulator at the time, the GSCC, later refused to register Victoria's social worker on the grounds of incompetence. While there have been many further examples of such perceived failures, Parton (2014) argues that the death of Peter Connelly in 2007 is the most significant, which again saw the individual social workers, along with the head of the organisation, being targets for episodic shaming by politicians and journalists and again removed from their posts (Jones, 2014; Shoesmith, 2016).

Such shaming has had two consequences. The first has been that social workers received a message that they are not good enough. The majority message has been that social workers have been overly optimistic and have failed to protect children by doing too little too late and, therefore, need to use their authority to intervene in the lives of families to prevent such tragedies ever happening again (Ferguson, 2011; Parton, 2014; Warner, 2015). The minority message has been that they should not get this wrong, increasing the systemic feeling of self-consciousness while practising. These new systemic boundaries for practice refashioned the therapeutically informed, socially conscious, form of practice as inadequate, inappropriate and dangerous, reconstructing social workers' sense of shame and pride by ensuring that they knew what they would be shamed and praised for. The second consequence was a perception that greater control was needed over what social workers did and how they did it.

Following the death of Maria Colwell, social workers were placed under unprecedented levels of management oversight through extensive administrative procedures that were set up to monitor their work, including multi-agency child protection conferences and a register to keep a record of children considered to be at risk of non-accidental injuries (Payne, 2005). After the death of Victoria Climbié, the Children Act 2004 was brought in to 'sharpen accountability' (Parton, 2014: 50) of all agencies that came into contact with children, which involved significant organisational changes. These included the dismantling of the generic local authority social work service that had been in place since 1970 and the creation of new local authority departments for children's and adults' services. It further included the dismantling of CCETSW and the creation of the GSCC, which not only took over the responsibility for regulating social work education, but was also provided with increased regulatory control over the workforce. The GSCC set the standards for practice, which social workers had to demonstrate that they met to be able to register with them to practise. McLaughlin (2007) argues that these standards were devised in the context of a lack of trust of laypeople and professionals, and, therefore, framed social workers' role as one of preventing abuse and the regulator's as preventing social workers from abusing. Within these new arrangements, he argues, 'whether at work, home or leisure, the message to the social worker is clear: "You are being watched"' (McLaughlin, 2007: 1275). Further control measures were implemented through the use of technology to store and retrieve information, which, as White et al (2010) observed in their ethnographic study of practice, forced social workers to follow a specific workflow of documents within a specific time frame. Indeed, Wastell et al's (2010) study argued that practice revolved around the computer system in an atmosphere of performance management, with highly formalised rules and procedures, an empowered management system, and diminished professional discretion.

This latter point is associated with the final component of the discourse of derision, that social work services are not fit for purpose. Satyamurti's (1981) ethnographic study of the newly created social service departments in 1970 highlighted an uneasy relationship between the social workers and the new administrators. Through the discourse of neoliberalism, however, such arrangements were viewed as inefficient, ineffective and not value for money. Such a perspective was only reinforced by the wider economic problems of the 1970s, the ongoing critiques of public services and the specific tragedies of child deaths. In order to ensure that public services were reformed in line with neoliberal principles, Power (1997) argues that governments developed forms of checking to ensure that the workers were doing what they were 'supposed' to be doing. By making organisations, and therefore the individuals within them, account for what they do, governments could ensure that professionals were 'accountable' to those who funded the service. The Audit Commission was, therefore, established in 1982 to fulfil this function, with a principal aim of being the driving force in the improvement of public services (Munro, 2004). The objectives and standards for practice, and indicators of good performance, were defined so that the auditors could use them to make a judgement about the organisation. This imposed a standardisation on social work the likes of which the profession had never seen before, which Munro (2004: 1083) states was based on 'a number of theoretical assumptions that have no clear authority from empirical research or professional consensus'. Nevertheless, the judgement of the auditors was trusted, despite questions about the process and results of such judgements, elevating the audit process to the status of highest importance (Power, 1997). Legitimacy as an organisation, and therefore pride in one's profession, required a positive judgement.

For organisations to be able to provide the evidence that the auditors needed, they had to implement new policies, procedures and internal monitoring, recording and data-management systems in order to control what its employees did. Power (1997: 51) argues that through a process of regulating and policing these structures, the auditors control the control systems inside organisations, resulting in organisations being 'constructed around the audit process itself'. Such moves deliberately sought to challenge the organisational power and discretion of the professionals that had developed over the post-war period in order to provide the government with more control of what professionals did and how they did it (Power, 1997). Under the guise of creating greater effectiveness, efficiency and value for money, local authorities were encouraged, through the audit process, to move away from the generic model of social work services to provide more specialist services, which saw the proliferation of teams that worked exclusively with children and their families and those that worked with vulnerable adults, while separating the commissioning from the delivery of services (Parton, 1996; Munro, 2004). Parton (1996: 12) argues that through this process, 'no longer are social workers constituted as caseworkers drawing on their therapeutic skills in human relationships, but as care managers', monitoring and reviewing the packages of care that they have put in place.

Gilroy (2004) outlines how the work of the inspectors took on the methods of auditing and began to change from one of inspecting the professional practice of social work to auditing the management, organisation and delivery of the services. Indeed, Power (1997) argues that inspections have simply become audits with the power for independent escalation. Perhaps unsurprisingly, the work of the Audit Commission and the inspectorate began to overlap and they began undertaking joint inspections from 1996 (Gilroy, 2004). Munro (2004) argues that these developments only intensified under the new Labour government elected in 1997. 'Performance', 'outputs' and 'outcomes' were further quantified to drive and measure improvement through audit and inspection, which produced for the first time a grade for the local authority, a league table and the possibility of being placed in 'special measures'. Such measures could be seen to formalise and embed the systemic shame and pride for social work as those within and outside the organisation now knew the boundaries for shameful or praiseworthy behaviour, which legitimised the episodic shaming and praising of organisations that were considered to conform to, or transgress, these boundaries.

Under the auspices of transparency, following the death of Peter Connelly, serious case reviews (SCRs), that is, reports on what went wrong in cases of a child death or serious injury, were required to be made public, which, while explicitly not about apportioning blame to individuals, served to highlight the most serious mistakes in child protection. Furthermore, the inspection regime was reformed, introducing unannounced inspections, while making it more difficult to attain the higher categories in a new grading system: Inadequate, Requires Improvement, Good and Outstanding (Ofsted, 2015). While the inspection regime provides a public statement about whether the organisation meets national standards, shaming those who do not and praising those who do, Perryman's (2007: 177) study of teachers' experiences of inspections identifies the panoptic and disciplinary force that they provide through 'fear, panic and loss of self'. Indeed, the inspection is symbolic of the systemic shame and pride in operation, heightening one's sense of shame during periods of increased scrutiny through knowing that one could be shamed for failing to conform to legitimised practices. The introduction of unannounced inspections, by this stage undertaken solely by the Office for Standards in Education (Ofsted), only served to place all local authorities under an atmosphere of continuous inspection (Perryman, 2007). Furthermore, the language of partnership, inherent to the therapeutic and socially conscious representations of social work practice, was absent from the renewed statutory guidance, and in its place was the idea that social workers should 'rescue children from chaotic, neglectful, and abusive homes' (HM Government, 2013: 22), more familiar to the social policing representation.

Resisting the neoliberal re-conceptualisation of child and family social work

Those committed to the neoliberal discourse had to establish it as the dominant discourse among the communities and constituencies with power and influence by competing with alternative ideas, meanings and representations. The Barclay Report (1982: vii), for example, commissioned by the government to address what was seen as a growing crisis in social work towards the end of the 1970s and early years of the 1980s, opened with 'too much is generally expected of social workers. We load upon them unrealistic expectations and we then complain when they do not live up to them'. The report recommended an alternative direction for social work practice based more on community engagement and social action than the more individualised forms of practice advocated by proponents of neoliberalism, along with greater levels of trust in and autonomy for social workers to perform their work. While such proposals were not enacted by the government, competing discourses continued to challenge neoliberal hegemony.

The Children Act 1989 is a good example of competing discourses coalescing to create a wider consensus in relation to the support and protection of children and their families. In the context of a number of child abuse inquiries and wider concerns about state intrusion in family life, Parton (1991) argues that the Children Act was an attempt to consolidate and reform the range of legislation and statutory responsibilities in relation to children and families. On the one hand, some key themes of the neoliberal discourse can be seen in the foundational debates that formed the Act and in the Act itself. Issues of individual responsibility and accountability were central, as were limiting state intervention unless necessary on the grounds of harm; however, so were issues related to parental and children's rights and a collective responsibility to provide support to children and families who were in need. Parton (1991) outlines the dominance in the majority message leading up to the creation of the Act for the need to protect children, with the need to provide support being a minority message. Winter and Connolly (2005), meanwhile, argue that the mistrust of social workers provided a clear motivation for the government to restrict and prescribe their role and functions within the new Act. So, while Parton (1991) argues that the formal regulation function provided by the new Act was inclusive of competing discourses, re-establishing confidence in the public service by balancing the need to provide family support with that of protecting children, the discursive strategies employed by neoliberal advocates regulated the emotions of the social workers. Indeed, Ferguson (2011: 35) argues that despite the balance within the Act, 'the impact of child deaths and the pressure to avoid making mistakes and blame led to the work being dominated by child protection concerns'.

There were further competing discourses outside of the profession that challenged the legitimacy of neoliberalism. Sieber (1981), for example, argued that neoliberal measures to manage and make accountable public service organisations would create a 'fatal remedy' through the construction of a dysfunctional system set up to satisfy the auditing system rather than the people it was intended to serve. Indeed, Power (1997) refers to this as 'colonisation'. Furthermore, the methods of auditing were criticised by some (eg Cutler and Waine, 2003), and the Audit Commission (2002) itself identified that social workers were leaving the profession because of bureaucracy, paperwork, targets, lack of autonomy and unmanageable workloads. Further evidence was created within the field of social work for the failure of the neoliberal reforms to produce the results that it had claimed it would (eg Baginsky et al, 2010; White et al, 2010). Furthermore, the Laming (2003) inquiry set up after the death of Victoria Climbié, and the Social Work Task Force (2009) set up after the death of Peter Connelly, both identified procedure, guidance and targets as barriers to effective practice. The Social Work Task Force, and the subsequent review of child protection (Munro, 2011), both challenged the discourse of derision of social work by reaffirming the importance of the profession and setting out a vision for an improved system with professional expertise and relationships at its heart. Yet, despite the growing wider critique of neoliberal discourse and reforms (eg Plehwe et al, 2007) and the more specific critique within social work (eg Harris, 2003; Garrett, 2010; Houston, 2013; Gray et al, 2015), it remains defended, supported and promoted in the communities and constituencies with power and influence. Challenges to neoliberal ideology for social work services have been diverted by blaming social workers and social work organisations, and eclipsed by presenting a version of events that evokes shame in the profession, rather than identifying problems within the wider system.

Summary

Child and family social work can be seen within the wider professional project of social work that has attempted to create and maintain social work as a legitimate profession, creating practitioners with expert knowledge and skills in the field of working with social problems. Competing discourses, however, provided a range of pressures in which to establish the professional project. By providing alternative shared understandings for what is praiseworthy and shameful behaviour, these discourses regulated the emotions of practitioners. Such systemic boundaries, supported by evoking, eclipsing and diverting pride and shame in particular ways, constructed contextually specific representations of practice as certain communities sought to attract praise and avoid being shamed. Hence, child and family social work practice developed out of, and was shaped by, the emotion regulation of those outside the profession and the emotion work of those within it. The utility and value of the resulting orientations to practise were then seen within different communities and constituencies who promoted and supported them, achieving legitimacy, acceptance and state sponsorship within the bureaucratic field.

The boundaries for praiseworthy and shameful behaviour were, however, revised and refashioned, placing new regulatory pressures upon the profession. The discourse of neoliberalism advocated for the destruction and reformation of certain established social, political and economic institutional arrangements in order to construct and embed new ones in attempts to create, expand and develop markets, and facilitate individuals who can engage in them. The state, state apparatus, state employees and even citizens have been re-conceptualised through the discourse of neoliberalism to achieve these aims. Services have been encouraged, or forced, to implement business processes, with praise for compliance and shame and humiliation for resistance, fracturing social work into different areas of practice and divorcing the purchasing from the delivery of services. The therapeutic and activist representations of practice have been shamed, the administrative and policing representations have been praised, while practical help is considered to be best provided by non-social workers, usually through commissioned services. Indeed, children's services are provided with a positive inspection grading if they can demonstrate good administration and are seen to be keeping children safe. While the following chapters will demonstrate that there are many different ways in which social workers engage in their everyday work, the result of the institutional changes has been a reconfiguration of child and family social work services within the neoliberal agenda (Garrett, 2009; Woolford and Nelund, 2013; Featherstone et al, 2014; Gray et al, 2015; McKendrick, 2016).

FOUR

Pride and shame in the creation of the 'appropriate' organisation

As Chapter Three indicated, the professional struggle to gain cultural legitimacy within the bureaucratic field is inherently tied up with the struggle by organisations that provide child and family social work services for social acceptance. With most social work service organisations being constituted not only by the profession of social work, but also by the state that owns and runs those services, the changing circumstances, pressures and contexts, both within and outside of such organisations, means that achieving and maintaining acceptance and legitimacy becomes a never-ending process of change and renewal. Indeed, there is a range of representations of public service organisations, which are themselves eternally evolving.

This chapter argues that the different communities and constituencies interested in statutory child and family social work services impose competing representations of what organisations that provide social work services are and do. These representations provide conflicting sets of standards, ideals and goals, which can be understood as institutional logics. These multiple institutional logics imposed on social work services set the boundaries for pride and shame for an organisation, thereby directing and shaping its identity. Within this context, this chapter introduces the idea of organisational emotional safety, in which organisations are constructed to avoid organisational shaming and rejection, on the one hand, and attract pride and acceptance, on the other. In an attempt to manage its image and reputation, organisational leaders engage in this form of emotion work to navigate the competing and conflicting pressures, demands and expectations in order to create and maintain a consistent set of organisational actions which ensures that it is safe from episodic shaming, while evoking pride within the organisation and acceptance without.

A case example is provided to illustrate the argument that pride and shame play a significant role in the creation, maintenance and disruption of child and family social work services. This illustration enables a detailed look at the processes through which pride and shame influenced, shaped and guided the thoughts, actions and feelings of organisational leaders and actors in attempts to create, embed and maintain what was perceived as the necessary changes for the organisation to verify its identity as a high-performing child and family social work service. This demonstrates how pride and shame were at the heart of drawing on the social administration and social policing representations of practice by changing the normative associations and rule systems that provided status within the organisation. While this created organisational emotional safety, enabling the leaders to claim that they had achieved their stated aim of being one of the best-performing local authorities in the country, it demonstrates how such changes refashioned the service within the neoliberal re-conceptualisation of public services. The result was a child and family social work service that was perceived as the 'right' kind of institution, similar to Rorty's (1989) notion of the 'right' kind of human being. It was doing the 'right' kind of things, in the 'right' kind of ways, in the eyes of those with the power of definition.

Part one: theorising pride and shame in the creation, maintenance and disruption of child and family social work services

The idea of institutional logics was introduced by Friedland and Alford (1991) but has since been developed by a number of scholars. Thornton and Ocasio (1999: 804) provide one of the more widely used definitions, considering them to be 'the socially constructed, historical patterns of material practices, assumptions, values, beliefs, and rules by which individuals produce and reproduce their material subsistence, organise time and space, and provide meaning to their social reality'. So, while we can conceive of communities of people holding social representations of socially constructed objects (Moscovici, 1961), where these objects are institutions, such representations can be considered to be constituted by a certain logic (Friedland and Alford, 1991). Representing social work as a profession, for example, would involve the logic of professional knowledge, expertise, autonomy and a commitment to public service, and given such a logic, the academic and social work communities expect organisations that employ social workers to facilitate their ability to achieve these professional aims.

For child and family social work services within the UK, however, the success of the professional project has been to achieve state sponsorship, resulting in practice now being performed mainly within statutory local government organisations. So, while social workers within the UK have certain expectations of statutory organisations, such organisations have additional pressures, demands and expectations placed upon them as a consequence of different communities and constituencies subscribing to alternative discourses and representations of them. While there are many views about social work services and what they should do, the political and public administration community consider statutory organisations as administrators of public policy. This latter view brings a logic of the state that rationalises and regulates human activity through legal and bureaucratic hierarchies (Friedland and Alford, 1991). Furthermore, with modern-day state organisations being re-conceptualised through the discourse of neoliberalism, they are also founded in the logic of capitalism and business practices that aims for the imposition of markets and the creation of effectiveness, efficiency and value for money (Power, 1997; Courtney et al, 2004). Statutory social work services are, therefore, expected to be different things to different people, and such external pressures and expectations place competing and conflicting systemic boundaries for praiseworthy and shameful behaviour on such organisations. Indeed, they can be considered to be institutionally plural organisations in that they have more than one ascribed identity and more than one societally sanctioned purpose (Kraatz and Block, 2008).

Organisational leaders are required to navigate these systemic pressures, satisfying the different communities and constituencies involved. As Selznick (1957) argued in *Leadership in administration*, leaders have to appeal to different interests, values and ideals within the organisation, as well as having to make deals, build coalitions and take pragmatic action in order to effectively lead the organisation. He argued that in satisfying the different constituencies' needs, these different purposes are knitted together, creating a coherent structure that organisational leaders seek to maintain. Such institutional work embeds these competing and conflicting institutional logics into the fabric of the organisation (Thornton and Ocasio, 2005), creating what Albert and Whetten (1985) termed an 'organisational identity', which they define as the collective understanding by members of the organisation of its central and enduring attributes, and that distinguishes it from other organisations.

While organisational leaders are constrained by the competing range of systemic boundaries for shame and pride that operate in social work services, however, they are not so constrained that all services are created the same. Each social work service has its own identity that seeks to efficiently administer public policy, perform good social work practice and provide effective services to children and families. The historical, national and local pressures and expectations provide different contexts for each local statutory service to create their own organisational identity claims that construct a set of standards through which organisational leaders manage the organisation. Any action that confirms and reaffirms the organisational identity attracts praise, while any action that threatens the organisational identity becomes a target for episodic shaming.

Organisational identities, however, require formation, reformation and ongoing maintenance, which Whetten and Mackey (2002) define as the organisational management project. The actions of employees project an image of the organisation to the different interested communities. These interested communities then provide feedback to the organisation, defining its reputation. Whetten and Mackey (2002) argue that much of the work of organisational leaders can be considered to be a process of managing the identity of the organisation by regulating and controlling different internal groups of organisational actors so that identity-congruent messages are provided to outsiders, while seeking to regulate and control the feedback of outsiders so that the credibility of the organisation's self-definition is upheld, as illustrated in Figure 4.1. The role of emotions in this process, however, has not been well articulated or illustrated. Yet, with systemic forces imposing a set of boundaries for praiseworthy and shameful behaviour, and an internal set of standards associated with the identity of the organisation, pride and shame can be considered at the heart of the processes by which organisations are created, shaped and maintained.

The praising and shaming of organisations by politicians and journalists evokes pride and shame in those responsible for the creation and maintenance of the organisation. Through developing knowledge

Figure 4.1: The organisational identity management project

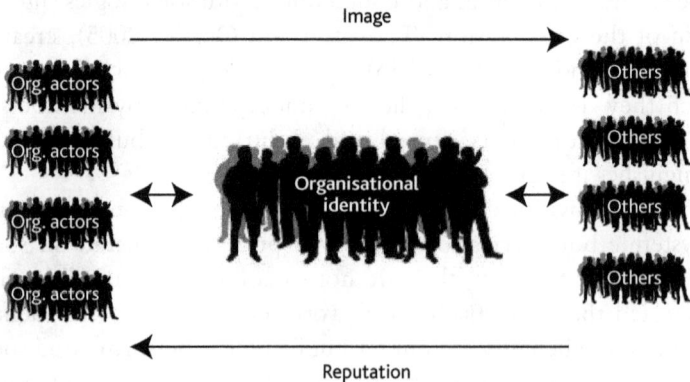

Source: Adapted from Whetten and Mackey (2002: 407)

and experience of being praised and shamed, leaders and managers seek to protect their organisation from being shamed, on the one hand, and attract praise, on the other. This form of emotion work can be conceptualised through the notion of organisational emotional safety. Created by Catherall (2007), the concept of emotional safety has been confined to romantic relationships and defined as a shared belief that there is no threat to the identities of those within the relationship or to the relationship itself. He argues that shame is at the heart of experiences of identity and relationship threats and that feeling protected from shame results in increased trust and greater benefit of the doubt in questionable situations. Where a person feels that their identity or the relationship is threatened, however, Catherall (2007) argues that those in the relationship feel vulnerable to being shamed and, therefore, emotionally unsafe. Under such circumstances, the individuals in the relationship become more suspicious and distrustful of the other's actions and motives.

Applied to the field of organisational studies, emotional safety can be seen as a feeling within the organisation that any threat to its identity is minimised, protecting organisational actors and leaders from episodic shaming. Given sufficient threats to an organisation's identity claims, leaders and managers can feel vulnerable to being shamed and will seek to create emotional safety. Indeed, organisational leaders have long been observed to physically, psychologically and symbolically distance organisational actors from anxiety-provoking emotions that might arise as a result of performing legitimate organisational activities (eg Jaques, 1955; Menzies, 1960). Such emotion work protects the organisation from internal threats to its identity. As leaders respond to feedback, however, they may also seek to refashion and reconstruct the activities of organisational actors by changing what is praised and what is shamed, thereby altering professional practice and protecting the organisation from external threats.

Given the range of pressures and expectations placed upon statutory social work services, however, competition emerges within the bureaucratic field to get specific sets of concerns, objectives and values addressed. Those with more power and influence are able to exert a greater threat of an organisation being shamed and rejected, resulting in certain discourses, representations and specific shared ideas of what constitutes praiseworthy and shameful behaviour being prioritised over others. While Oliver (1991) argues that organisations may seek to acquiesce to external expectations, compromise on some demands, avoid or defy certain pressures, or even seek to manipulate the source of any external force, some concerns will have greater salience, prominence and commitment within the organisation than others, providing a hierarchy of organisational standards. While it is possible that a social work organisation may defy the political and public administrative pressures placed upon them, the political and public administration constituencies have greater power and influence to evoke shame and pride in social work organisations through messages promoted in the media, the issuing of certain inspection ratings and threats of having leaders and managers replaced, or even services taken over by new organisations. Such regulation of people's emotions evokes pride and shame in certain practices, eclipses any shame or guilt felt from prioritising political and public administration agendas, and diverts any feelings of pride experienced from professional practice frowned upon within the dominant discourses. It is this process that enables the ideas of neoliberalism to be imposed and embedded within statutory child and family social work services.

This process can be summarised as follows: individuals, groups and communities develop shared ways of understanding and communicating about institutions. With differences in how statutory public service organisations are represented within different groups, different ideas about what such institutions are, what they should do and how they should do it are imposed on the organisations, placing competing and conflicting pressures, expectations and demands upon them. By episodically shaming and praising individual organisations, how organisational leaders and managers define, construct and manage professional practice can be disrupted, influenced and altered. In attempts to achieve legitimacy, stability and a positive reputation, leaders and managers engage in emotion work to avoid being shamed and attract praise by creating and maintaining organisational identities within the confines of the boundaries for shameful and praiseworthy individual and organisational behaviour. This results in an organisational identity that is 'appropriate' to the context, with central, enduring and distinctive attributes about what the organisation is and does. These attributes serve as a guide to evaluate and adapt the individual and collective actions of those within the organisation in attempts to project an image consistent with its identity claims and manage its public reputation. The self-conscious emotions of individuals within the organisation are, therefore, regulated according to these standards. This process is illustrated by the following case example.

Part two: a case example

While individual case examples do not prove anything, they do provide the opportunity to illustrate theory in practice. The case example used here is of a child and family social work service in England. Of course, not all child and family social work services within England are like this one. The knowledge and processes exemplified within this case, however, may be useful to understanding them in other contexts (Thomas, 2010). Details of the research from which this case and these data are drawn were outlined in the introduction. The focus of this part of the chapter is how the organisation, referred to as the Council, had created an identity within the confines of previous governmental reforms, but with changes to the external pressures and expectations, regulatory pressure was applied that required significant changes in order to maintain its identity as a high-performing, innovative service. Indeed, the recreation of the service can be seen as a response to being shamed by Ofsted by being given a poor inspection grading, resulting in reforms intended to create emotional safety in order to protect the organisation, and those within it, from further shaming. This was achieved by changing the context for child and family social work practice, constructing policing and administration as good social work practice, changing the boundaries for membership within the new service, and refashioning the rule systems that praised and shamed practitioners so that they were in line with the new intentions. Together, these show one example of how pride and shame can be used as political and cultural resources in creating organisations that are seen as 'appropriate' to the context by those with power and influence, which, in this case, was to further construct the organisation along neoliberal lines.

Creating and maintaining an organisational identity

In 2007, the Council's services for children were successfully organised according to the national reforms imposed following the death of Victoria Climbié. As an institutionally plural organisation, the logic of the state had conceived the Council as a bureaucratic hierarchy, the logic of professionalism had embedded the idea of professional expertise and the logic of local authorities as businesses had embedded the idea of competition and innovation into the identity of the organisation. The central message from the leaders and senior managers of children's services within the Council from 2005 was, therefore, that they were providing high-quality, innovative services to children and young people and were performing better than many local authorities, as the leader of the Council stated in 2007:

> The good news is that the information paints a very positive picture. It tells us that we are improving our performance faster than other Councils … and children in [the Council] now have access to a range of improved services appropriate to their needs. (Council meeting minutes)

Such identity claims were routinely verified by Ofsted, who generally graded them as providing good services to children and young people. The resulting legitimised organisational identity was then used to reinforce a positive image of the organisation, both internally and externally. Press releases were provided to the media and the Director used these judgements in reports to local councillors and communications with front-line staff as evidence that they were 'making a real difference to children and families' (Council meeting minutes). Such validated and legitimised claims created and supported a shared belief that the Council was doing a good job and was a good place to work. The result was that the Council developed a positive reputation within the field, as Lucy, a social worker within one of the teams, stated: "To me, the reputation of [the Council] has always been very good but I come from [a] university where [the Council] was thought of as a good local authority" (interview data).

In 2008/09, however, significant changes were taking place in the circumstances and dominant discourses in the fields of both social work and public administration. These new conditions laid the foundations for the deterioration of the consensus within the Council around the value of the current arrangements, which now posed a threat to the Council's organisational identity. Indeed, the Director wrote to local councillors in 2010 stating that 'doing nothing or staying as we are currently is not a viable option' and arguing 'that there needs to be a new paradigm to improve outcomes for [the Council]'s children and young people' (Council meeting minutes). A proposal was made to the councillors for a 'transformation and radical reshaping of existing provision' (Council meeting minutes). Two separate arguments were presented by the leaders of the organisation to the local councillors and Council employees for the rationale for these changes. The first was that there was a need to 'improve services for children, young people and families', while the second was that there was a need to 'achieve financial savings' (select committee meeting minutes).

Disrupting and creating new professional identity claims

The political and media fallout following the court case into the death of Peter Connelly in 2008 evoked shame within the nation in child and family social work practice (Jones, 2014; Warner, 2015; Shoesmith, 2016). This imposed significant mounting social pressure on all local authorities to demonstrate that they were competent at protecting children. While the organisational arrangements in place in 2008 had been designed exactly to prevent such perceived system failures, this new systemic pressure eclipsed the pride that organisational leaders felt in the service by casting doubt over whether the established arrangements were appropriate for the task of protecting children. Observing the episodic shaming of specific social workers and organisations nationally, the leaders and senior management team sensed the possibility of being shamed themselves and classified all their social workers as 'an "at risk" staff group' (Council publication), supporting the perceived need to change the established arrangements. Towards the end of 2008, the political leaders of the Council were arguing in meetings for the greater integration of services for children and young people, and a consultation was opened on a new model for integrating and improving services. At the same time, the Social Work Task Force and Munro review of child protection, while casting further doubt over the established arrangements following the reforms after the death of Victoria Climbié, evoked pride in professional practice by reaffirming the importance of the profession and setting out a vision for an improved system (Social Work Task Force, 2009; Munro, 2011).

In seeking to protect the organisation and those within it from being shamed, the Director drew on the social worker-as-therapist representation to set out the aims for the new service, claiming that it would address the complexity of social problems through a 'whole family', early intervention approach, being informed by national research. The leaders of the new service worked with a national children's charity to develop the vision and plan for the new service, and family group conferencing was included as a significant tool for intervention and support. In further appeal to the social work constituency, it was argued that the teams would be 'remodelled', providing 'a manageable caseload supported by consistent reflective supervision' and enabling social workers 'to take responsibility for planned interventions' (Council meeting minutes). This would be achieved by returning to 'patch'-based services (see Barclay Report, 1982), with teams being responsible for a specific area, and investing in family support services to work with families before they reach the 'threshold' for social work services. Furthermore, the signs of safety approach to child protection social work (Turnell and Edwards, 1999), an approach grounded in the therapeutic representation of practice, was implemented in the service. While the rationale for the new service was framed positively, the systemic shame that contributed to the disruption of the current arrangements was evident, being outlined by the Director as a risk to the Council:

> A potential failure to intervene at an earlier stage would have very high risk consequences for the child(ren) involved, the reputation of the local authority and poor Ofsted inspection results. Whilst it is never possible to prevent all injuries inflicted upon children and young people by their carers, the local authority aims to minimise the likelihood of an avoidable child protection failure by ensuring that it has skilled, resourced and well-scrutinised robust services for children, young people and families. (Council meeting minutes)

The political community clearly placed the responsibility for the death of a child at the hands of their carers at the door of the local authority. Such a standard was internalised into the identity of the organisation, leading the Director to believe that a child being harmed equated to a failure of the new system, jeopardising the legitimacy of the whole organisation.

Disrupting and creating new public administration identity claims

Meanwhile, functional pressures in the economy, following the fallout of the financial crash of 2007/08, created a new national political context of austerity. The first budget of the new government in 2010 meant that local authorities were facing a reduction in funding by about a third (HM Treasury, 2010), making it a political necessity that all local authorities reduced their spending. While the Council considered itself to be 'well managed and financially sound' (Council meeting minutes) in 2007, following this budget, there was an admission that 'there would be considerably less funding available to the Council over the next few years and that the Authority needed to take urgent action to deal with this' (Council meeting minutes). The new emphasis in the dominant discourse for public services provided a new context in which the public administration organisational identity claims were being made. Saving money had become a new identity standard imposed upon the Council's services for children and young people as any part of the local authority that did not achieve these standards would be perceived to be failing the local authority. This potentially negative image of the service would directly threaten its claims to be a high-performing Council. Saving money was therefore perceived to be objectively correct and became a shared rule within the Council. A failure to achieve financial savings was, therefore, identified as a 'main risk' (Council meeting minutes) to the new service in the Director's report to the councillors. The Director, however, argued that the new service, 'In the long-term, is likely to achieve financial savings as fewer cases will require intervention from costly specialist services' (Council meeting minutes).

Additionally, the election of the new government placed further political pressure on local authorities to commission more of its services (Horton and Gay, 2011), and in line with its identity as an innovative organisation, the Council committed itself to becoming a 'commissioning orientated organisation' (Council report). The Council, therefore, sought 'to develop a robust joint commissioning process and to strengthen the role of the Third Sector to deliver services on behalf of [the Council]' (Council meeting minutes). It was believed that this would achieve some financial savings and improve services but that it required a cultural shift to achieve this. This imposed standard on the new service provided clear boundaries for systemic shame and pride: saving money for the local authority and commissioning services were necessary, with a failure to achieve this constituting shameful behaviour.

Recreating the new service

While the new service had been purposively designed to address the needs and concerns of the public administration constituency, the institutional logic of professions had been used to address these issues by grounding social work practice in the social worker-as-therapist representation. A significant amount of work was undertaken at an inter- and intra-organisational level to construct and promote the new service through consultations, briefings and communication with a wide range of staff and partner organisations. Furthermore, a significant amount of work was undertaken at a political level to define and promote the new service to local politicians and government departments, presenting an image of an innovative Council with a 'new way of working' (Council meeting minutes). However, a few months before the start of the reorganisation, Ofsted undertook an unannounced inspection that, as an acknowledged threat to the Council's reputation, heightened the sense of shame within the Council. As a team manager told me in her interview: "the nightmare here is that you fail Ofsted. If you were here at the time, you'd think everybody was going to have a heart attack" (interview data).

The Council was judged by Ofsted 'to be failing children needing help and protection' (Ofsted report) and the new service was graded as performing poorly, the lowest possible rating. This episodic shaming of the Council by Ofsted led to a failed identity claim, which was described as a 'shock' (Director's report) by the Director. In attempts to provide a positive organisational image and mitigate any reputational damage, the positive comments within the Ofsted report were highlighted and used for internal communication and press releases. The message was that many of the services for children and young people were, in fact, good; the problem was the social work service, a message that was received by all those working in that service, as one team manager commented: "the pressure, and it's because of the safeguarding. I get that. We're the problem but we're the bit that keeps the children safe" (interview data).

What started as episodic shaming of the Council by Ofsted led to episodic shaming of the social workers by the leaders of the Council. While the Council had identified the social workers as 'at risk' and had sought to design a system to protect them and reaffirm their professional status, this action of organisational self-protection had the effect of spoiling the social work identity within the Council (Goffman, 1963). The new service was always intended to verify the Council's identity; yet, with the shaming of the Council, it remained at risk of further shaming unless it could provide Ofsted with the evidence it required for a positive judgement. The Council's political leadership and senior management team, therefore, sought to protect the organisation from further shaming by providing time and resources 'specifically committed to address the issues identified by the inspection' (Director's report to local councillors). With the social work identity spoiled, greater emphasis was placed on the administrative component of practice to achieve the necessary results, as one team manager, reflecting on the new service, explained:

> "I think the loopholes have perhaps been tightened, but in terms of children, I think I would say we're probably less about children and more about performance and bureaucracy than we've ever been, although that's probably not the general tone being expressed." (Interview data)

Creating organisational emotional safety

The evoking of shame, and the threat of further shaming, heightened the sense of shame within the organisational leaders, who sought to change the system to protect them and others from further episodes of shaming. They sought to achieve this by redefining the context for practice, embedding social policing and social administration as social work practice, redefining the boundaries for professional membership, and reconstructing the rule systems that provided status within the organisation. How each of these was achieved is outlined in the following.

Defining the context for practice

The first step in creating this organisational emotional safety was to create new specialisms for different functions of the service. Early help and support for children and families were provided by an expanded family support service of practitioners without a social work qualification, leaving the work of the social workers almost exclusively related to safeguarding children. Situations in which a child or young person was perceived to be in need of care or protection were the domain of the social work teams, and situations in which children and young people were perceived to be in need of support and practical help were the domain of the family support teams. Cases were moved between these teams accordingly. This institutional work (Lawrence et al, 2009) can be considered to be located within the discourse of dangerousness and risk to children (Parton, 2011), defining the context for social work practice as responsible for ensuring that children were safe from harm rather than in need of more general support. Given that the risk to the organisation of further shaming lay with their ability to protect children, the social workers were effectively provided with the responsibility for the protection of the organisation from such a situation. Furthermore, this move elevated the representation not only of social work-as-social administration, but also of social work-as-social policing.

Constructing and embedding social policing

The death of Peter Connelly was described by a team manager as having an immediate and direct impact on front-line practice:

"you would have to really convince [the Assistant Director] if you needed a section 20 placement[1] and he would really put you through your paces ... there were occasions when they'd ask for a placement and it was refused, they wouldn't do it. When Baby Peter happened, all the senior managers reviewed all the child protection cases in late '09; the difference immediately was certainly very obvious to me. We'd send off an email, think 'Well yeah, we do need a section 20, we might have a bit of a fight on our hands to get it', placement agreement, two-line email, placement agreed on every case that I dealt with." (Interview data)

Following the death of Peter Connelly, the redefined systemic shame provided the Council with the message that their cultural practices associated with providing a child with accommodation (section 20 of the Children Act 1989) were potentially unsafe. The moral foundations underpinning these practices were therefore undermined and a new moral foundation put in place which suggested that a safe organisation always provided accommodation to a child where there was any doubt about a child's safety. The tension between this new practice and the expectations within the professional community that drew on alternative representations of practice, such as social worker-as-therapist, activist or practical helper, was evident in one team manager's comments:

"I think we were, all of us, from the highest levels down, saying 'You want a placement? Okay, let's do it, let's protect this child'. Is that a good thing? No, it isn't, because we're not questioning, we're not looking, I mean we've got the intensive prevention service that works to keep children out of care but I think our thresholds have come down." (Interview data)

Despite the tension, the desire to avoid being shamed provided a stronger motivation in decision-making, meaning that the 'threshold' for child protection intervention and for a child to come into the 'looked-after' system had been lowered. The leader sought to embed this new practice into the new service through remaking the moral foundations of these practices, as a team manager told to me:

"what [the leader] said about the increase of child protection plans surprised me somewhat because she said for years and years and years [the Council] were around 400, 420, 430 at any one time on CP [child protection] plans. It's now over 600 so there's been an increase there of 160, 170, something like that, and it's consistently now at that level. And [the leader's] take on it, I believe, is we were always too low compared to comparator authorities and what's happened is actually good, it's positive because this is the number of children you should expect in an authority of our size to be on child protection plans. I'm not sure about that." (Interview data)

The old practices were now cast as dangerous, arguing that they should have had more children subject to child protection plans all along, and now they have more children on child protection plans, the Council can be considered to be doing well. This conflicted with the team manager's standards for practice, leaving her in some doubt about whether to believe this, although the effects were still evident in her team having the highest number of children on child protection plans in the Council. Inevitably, the result of the increasing numbers of children subject to child protection plans and a lowering of the threshold for children to be looked after by the Council led to increasing numbers of children in care. Having had the old practices associated with removing children undermined, the moral and cultural foundations of these practices disappeared within the new service, as one team manager stated:

"with children in care, I can remember for years and years and years being told we've got to keep the LAC [looked-after children] population down, that's why we had family support teams set up in 2004, that's why we had [duty] teams in 2007, 'We've got to keep the LAC population down'. They were having kittens at headquarters when it went above 600 for the first time and now it's typically 969, 970, why I don't know, I'm not in a position where I can analyse all the data.... Numbers of proceedings I'm not sure, is it a key factor? Maybe, maybe it is, I'm not sure but some of the language that was used in years gone by about 'We must reduce our LAC population', I don't hear that language very much nowadays." (Interview data)

Constructing and embedding administration as ethical practice

The Council had to ensure that it was keeping children safe and that it could provide evidence of any work with families to Ofsted, which may choose any case to audit. The primary method for evaluating practice by the Council's management and Ofsted was through the recording on the computer system. Up-to-date and comprehensive recording of all activities was required, with failure to do this resulting in criticism and potential discipline. This systemic shame was embedded through the phrase 'if it's not written down, it didn't happen', which served to construct a significant component of social work practice as administration. Being a good child and family social worker was doing things to keep children safe, but if it was not recorded, then, in effect, they had not done their job, as Monica explained:

> MONICA: "If it's not written down, it didn't happen."
> INTERVIEWER: "What do you think of that statement?"
> MONICA: "It's true isn't it? It's a farce because … all my notes are all on my notepad, etc, so I do just need to transfer it on to the computer, but … if you were in court and it wasn't evidenced in a case note, then that's it. When I was at court for two days on that EDS [emergency duty service] work, I knew then I'd asked mum about where dad was, I knew that I had but I hadn't documented it and that I didn't trust myself to say in court because I was being criticised for not asking where dad was when we were doing the PPO [police powers of protection]… so I think that has changed the way that I practise … I just make sure that on a case note, I put in as much information as possible." (Interview data)

The threat of being shamed for not having undertaken the taken-for-granted practice of recording brought the phrase 'if it's not written down, it didn't happen' to life, with Monica acting in court as if she had not done what she believed she had. Further attempts were made by the leader to construct administration as social work practice, and, therefore, achieve greater acceptance within the professional community by linking it to the therapeutic form of practice that had greater legitimacy within that community, as illustrated by Amy:

AMY: "[The leader] said in the training, 'If you don't do your paperwork, you don't have empathy'. What the hell has paperwork got to do with your empathy?"

INTERVIEWER: "What do you think of that?"

AMY: "Well, she followed it by, 'You don't have empathy, so you shouldn't be here, and leave'. I just thought, my initial thought was, 'Fuck off', because paperwork is important, it's very important, but it doesn't mean you don't have empathy, it means you don't have time. I thought it was a disgusting statement, if I'm being quite frank. I thought it was disgusting." (Interview data)

Despite Amy's, and other social workers', resistance, within these new arrangements, administrative practice had clearly been set as a moral and cultural foundation for social work practice.

Constructing and embedding administration as performance

Those who had been practising for over 10 years frequently made comparisons between their experiences of practice some years ago and their experiences of practice today, as one team manager demonstrated in her interview:

"I mean, I can remember my first team manager, you'd go into his office, there'd be a pile of children's files on the floor and he'd say, it was a common phrase in that office, 'this case is on the floor', and it meant it hadn't been allocated, and he was saying his child protection cases come over from the child protection team, 'I'm going to allocate it to [name] maybe in two weeks' time'. Whoa hang on, if the child protection comes in here today, I've got to give it to somebody immediately but the timescales don't allow you to hang around." (Interview data)

In the 1980s and 1990s, it was not unusual to have unallocated child protection cases (see Secretary of State, 1993). This was argued by some to be safer than overloading social workers with cases as they could do their job properly with a manageable caseload, with the unallocated cases being monitored by the team manager (eg Hearn, 1991). The practice of having unallocated cases, however, has been criticised for leaving children in unsafe situations (Brandon et al, 2008) and the inspectorial regime reports on the number of unallocated cases, which can potentially lead to a negative judgement of the service (Ofsted, 2012). The Council therefore had a policy of having no unallocated cases. While the foundation of this policy was argued to me by the leader and senior managers to be a moral one, in that this ensured that children were safe, it also served as a form of protection against being shamed by Ofsted.

The normative association between the administrative practice of having all cases allocated to a social worker and the moral foundation that this was necessary to keep children safe was defined as 'performance' for the team manager. A team manager would not be performing adequately if they did not adhere to the policy. As discussed earlier, performance was monitored through regular ongoing audits, with failure to comply with the policy resulting in criticism and potential discipline, providing a boundary for the systemic shame for the team managers. The team managers were aware of these boundaries, which aligned their sense of shame and pride to them and made the need to allocate all cases seem objectively correct. With such moral and cultural foundations in place, the old practice of ensuring that social workers had a manageable caseload and having unallocated cases was now something to be shocked by, while the new practice, which turned this on its head, went unquestioned, as shown by one team manager's comments:

> "It's a bit of a difficult balancing act because … I will say to people 'You've got too much work on' but I also have to say 'I know you've got too much work on and I'm very sorry about this but here's some more' and that's not nice because if we could organise things, which we can't, completely rationally, I'd be saying 'Well, you might be on duty but I know you've got far too much work on', I'll do that occasionally but, in general, I can't because I've got to allocate." (Interview data)

The practice by the team managers was, therefore, to allocate any case that came into the team immediately. Social workers were then provided with set timescales to undertake the allocated work, which was defined as 'performance' for the social workers, as Carol stated:

> Carol: "We've obviously got to perform, haven't we … there's a requirement from the organisation that they're to be doing timely assessments. It's all right, it's all relevant, it's something I agree, that everybody agrees, with."

INTERVIEWER: "So, when people talk about performance, what does that relate to?"

CAROL: "Well, I guess the indicators, what they're measuring you by. It's the percentage of assessments that you do on time, how often you see children. Are you seeing them all the time in a timely manner? Are you giving reports out to parents? It's all that that's being constantly collected and collated." (Interview data)

As indicated by Carol, the social workers were keenly aware of the Council's auditing practices and that their 'performance' was being monitored. They were also aware that they would be criticised and potentially disciplined for not 'performing', providing a boundary for the systemic shame in place for them. Nationally, the timescales for undertaking a social work assessment have been changing, from seven working days prior to 2010 (HM Government, 2006), to 10 working days from 2010 to 2013 (Department for Children, Schools and Families, 2010), to 45 days from 2013 to today (HM Government, 2013). The Council had implemented a two-tiered system of assessments depending on the complexity of the situation, with less complex situations being given 20 days and more complex situations being given 40 days. With a boundary for the systemic shame in operation within the Council relating to meeting these timescales, being aware of these boundaries, together with a desire not to be shamed, the social workers aligned their sense of shame to them. The cultural practice of adhering to these timescales within the teams was, therefore, rarely questioned. What was questioned was the amount of work they had to do.

Defining the boundaries for membership

The leader of the social work service did not want just anyone in the service; she wanted people who could do what she considered to be the 'basic requirements', as a team manager stated: "I've found that if you do the basic requirements, as [the leader] calls them, and 'if you can't do them, please give in your P45' ... they tend to leave me alone more" (interview data). The term 'basic' served to make these expectations seem reasonable and achievable. Indeed, any person unable to meet them could be cast as not being competent and therefore not belonging to the new service. Such actions are defined by Crowley (1999) as the politics of belonging, a form of 'boundary maintenance' that is concerned with the boundaries that separate 'us' from 'them'. 'Us', in this case, was being compliant to superiors and providing the organisation with evidence that it is meeting the standards they are measured against, as Christine explained:

> "I'm doing a good job for the department if I'm ticking all the boxes. I'm doing a good job for [the team manager] if I'm keeping in all the timescales and that she can go through supervision and I've done everything she's asked of me." (Interview data)

Evidencing meeting these standards was most often an administrative exercise, meaning that a boundary for membership of the new service was having good administrative skills. Such a requirement for membership was intended to create a uniform service, where social workers provided the same standard of service no matter who they were so that the organisational identity could be verified and legitimised by Ofsted. This expectation was explained by one team manager:

> TEAM MANAGER: "I don't think everybody should be exactly the same because we're individual people and this dream that we're going to have 18 safeguarding units that perform exactly the same, the social workers are all exactly the same – it's ridiculous. We're all people and you bring yourself with you to work, don't you?"
>
> INTERVIEWER: "Is that the dream?"
>
> TEAM MANAGER: "Consistent service – everything's exactly the same standard by every single person. That's what they want." (Interview data)

The desire to avoid being shamed by Ofsted distracted those involved in the creation and maintenance of the new service away from the experience of the social workers and eclipsed their protestations that the new system, argued to be based on reasonable and achievable standards, was impossible to achieve, as Faye stated:

> "all [the leaders and managers] are concerned about is the statistics really, I think, and they just think that everything should be done on every case and then that's not always realistic due to the workloads that we have, and I don't know to what extent that is taken into consideration? So, I think they're very black and white about it." (Interview data)

The institutional work of defining the boundaries for membership provided a clear message to the social workers that a failure to meet the basic requirements would be grounds for criticism, discipline and potential dismissal. This ensured that the social workers developed an understanding of the conditions for being shamed, thereby aligning their sense of shame for the new context. This ensured that the organisation's priorities were attended to by ensuring that they acted in a manner that avoiding being shamed.

Reconstructing the rule systems that provide status

While the social workers were keenly aware of the formal hierarchy within the Council – as explained by one team manager, "[social workers] are under a hierarchy and they feel it from above" (interview data) – they were also aware of the informal status hierarchy that operated within the new service. The cultural practices within the teams were such that there was significant oversight of the administration of social work and very little oversight of the direct work with service users. Team managers not only had to read the paperwork that the social workers produced, but had to sign it off, confirming that it was of an acceptable standard. Team managers observed very little direct contact between social workers and children and families, and what contact they did observe was usually a situation in which they had a formal role, such as chairing a meeting. The result was that social workers did not think that the managers knew about their direct practice, as Lucy explained: "she [team manager] doesn't get to see the day-to-day practice and the engagement with children or anything like that. But what she does get to see is the written side of things" (interview data).

Earning status within the teams and the possibility of promotion, a stated aim of many of the social workers, was therefore directly associated with the production of timely outputs to satisfy the administrative constituency of the organisation. These boundaries for action were then embedded within a system of monitoring the 'performance' of each team through administrative devices known as the 'duty tracker' and the 'report card'. The 'duty tracker' was a spreadsheet of all the cases in the team linked to the allocated social worker, with information on whether they were within timescales or not. This information then went together with a range of other information from the computer system to make up the 'report card', as a team manager explained:

> She said there is a team 'report card' which details all the
> information about the team. This is circulated to all team
> managers in [the Council] so everyone can see everyone
> else's. The teams are ranked according to the data. It is
> colour-coded, with things highlighted in red meaning it
> was considered bad, and has a commentary from the area
> manager on the team performance. (Fieldnotes)

The effect of the duty tracker and the report card was to provide
a public league table that embedded the boundaries for pride and
shame in each team. The social workers and team managers did not
want to be at the bottom of the table, nor did they want a negative
judgement from the senior managers, and nor did they want to present
a negative image of their team to other teams. Equally, while not seen
to be as important, the social workers and team managers could take
some pride in being high on the table. The social workers and team
managers' sense of shame and pride was therefore heightened within
this context, making the timescales and paperwork a significant feature
of the work, if not one of the most important aspects of the work, as
demonstrated by Linda's experience:

> She said that she had had an email from [the team manager]
> which had told her to do less visits to families and do more
> paperwork. She said she was upset getting it. I asked her
> what the upset was about. She said "I work really hard
> at home to get my paperwork done".… She then shows
> me the 'duty tracker', a printout of all the cases in the
> team, which has the statistics of how in date or out of
> date assessments are in relation to the timescale. Her name
> was against two children's names, which said 'overdue'.
> (Fieldnotes)

In this case, the duty tracker was used as a mechanism for surveillance so
that Linda's behaviour could be regulated to remain within acceptable
limits. Deciding to spend her time with the families at the expense
of her paperwork received a message of disapproval from the team
manager, reducing her perceived status, which could only be regained
by refocusing her efforts on the paperwork. Such surveillance devices
not only enabled effective policing of the boundaries of pride and
shame in the teams, but also ensured that the social workers' sense of
shame and pride was aligned to these boundaries. The social workers
now knew the consequences for transgression and so could change

their own behaviour, embedding the neoliberal re-conceptualisation of public services and professionalism based on individualism, competition and auditability into the system, as demonstrated by Amy when she described how it felt to be close to having something out of timescale:

> AMY: "For me, I can go, 'Yeah, I've got five assessments to do. Phew, I've got two days. It's not gonna happen'. Done. And whilst making that decision, I'm like, 'Fuck it. I don't care', and then after I'm thinking, 'Shit, shit, shit, they're seeing that, shit. Right, [Amy's] name's coming up'. Do you see what I mean?"
>
> INTERVIEWER: "Who's they?"
>
> AMY: "[The leader], [the area manager], other teams, because of the bloody report card you get, which I think are absolutely ridiculous, that every other team manager sees. And, actually, that makes it dangerous because teams become competitive with one another, as opposed to supporting one another. So, when you go on training, 'Oh, you're from [team manager's] team. Oh, you've got such and such percent'. It makes people – because we are a well-performing team – it makes people, because of the duty tracker and the impact it has.... So, it brings, like, a professional jealousy to it, and it stops teams from helping one another." (Interview data)

The new child and family social work service

It was envisaged that the practices of the social workers within the new service, and the moral and cultural foundations of those practices, would be founded within the therapeutic tradition of social work. Indeed, this was argued to be vital to improving the services to children and young people. The national and local social, political and functional pressures in place at the time, however, created a systemic force that posed an ever-present threat to the Council's identity. As this threat came from the political and administrative constituencies, the logic of bureaucracy and markets dominated the thinking of what was needed to avoid organisational shaming. This refashioned the organisation's identity in the eyes of the leaders, who then sought to reconstruct the activities of social workers accordingly, thereby aligning the organisation along neoliberal principles. These changes were felt by the social workers as an anxiety that one could be shamed for not meeting the new standard, as Carol suggested:

"I do think they don't care. You've got to do it. That's it. You know the practice, you know the policy, you've got to do it. But what do they care about why you can't do it? I don't know. And that's not a helpful feeling, really, because that doesn't do anything to reduce your anxiety." (Interview data)

Rather than draw on the therapeutic representation of practice as intended, the new service had been coerced into drawing on the policing and administration traditions of the social work profession. The result was that the new service was able to verify the Council's identity, being graded as 'good' in their next Ofsted inspection. The Director could now claim to the local councillors that "The Local Authority has developed effective services to investigate and manage both referrals and established concerns about harm to individual children and young people" (Council meeting minutes). The senior managers and team managers praised their staff for achieving this result, as I observed in a team meeting:

The team manager then asks for a review of the year and opens this by praising everyone for their hard work over this period and stated that Ofsted had been in and they got a Good rating, which was one of the best Ofsted have given all year. (Fieldnotes)

As a consequence, the social workers could feel proud of the result:

INTERVIEWER: "How did it make you feel that [the Council] got good in the Ofsted inspection?"
LUCY: "Proud. I did feel proud." (Interview data)

Summary

All organisations can be conceived as having a shared set of central and enduring attributes that distinguish it from other organisations, that is, an organisational identity. Given the competing representations of social work services, with different perspectives on what is praiseworthy and shameful behaviour, organisational leaders can be seen to navigate such complex social terrain to create, maintain and disrupt the organisational identity. Pride and shame can, therefore, be placed at the heart of such institutional processes. Leaders can feel proud as a result of their organisation fulfilling its identity claims and ashamed by it failing to meet its identity standards. Equally, leaders can feel proud of their organisation being praised and accepted, and shamed as a result of criticism and rejection. Leaders, therefore, seek to manage the organisational identity so that organisational actors present identity-congruent messages to others and that feedback verifies the organisational self-definition.

The boundaries for praiseworthy and shameful organisational action, however, are open to negotiation and manipulation. Those with greater power, status and influence are able to exaggerate certain concerns, evoke shame in certain practices and gain support for their definition of the problem and their solutions to resolve them. With changing systemic pressures, old organisational arrangements and practices can be cast as failing to deliver on the organisation's identity claims, placing the organisation, and those within it, at risk of being shamed and rejected. It is possible that some organisational leaders may resist such systemic pressures, or even episodic shaming. Given the consequences, however, it is often that efforts will be made to create organisational emotional safety by reconstructing the arrangements, relationships and structures within the organisation. This creates an 'appropriate' organisation for the time, context and location, with new boundaries for feeling pride and shame.

Note

[1.] Section 20 of the Children Act 1989 provides the local authority with the power to accommodate a child in their area with the consent of all those who hold parental responsibility.

FIVE

Pride and shame in the creation of the 'appropriate' professional

Chapter Four outlined the role that pride and shame played in the creation of 'appropriate' child and family social work services. In the government's attempt at control, the emotions of organisational leaders and managers are regulated by evoking, eclipsing and directing experiences of pride and shame so that delegitimised practices are disrupted and new, more legitimate, practices are created and maintained. Given the systemic boundaries for praiseworthy and shameful behaviour, along with mechanisms of policing these boundaries through inspection and public grading, leaders and managers engage in emotion work in attempts to avoid being shamed and attract praise. Consequently, attributes of the organisation, that is, components of its identity, are altered. The success or failure of a child and family social work service to meet its new objectives, however, lies in the day-to-day work of the social workers. What the social workers do and how they do it is, therefore, considered a legitimate target in organisational attempts at control.

This chapter extends the theory of pride and shame in professional practice by considering how pride, shame and other self-conscious emotions are strategically used to regulate the emotions of the social workers to alter not just what they do and how they do it, but also who they are. While this chapter draws on social representation theory (Moscovici, 1961, 1981, 2001), and specifically how social groups ascribe, promote and support meanings and standards for the group (Breakwell, 2001; Duveen, 2001), it further draws on identity theory (Burke and Stets, 2009), the major theory of identity in sociological social psychology, which provides an explanation for how individuals come to develop and attach meaning to who they are, what they do and what groups they belong to. While these theories provide a framework to understand the interaction between the shared ideas within the social group and the personal ideas about identity, the role of pride and shame in these processes has received limited theoretical and empirical attention.

This chapter, therefore, develops the idea of organisational control by conceptualising pride and shame as central to this process. Rather than control being achieved through the regulation of employee identity, as has been argued in organisational theory (eg Alvesson and Willmott, 2002), it is argued that it is through the regulation of employee emotions, and specifically through self-conscious emotions, that what people do, how they do it and how they define themselves can be shaped, influenced and manipulated. It details how organisationally sanctioned discourses are used to refashion and reconstruct the social representation of a social worker within an organisation, providing locally specific systemic boundaries for praiseworthy and shameful behaviour for employees. Such a process not only defines what is considered 'appropriate' within the organisation, but also legitimises attempts to shame and humiliate those who transgress such boundaries. Thus, organisational leaders and managers can be seen to regulate the emotions of the social workers directly, and therefore their identities indirectly, so that they perform the 'appropriate' tasks, in the 'appropriate' way, at the 'appropriate' time.

After considering the theory of regulating the emotions of social workers, this chapter returns to the case example used in Chapter Four to take a deeper look at these processes in practice. How pride and shame were used to refashion the social work role by setting administration as the primary task, policing as the primary function and individual responsibility and compliance as primary expectations is discussed. Furthermore, the role that pride and shame played in the construction of a moral, resilient and competent community of practitioners to define the characteristics of the social group is explicated. Together, these provided the boundaries that were used by organisational guardians to police and deter transgressions from the organisational representation of a social worker through shaming and humiliating practices. This case demonstrates how the wider neoliberal agenda became embedded within the organisational constructions of social work identity, which were then offered, imposed and enforced onto the social workers.

Part one: theorising pride and shame as mechanisms of organisational control

As Chapter Three outlined, a social worker can be considered as a socially constructed object, which groups of people attach ideas, values, beliefs and practices to. These representations of social work provide concepts for what a social worker is and does, or what a social worker should be and should do. As the self is reflexive, in that it can take itself as an object (Mead, 1934), a person can categorise themselves with established social representations, such as that of a social worker (Breakwell, 2001; Duveen, 2001). This process of self-categorisation is termed 'identification' within identity theory (Burke and Stets, 2009) and this identification creates a person's 'identities' (Stryker, 1980). Given the complex nature of social life, we not only develop identities that define us as unique individuals, creating 'person identities', but may also identify with particular societal roles, creating 'role identities', and particular social groups, creating 'social identities' (Burke and Stets, 2009). Once formed, an identity can be understood as the set of meanings that one holds for each of these 'internal positional designation[s]' (Stryker, 1980: 60). Such identity meanings are not static, however, and are subject to revision, reformation and reparation (Burke and Stets, 2009), which Alvesson and Willmott (2002) define as identity work.

The social representation of a social worker can be considered both a role identity, in that it provides a set of meanings to guide how to carry out the task of doing social work (McCall and Simmons, 1978), and a social identity, in that it provides a set of characteristics that are considered necessary to undertake social work (Hogg and Abrams, 1988). While Thoits and Virshup (1997) argue that the boundary between the two is a fuzzy one as in real-world situations, people are usually in a role and a social group at the same time, an analytic distinction can be made between the two depending upon the context and the primary focus of the person in that context. The expectation of what a social worker should do (role identity), for example, can be distinguished from what characteristics social workers are expected to possess (social identity).

While there may be core elements to what it means to be a social worker generally, there may be differences and deviations between representations held by different communities and constituencies (Deaux and Philogène, 2001). Indeed, how professional representations of social work, such as social administrator, social police, therapist, activist or practical helper, are interpreted and enacted varies according to the community context in which they embed (Moscovici, 1981, 2001). Different contexts, such as geographical, institutional or organisational location, may construct locally specific ideas of social work that draw on the range of professional representations available to create an organisational representation that deviates from such ideal-types.

A child and family social worker enters the profession with general values, meanings and ideals of what a social worker is. Such general views, however, are expanded, adapted and changed through social engagement within their employing organisation. How a social worker constructs their professional identity is, therefore, an ongoing process of accepting and rejecting the meanings and expectations that are provided to them about their work, their role and themselves (Miller, 2010). Given the pressures placed on organisations, Alvesson and Willmott (2002) argue that leaders, managers and others act more or less strategically to introduce, reproduce and legitimise the presence or absence of particular discourses with the intention of attempting to influence, manipulate and control these individual identity processes. As Deetz (1995: 87) stated: 'the modern business of management is often managing the "insides" – the hopes, fears, and aspirations – of workers, rather than their behaviors directly'. Such attempts to gain organisational control have been termed 'identity regulation' by Alvesson and Willmott (2002: 625), who define it as 'the more or less intentional effects of social practices upon processes of identity construction and reconstruction'. While there has been empirical attention to the processes and practices of identity regulation (eg Alvesson and Willmott, 2002; Sveningsson and Alvesson, 2003; Kärreman and Alvesson, 2004; Roberts, 2005; Fuller et al, 2006; Kreiner et al, 2006; Sluss and Ashforth, 2007; Nair, 2010; Pezé, 2013), and there has been empirical and theoretical attention to the processes of identity development within social work (eg Bogo et al, 1993; Miehls and Moffatt, 2000; Miller, 2010; Leigh, 2013), the role of pride and shame in these processes has largely been neglected.

As leaders and managers seek to fulfil organisationally defined objectives, shared ideas develop about what employees should do, how they should do it and what kind of characteristics are required to undertake such tasks. By creating and embedding a particular interpretive framework that supports such a conceptualisation, a new set of systemic boundaries for what is shameful and praiseworthy behaviour is established. Organisations can, therefore, be seen to purposively reshape and reconstruct the meanings associated with an organisational representation of a social worker. Particular discourses are then promoted and embedded to evoke pride in the individual for compliance, and shame for failing to comply, with such a representation. Furthermore, discourses can be used to eclipse any concomitant negative self-conscious emotions, such as feeling ashamed, guilty or embarrassed, as a result of undertaking organisationally prescribed and accepted practices, along with diverting them from organisationally unacceptable activity. Given the new conceptualisation for employees, it becomes legitimate to shame and humiliate any transgressions in order to police the boundaries and deter others from deviation. By learning what is praised and shamed within the context, employees adapt their sense of pride and shame accordingly, enabling them to know how to avoid being shamed and rejected, and create the conditions for experiencing pride and acceptance.

By attempting to regulate the self-conscious emotions of the social workers, what they do and how they do it can be shaped, influenced and manipulated, providing greater control over professional practice. As Alvesson and Willmott (2002) note, the presence and promotion of particular discourses does not necessarily mean that they will influence the identity work of employees to become embedded into their identity standards. Evoking pride and shame, however, which are inherently related to a person's idea of who they are and their relationships with others, provides a greater chance of embedding organisationally sanctioned meanings and expectations into their identity construction. Regulating the emotional experiences of pride and shame not only prompts the emotion work of employees to alter what they do, therefore, but can also be seen as the mechanism by which established identity meanings are disrupted and new, 'appropriate', meanings, standards and expectations for a good employee in an organisation are created and maintained, as illustrated in the following case example.

Part two: a case example

Chapter Four detailed the pressures and expectations placed upon the Council's child and family social work service and outlined how pride and shame were strategically used to disrupt established organisational arrangements and construct and embed new ideals, objectives and practices into the service. This chapter now considers how the leaders and managers of the service sought to achieve their new aims by strategically using pride and shame to refashion the organisational representation of a social worker. Indeed, this case example shows how pride and shame were used to reshape the social work role in order to set administration as the primary task, policing as the primary function and personal responsibility and compliance as primary expectations. Furthermore, it shows how pride and shame were purposively used to construct a community, or an 'in-group', of practitioners undertaking moral work, with praiseworthy characteristics for such work being resilient and competent. Deviation from these tasks and attributes is shown to be policed through shame and humiliation, embedding the new organisational representation of a social worker into the service.

Refashioning the organisational representation of the social work role

A role identity consists of the central features, meanings and expectations of the role (McCall and Simmons, 1978; Stryker, 1980). In order to influence the social workers so that they performed the role as required and expected within the Council, the leaders and managers evoked pride and shame in particular ways so as to make the boundaries for the role clear, eclipsed other emotions that may motivate social workers to practise contrary to expectations and diverted their attention towards performing the role as required. Such emotion regulation prompted the emotion work of the social workers to seek to feel proud and avoid or change the experience of shame and humiliation. Such emotion work affected their practice, aligning it with organisationally acceptable standards.

Using pride and shame to set administration as the primary task

Given the changes in the new service, as outlined in Chapter Four, we can understand a primary expectation of a child and family social worker within this new service as undertaking administration, as demonstrated by the following experience:

> [Jane] tells me that I should have been here last week when they got an email from [the leader], she said they were "not happy" and "it went down like a lead balloon". [Jane] and [Jemma] explained that [the leader] had sent an email to all teams in [the area] that their statistics were not good and it stated that 'this will be addressed'. [Jemma] said that it was not the statistics, but the tone of the email that upset them. She said [Christine] has been coming in at 5.30am, [Monica] and [Julie] have been working late, and everyone else has been taking work home. (Fieldnotes)

All of the teams in that area of the service had been shamed for their poor 'performance', and in efforts to avoid future shaming, the social workers sought to improve their statistics, which primarily involved administrative methods, such as recording on the computer when visits had been conducted, writing up notes, minutes or assessments, or completing the paperwork required to close cases. The shaming of poor administrative practice was further embedded into the service during formal meetings, such as child protection conferences or looked-after child reviews, which were chaired by independent reviewing officers (IROs). Indeed, the IRO-as-shamer was made explicit by Knowles and Sharpe (2012: 1381), who stated that 'the point needs to be made clear to all concerned: the IRO is someone who not only carries a big stick but also has direct access to those whose sticks are even bigger'. Within the Council, the IRO service had co-opted Ofsted's rating system to grade cases, which social workers experienced as the IRO grading them personally, as Helen explained:

> "if you get an 'inadequate', you feel like you've done a crap job then…. If it was an 'inadequate', they always email it to your manager, with you cc'd into it, to say this is why I scored an 'inadequate'. But even if you just get, if you put your heart and soul into a report, and you get a 'good', sometimes I just think, 'I want an outstanding, because I've done everything that you've asked me to do. What do I need to do?'." (Interview data)

Cases could be graded as 'inadequate' for such things as one visit being one day out of timescale or a report not being provided to the family or the IRO within timescale. To avoid being shamed, the social workers organised their time to ensure that they did not miss a deadline, embedding administration as a primary task of the social work role, as Lucy explained:

> "I'd like to spend a lot more time actually doing social work rather than typing minutes, typing reports, writing case notes, especially the direct work with the children. I think we all find that the hardest to fit in because for everything, there's a deadline or you're graded or you're marked on it, so we all prioritise trying to meet 'stat' [statutory] visit requirements or requirements for your conference report to be in on time. So, we all focus on those tasks because we're told that's what we need to do. So, sometimes, the things that get missed are the real social work bits of working with the children in school. We don't have indicators or targets to do that." (Interview data)

Despite the desire to undertake 'real' social work by directly interacting with children and families, the consequence of evoking shame and pride in administrative tasks embedded a clear expectation for what it means to be a social worker within the Council.

Using pride and shame to set social policing as the primary function

The death of Peter Connelly was used by politicians and the media to evoke shame in child and family social work services (Jones, 2014; Warner, 2015; Shoesmith, 2016), thereby serving to promote a discourse of dangerousness that placed pressure on social work services to demonstrate competence and legitimacy. While the social workers within the service were already investigating and assessing the level of risk to a child's safety, the expectation that social workers protected children from harm was heightened through the discourse of dangerousness and risk to children (Parton, 2011). This was achieved by making specific stories of child deaths, mainly Peter Connelly, and generalised stories of harm to children, mainly through reference to serious case reviews, readily available. These served as a reminder to the social workers of the link between being shamed and children being harmed, and being praised and protecting children from harm. The organisational leaders and managers further defined this interpretive framework by embedding the removal of children as a symbol of protection. Social workers and team managers were praised for removing children into state care, as Paula, a social worker, explained:

> "the other night, when we did the removal, the next morning, we all had an email [from the team manager] saying 'Thank you so much for what you did last night. It can't have been easy. It's a very difficult thing to do, but well done, and thank you. These children are safe now'."
> (Interview data)

In contrast, social workers and team managers could be shamed for failing to remove children considered at risk of harm, as one team manager explained:

> "I'd been to the adoption panel on a particular case and the lay member of the adoption panel had said 'Why didn't you remove these children earlier?'.... That comment then made all its way to [the strategic lead] and she then told the [area] manager, who said to me 'Why aren't you

removing more children? I'm hearing that you're not removing enough', and I said, I was absolutely stunned by this and I said 'We remove more than any other team'....
I made a very robust defence of this and I put together an email and said 'These are the children we've removed in the last 12 months, loads of them, there's no other team in the [west] of the county that's removed anything like that number of children, you ought to know this stuff so please take account of this and don't ask ...', I don't think I said don't ask me silly questions, but I defended myself very strongly." (Interview data)

The practical effect of evoking pride and shame in such a manner was to provide a regulatory force to the social workers' developing sense of a professional self (Alvesson and Willmott, 2002). The tenets of policing were, therefore, promoted and embedded as standards for the role. Hence, the team manager sought to defend her actions against the accusation that she was not performing her role appropriately by arguing that she had removed a sufficient number of children rather than attacking the notion that removing children was morally right and defending the decision of not having removed others. Good investigation skills, for example, were valorised, as shown by Donna's explanation that "the reason [the team manager] wanted me as a social worker is because I'm so good and so investigative" (interview data), and state intervention was approved of, as Jane explained:

"you're going into a child protection conference or you're going into a court arena, and I know it's heart-wrenching, you know, but we have to do these things, and at the end of the day, if you get what you need, you know, you're doing a good job, like if you put an ICO [Interim Care Order] in place or a child on a child protection or a child's had to be removed and placed in foster care, you know at the end of the day the child's safe and that, that for me, that's a good job." (Interview data)

The social work-as-social policing representation conceptualises practitioners as seeking to protect a victim from danger, or, more usually, protect a potential victim from potential danger. While the social workers all stated that they valued and sought to develop positive relationships with the people they worked with, given this conceptualisation of practice, developing a positive relationship was not always seen as possible or even desirable. Indeed, where the danger was perceived to be the parent, an interpretive framework was provided that normalised the absence of a working relationship, as demonstrated by the following observation in the team room: '[Amy] tells [the team manager] she is going to see the mother with the alcohol problem later and [the team manager] says "we're not paid to be liked but we like each other so it's ok"' (fieldnotes).

Furthermore, social workers could be praised for receiving hostility from family members, as shown by Donna's comment that "[the area manager] said I must be a good social worker because [the father] wants to change his social worker" (interview data). Such discursive practices evoked pride in this form of practice and eclipsed and diverted from the more difficult emotional experiences that resulted from such practice. For the uninitiated, however, such messages came as a shock, as demonstrated by Melanie:

> "I remember being a student and a social worker said to me, 'You know, you're not, you're not doing your job until you get a complaint'. They actually said 'You're not doing your job properly until you get a complaint!'." (Interview data)

The message that the social workers received was that a successful identity performance of the social work role required a neutral or negative relationship with a parent or carer. Developing a positive relationship was, therefore, grounds to question one's role and competence, as Mandy explained: "I suppose I always worry when [parents] do like me because I'm not really meant to be liked and then I start thinking 'Am I doing this right?'" (interview data). The result was a conceptualisation of practice as transactional, rather than relational, interested in discrete transactions for the purposes of collecting information or ensuring that agreed obligations had been met as laid out in some procedure or plan.

Using pride and shame to set responsibility as a primary expectation

Individual responsibility as a principle was embedded within the new service. Work was divided and allocated to specific individuals and an expectation was provided that they accepted responsibility for this work. Through mechanisms of monitoring and surveillance, brought about by administrative processes, individuals could be held to account if the work was not completed within the expected time frame or to the expected standard. This expectation was embedded into the social work role at the birth of the new service, with a team manager explaining the effect of the reorganisation:

> "within a week of the new system, we were being flooded, we were getting 100 referrals a month ... it was absolutely terrible, you know, people had caseloads of, [Donna] was on 88, 89, [Christine] was on 80, it was a nightmare, it was an absolute nightmare." (Interview data)

While the team manager perceived this situation to be a result of the new system, and consequently felt no responsibility for the dire situation in which she found herself and her team, the senior management considered it a failure by the team manager and the social workers to perform their roles appropriately, as the team manager described:

> "I just thought, 'whoa', there's a different perception here, I'm saying we're struggling because our new system isn't working, you're saying we're struggling because we're struggling and the inclination is that maybe this team manager isn't on top of it, isn't equal to the task. And it was never said explicitly but you can read between the lines, you've got to be very sensitive in this job ... and when [the leader] said once, 'I lose sleep over the [west] team', I thought I need to watch my step." (Interview data)

Despite the origins of the problems being systemic, the responsibility for these problems was individualised by threats of being labelled as incompetent. With a reputation for shaming social workers, the leader could then be used symbolically by the team manager to promote and embed the expectation for responsibility in the social workers, as demonstrated by Donna's conversation with her team manager about outstanding work:

> [Donna] said she has so many cases she can't possibly get everything done and so it is the "organisation's fault not mine". She said she felt "panic" because "what about all the other things I've not done" and so she felt on her own. [The team manager] said that if [the leader] were here, she would ask very direct questions about what has been done and she would "erupt like a volcano" if things weren't done. (Fieldnotes)

In a parallel process to the team manager's experience, Donna defended herself against the accusation of incompetence by placing the responsibility for not having done her work onto the organisation, an attempt at emotion work to protect herself from being shamed. Donna stated in her diary entry of this conversation, however, that the team manager's response left her feeling rejected, humiliated, embarrassed and angry. Conversely, those who were perceived to take responsibility for their work were praised, as Sally described:

> "[Team manager] is always telling me that I'm one of the most organised, and that, you know, she thinks I keep my work up to date. We recently had the performance conversation and when we were discussing, you know, how I was performing, she said that, she felt that I was achieving and excelling in some areas, so that obviously was pleasing to hear." (Interview data)

Evoking pride and shame in such a fashion successfully embedded the expectation that social workers 'take' responsibility for 'their' work, as Julie explained:

> "The expectation is that you work your arse off into the ground and you do it until your work's up to date, and if your work isn't up to date, then sod you. But nine to five, it's not possible, or eight thirty to five, it isn't physically possible to do what's asked of us." (Interview data)

Using pride and shame to set compliance as a primary expectation

Scott (2014) argues that institutions are constituted through regulative and constitutive rules that provide a 'right' way of doing things. Consequently, a corollary to being individually responsible for any allocated work was the presumption that employees comply with such rules and expectations. Through messages in the media and the promotion of particular discourses within the organisation, employees knew that failures to adhere to professional and organisational rules and expectations provided legitimate grounds for episodic shaming. This provided a constant threat of being shamed that heightened the self-consciousness of employees when performing their role within the organisation, as explained to me by a team manager:

> "I feel it strongly there's a big change and it's, and I say, 'accountability' because that's how I feel, you know, if I do something wrong, they'd sack me. I don't feel secure in this job anymore ... I don't know if it's come from the government or what, but this pressure that you're always being looked at to be sure you're doing it good enough, you know." (Interview data)

Such heightened self-consciousness and anxiety about being shamed served to embed the expectation for compliance with organisational rules, prescriptions and directions. In attempts to avoid being shamed and gain social acceptance, employees complied, as exemplified by one team manager's experience:

> "I certainly thought I'm under the microscope and I need to be seen to be complying with what's going on. So, when new ideas come up ... I just thought, 'Yeah, we need to try everything here, you want a "duty tracker"? Bring it on, let's have a look at it'. I don't think it was going to make any difference really, but I wasn't going to say that. So, yeah, I looked at new ideas and I welcomed them and I think, sometimes, when you're seen to do that, that pleases people who are making the decisions." (Interview data)

Having understood the expectation for compliance, the team manager then relays this message to the social workers, as demonstrated in a supervision session where a team manager tells Donna, "we have to do what those from on up high tell us" (fieldnotes). Such messages embedded compliance as a standard into the organisational representation of a social worker, which was then reflected back by the social workers themselves, as Melanie explained:

> "it's coming from the top down, you know, what's expected, what isn't expected, what's acceptable and what isn't. It's process-driven, isn't it? You know, you have supervision, you talk it through, 'Ok, what's next? Right, we've got to do this'." (Interview data)

Compliance with organisational rules and expectations then attracted praise from the leaders and managers of the service, providing further emotional and social incentives to reproduce the new cultural practices of the social work role. The evoking of pride in organisationally approved ways of being, however, further heightened the self-consciousness of the employees, who knew that praise and acceptance was conditional upon a successful role performance by complying with organisational expectations, as Mandy's experience showed:

> "[The team manager] thinks that I'm a good duty social worker, yeah, she does, she thinks, she tells me that she thinks highly of me and values me, which is good ... that's pressure, yeah, that's pressure that I put on myself. If my manager is telling me that she thinks I'm a good duty social worker, then I must be doing something and I've got to continue what I'm doing to be a good duty social worker, but I don't know what I'm doing because there isn't one single element I could pull out and think, yeah, that's why she thinks you know, that I'm a good duty social worker." (Interview data)

Refashioning the characteristics of the organisational representation

A social identity consists of the characteristics that members of the group possess while those outside of the group do not (Tajfel, 1981). Such shared personal characteristics provide individuals with a sense of belonging, which Tajfel (1981) argues provides an important source of pride and self-esteem. In seeking to influence the processes of identity formation, maintenance and transformation within the social group, organisational leaders and managers can provide particular interpretive frameworks that define the standards for the social identity (Alvesson and Willmott, 2002). Constructing and embedding particular community characteristics redefines the systemic boundaries for shameful and praiseworthy behaviour. These boundaries were created and maintained through regulating experiences of pride and shame in relation to the required characteristics, which were a community with a moral cause, with emotional resilience and with competence.

Constructing a moral community

Dwyer (2010: 181) argues that children should be ascribed the highest moral status in society because they are perceived to be 'more innocent, more beautiful, more full of potential, and on the whole simply more empathy provoking and awesome than adults'. A number of scholars have highlighted the evolving trend within Western cultures to recognise and seek to protect children's rights, with tragedies relating to children today provoking highly emotional responses (Payne, 2005; Ferguson, 2011; Parton, 2014; Warner, 2015). Indeed, Warner (2015: 7, emphasis in original) argues that 'children are *the* moral referent' in Western society, providing a moral settlement that considers prioritising children's needs as the 'right' thing to do. Certainly, in all matters relating to the Children Act 1989, the primary piece of legislation governing the work of child and family social workers in the UK, the court is compelled to consider the child's welfare as the paramount consideration (section 1(1)). Consistent with these changes, Featherstone et al (2014) and Parton (2014) argue that the dominant discourses within the field of child and family social work have become child-centric. Indeed, the new service was constructed within this context, with those within the teams considering themselves to belong to a community of practitioners with a moral foundation, as a team manager explained:

> "we're here doing good in a moral sense and that pleases me and I'm glad I'm part of it. Yeah, definitely, I've never lost sight of that, I'm not burnt out, I believe in what we do, the way we do it can drive you to distraction but I believe in what we're doing definitely." (Interview data)

Larson (1977) argued that professionals receive the equivalent social status as their clients. As social workers have historically been considered to work with those in poverty (Woodroofe, 1962), given the widespread negative attitudes towards those in poverty, some social workers have felt ashamed to tell others that they are social workers (Walker, 2011). By creating a moral community based on working with children, the principal client base of the social workers was refashioned away from people with low status towards the high status of children. This was explained to me by a team manager who stated that "social work doesn't only apply to the poor; it's a misconception" (interview data). As Warner (2015: 7) argues, 'the face of the child has the ultimate power to transcend boundaries between "us" and "them"', making the social work identity not only a morally important one, but also a socially acceptable one. By evoking pride in working with children, rather than those in poverty or the adults who pose a risk to children, the social workers could legitimately feel proud of who they were, as one team manager said: "I do actually feel proud to be a social worker" (interview data).

Such emotion regulation was demonstrated by the leader of the service, who would seek out good examples of work that was child-focused and would praise the social worker and occasionally send it around the service as a good example. This provided support for the belief that 'they' were there principally for the child and not the parents, carers or wider family. With knowledge that being child-focused received praise and acceptance within the group, social workers sought to consciously develop an 'acceptable' attitude, as Jane explained:

> "I try very hard to focus, as is my job, to focus on the children, and not just on what the parents are telling us. Because I think there is a danger, that working in child practice, that you can get, sort of, veered more towards the parents than you can, sometimes, towards the children. And I think I do subconsciously try to make an effort to not let a parent's views overtake the views of the children. And I think I'm quite conscious of that." (Interview data)

Given that social work can operate in morally ambiguous situations (McDonald, 2006), where the social workers have to navigate complex moral questions about the right course of action, they often experienced what Dahlqvist et al (2009) refer to as a troubled conscience. However, consciously invoking the moral supremacy of children constructed a vocabulary of motives (Mills, 1940) based on 'the child's best interests'. This served to resolve such complex moral questions, thereby alleviating their troubled conscience, as demonstrated by Paula's first experience of applying for an Interim Care Order (section 38 of the Children Act 1989) with the intention of removing the children from their mother:

> She said the solicitor is moving things too fast and she is not comfortable with it. She began to cry and reached for a tissue. She said she is not sure it is the right thing to do. During this conversation, [Faye] had come in and sat down next to [Paula] and she tried to comfort her by saying that you always question if you're doing the right thing even when you know it is in the best interests of the children. [Paula] said "Really?" and [Faye] said "You have to keep the best interests of the child at the centre". (Fieldnotes)

Faye was able to alleviate Paula's anxiety about doing the wrong thing while, at the same time, reinforcing the message that to be one of 'us' is to keep the child at the centre. Such consistent messages ensured that the social workers knew the conditions to be praised and aligned their sense of pride accordingly. For those who had done so successfully, it was both important and natural to remain 'child-focused'. Consequently, pictures that children had drawn for them were proudly displayed on the walls by their desks, as demonstrated by Jane: 'she said she "loved" the pictures from the children she works with and tapped a new one that was not up last time I was there' (fieldnotes).

For the newer members of the community, however, it took time to align their sense of pride to the systemic boundaries within the service through the conscious application of the interpretive framework. This was demonstrated by Paula's first experience of removing a child from their parents:

> PAULA: "I can remember that as we – there was [sic] three social worker cars, and we drove over the bridge, to head towards the address – and I can remember thinking, 'child snatcher'. Because we were all in convoy, one car after the other, I really felt like I was living up to that image of a child snatcher."
>
> INTERVIEWER: "What did it feel like when you thought that you were living up to this idea of being a child snatcher?"
>
> PAULA: "I felt an element of shame and, sort of, 'Well, what would my next-door neighbours think of me, if they knew I was doing this? And my friends, what would they think? You know, they're mums themselves and what would their perception of me be?'." (Interview data)

Being a newly qualified social worker, Paula's sense of shame and pride were not fully aligned to the systemic boundaries within the new service. She therefore felt ashamed about living up to the negative external image of social workers as child snatchers. The construction and application of the interpretive framework that prioritised children's safety above all other considerations, however, provided an internal image of social workers as undertaking morally important work. This served to regulate the emotions of social workers, and Paula was able to turn her shame into pride, as she went on to say: "although it wasn't easy to remove the children, it made me feel quite good, in knowing that, now, these children were going to be in a place of safety" (interview data).

Constructing a resilient community

The social workers reported emotional distress in having to hear stories, and see the effects, of abuse and neglect, as Carol described:

> "neglect, the abuse and listening to the trauma. And not just listening to the trauma, it's seeing the impact of the trauma. Witnessing it, I guess, about abuse. Witnessing the effects of abuse on a child and listening to adults talk about – it's not just children, is it, but parents can be victims and it's listening to their traumatic history as children themselves and what kind of life experiences they've had. And when you listen to that, that's not particularly very pleasant." (Interview data)

The leader told me that it takes a particular sort of person to be able to do safeguarding work and one area manager told me that she believed the social workers needed "emotional continence" (fieldnotes) to do the work effectively. Indeed, not being affected by difficult emotional situations was considered a necessary characteristic for child and family social workers. Failure to demonstrate such a characteristic provided legitimate grounds for episodic shaming by presenting the social worker as incapable, as demonstrated by Donna's experience of a conversation she had with her team manager:

> "Ever since this, 'it's been noted that you're struggling and you've lost your emotional resilience and you're not who you were and you're always down', and this, that and the other. And I find it quite offensive to be told that you've lost your emotional resilience.... I think what was a response to feeling really frustrated about a case and not being able to do anything for the kids [that] got '[Donna]'s weak and she's emotionally unstable'. I can't stop thinking about that comment and it will haunt her [the team manager] forever because it just makes me feel really small and depressed." (Interview data)

Such experiences served to provide not only Donna with the standards to be considered a legitimate community member, but also all those who heard about this experience. This embedded the characteristic of being 'resilient' to highly emotional situations as appropriate and necessary for the professional identity, as Carla's experience showed:

> [Carla] turns around on her chair to talk to [Amy] and says she has just been out on a duty case and spoken to a teenage girl who told her about the domestic abuse her father gives to her mother. She said this is the one child who has really touched her and it makes her feel sad. She said "I felt like crying but I had to remain professional". The girl had disclosed the father strangling the mother and hitting her since the girl was three years old. (Fieldnotes)

Despite feeling moved by the suffering of another, Carla demonstrates the intentional emotion work she undertook in her attempts not to feel upset and, therefore, to remain 'professional'. While she acknowledged that she did actually feel upset, however, the retelling of the story presented a picture of herself as someone who was able to endure emotional hardship and still demonstrate the appropriate characteristics to claim community membership. Indeed, being upset was seen within the teams as a weakness, as Monica showed when she told me, "I'm not usually a weak person, please let me just tell you this, it is very rare that I get upset" (interview data). The organisational message that to be one of 'us', one must be able to survive adversity constructed the conditions for worthiness, as Paula explained:

> "when you come into this, there you are, you're a newly qualified social worker, and, okay, you get some guidance, but it is very much about learning about yourself as you go along, and that does help you to just … help you to feel that you're better in – not better in your practice – but that you're a worthy individual, of being a social worker, and I imagine that when you get some really difficult stuff to cope with, that that's really essential, that you feel that you're good enough to be there." (Interview data)

Having aligned her sense of shame and pride to the organisational boundaries for being shamed and praised, Paula only felt an authentic member of the group, a sense of worthiness or of being good enough for the group if she thought that she could face and cope with difficult emotional situations. This message that emotional resilience was necessary permeated the conceptualisation of what it means to be a social worker within the service. Becoming distressed and upset was, therefore, grounds to question a social worker's suitability to the work, as demonstrated at the end of a working day as I walked with a group of social workers from the building and was party to their conversation:

They then start talking about [Faye] and said that she came back from leave on Monday and sat at her desk and burst into tears while reading her emails.... [Linda] said she has told [Faye] to get out of safeguarding and they discussed that she may be better off in adoption as she is good with children. (Fieldnotes)

While Faye was seen to *be* a social worker (social identity) *doing* social work (role identity), her claim to *be* one of 'us' was in question as she was not perceived to possess sufficient emotional resilience.

Constructing a competent community

The leader was considered within the teams to be a very competent person, as were the team managers, and competence was considered a necessary characteristic for the social workers, as one team manager demonstrated:

"there's no case that comes through here, that is, even the most complicated, messy, bizarre, horrible ones, there's no case that we can't deal with. We know what to do, I know what to do, the social workers know what to do." (Interview data)

Being competent meant being able to work on your own, as Faye stated, "[area managers] sort of think you should be able to manage your caseload and just get on with it" (interview data), while Paula commented, "if you took a worker with you to every single appointment, you'd never get anything done" (interview data). A competent social worker was, therefore, someone who knew what to do and how to do it, and usually one that they could do this without much support. To be able to achieve this, an expectation was embedded that social workers were authoritative, as shown by Paula:

"I feel that I can ask virtually any question without feeling embarrassed or worried about saying something. I can be very direct. I speak as I find, to some degree, obviously, with restrictions, because of the profession. But, you know, I can be very open with people. And I can say, 'Okay, so why are you doing that?', and 'Why are you in a relationship with this person?', you know, sort of, sometimes difficult questions that we might, generally, as people, find difficult to ask." (Interview data)

Being a 'social worker' enabled Paula to ask, with pride and confidence, questions that would not be asked, or would be embarrassing to ask, as a 'person', that is, not a social worker. Pride was evoked in such authoritative practice through stories told within the teams, making it seem an important and natural thing for a social worker to do, as demonstrated by one team manager's story to me in front of others in the team: '[the team manager] tells me she had to lock the building when the mother was here to prevent her from running away with her baby. [The team manager] said she took the baby off her there and then' (fieldnotes).

While the display of authoritative practice was sometimes resisted, not displaying such in-group characteristics were grounds for self-doubt about whether one measures up sufficiently to the in-group, as Monica demonstrated: "I do worry that I'm not authoritative enough, but then the families make the changes that they need to, so I suppose you don't have to speak to people like shit in order to get your message across" (interview data).

Policing and deterring deviation from the organisational representation

The primary mechanism for organisational reproduction was through the work of the social workers. By seeking to regulate the emotions of the social workers, the organisation could influence how the social workers conceptualised themselves and their work to be congruent with managerially defined objectives. Using discursive strategies to construct an organisational representation of a social worker, and using episodic shaming and praising to support and embed this representation in the organisation, the social workers learnt the conditions for being shamed or praised, aligning their sense of shame and pride to these conditions. In attempts to avoid being shamed, and seek to be recognised and accepted, the social workers operated within the confines of these boundaries, thereby becoming 'Council social workers'. Lawrence and Suddaby (2006: 229), however, state that 'relatively few institutions have such powerful reproductive mechanisms that no ongoing maintenance is necessary'. They argue that policing established arrangements and deterring change are necessary tactics used by institutional guardians to maintain an organisation. Given that the primary mechanism for organisational reproduction was what the social workers did, this meant policing the boundaries of what they did and deterring deviation from such requirements.

Policing the social workers can be marked out as distinct from regulating the emotions of the social workers on the basis of it being a much more humiliating experience. As humiliation is generally a much more public experience, the purposive attempts to humiliate social workers who were perceived to have transgressed 'acceptable' boundaries of behaviour and character served the dual purpose of reinforcing the organisational representation of what it means to be a social worker, not only to the target of humiliating efforts, but to all those who witness such humiliation. Donna recalled such an experience in a team meeting, where the health and safety officer had attended to talk the team through the Council's occupational stress risk assessment form. While the specifics of Donna's experience were not typical, the process was:

> [Donna] explained to the health and safety officer that "I had 88 cases and I worked 9 til midnight every day".… She said at that time an email went round with a list of all the social workers' names on with the number of cases they had.… She said her name was on the top of the list highlighted in red and that she was told that she had too many cases because of her time management so she had to photocopy her diary and account for every minute of her time. She spoke with a slightly raised voice and spoke quickly and forcefully. She said "it was the most humiliating experience of my professional life" and said "it feels like being punched". She said she acquired 300 hours' toil [time off in lieu] during this time, and one day when she was not at work, "I was called and someone told me to cancel my 300 hours toil because how dare I have that amount of toil with 88 cases", implying that it was her fault she had too many cases, therefore she was not entitled to the toil she had accrued. She stopped talking, stared into space, bit her top lip and her eyes welled up. No one asked her about how she was feeling or attempted to comfort her. She said "I was put on medication". (Fieldnotes)

Donna's claim was that the effects of the reorganisation had meant that she could not live up to the standards that had been set for social workers within the Council. This, however, was turned on its head by the managers, who placed the responsibility for the failure on Donna. Donna's identity as a responsible and competent social worker was, therefore, publicly denounced in such a manner as to be a painful humiliating experience, constructing a new spoiled identity (Goffman, 1963) that was not one of 'us', as Donna explained in her interview: "your name goes round on a blacklist round [the Council] and that's how you're introduced to team managers, as the person in [the Council] with the most cases" (interview data).

Donna's options to validate her professional identity were either to leave and work for a different local authority, or to comply with the expectations and standards within the Council in an attempt to earn sufficient social acceptance and status. The systemic shame within the Council had been asserted and Donna's sense of shame aligned accordingly. Not only was the effect of this humiliation observed by others at the time, but the retelling of the story further embedded the message that transgressions from managerially defined standards will be policed and deterred through humiliation.

Humiliating experiences were reported by social workers to involve being shouted at in front of others in their team room, being placed on disciplinary procedures and being restricted to what work they could undertake. Christine, who had a high caseload and was behind on her administration, was threatened with disciplinary procedures and sent to occupational health for a cognitive functioning test to identify if the reason for her inability to adhere to the standards was due to some personal impairment. She said this experience had made her feel "worthless" and "hurt", and told me she felt "humiliated". To prove her worth to the senior managers, Christine worked long hours, which took a significant personal toll, with her saying that she could not eat or sleep and that she dropped a dress size in a week. All those in the team were aware of this humiliating experience, ensuring that everyone knew that the boundaries for action would be policed through shame and humiliation, and that all employees produced work to an 'acceptable' standard, in a 'professional' manner.

The organisational representation of a social worker

Bourdieu and Wacquant (1992) argue that identities describe the relationship between the actor and the field in which that actor operates. By evoking pride, shame and humiliation, organisational leaders and managers could define the relationship between the social workers and the field in which they operated, constructing and embedding an organisationally approved set of characteristics and standards for the social workers within the Council. For some, such as Christine, this new imposed identity was seen as in conflict to her idea of what it means to be a social worker, as she explained:

> "my ideal social worker is [Alice] on the [other] team. She is a social worker's social worker. She's somebody who would put aside paperwork and spend time, at her own detriment, really … she's old-style social work, where she'll go in and she'll spend the time, and she'll have a phone, and she's on-call to the family, if needed, you know, 24/7. And, you know, we've moved away from that. We can't be like that anymore." (Interview data)

Christine highlights not only that the new arrangements prevented social workers from practising in a manner consistent with her idea of social work, but also that *they* were no longer able to *be* the type of social worker that would practice that type of social work. For others, however, the new imposed identity had highly defined boundaries that could easily be articulated, creating a Weberian ideal-type (Weber, 1978), as one team manager outlined:

> INTERVIEWER: "If you were to describe the ideal type of social worker that you think the organisation wants, what would that look like?"
>
> TEAM MANAGER: "Somebody who ticks all the boxes and meets all the timescales, makes all the deadlines, satisfies the performance indicators, can work 60 hours a week and not get ill or complain they're tired, somebody who isn't affected by their emotions and their dealings with human nature. I think somebody robotic really … if you appear to meet all your timescales and you appear to be fully compliant and doing everything quietly, without complaint, not causing any problems anywhere, then you're pretty much what's required." (Interview data)

Self-conscious emotions can be considered to be at the heart of the institutional processes of emotion regulation, which influenced the identity construction and reformation of the social workers, and created and maintained the desired institutional arrangements, actions and practices. The implication of this new context was that anyone who failed to develop an adequate professional identity in the eyes of the organisation would not be able to do what was required in a manner that was considered appropriate or professional.

Summary

The general theory of pride and shame in social work can be seen to operate within organisations, where pride and shame can be strategically and purposively used in attempts to gain organisational control over employees. Systemic boundaries for praiseworthy and shameful behaviour are set by organisational objectives and expectations. These construct the shared understandings of what it means to be a social worker within the organisation, which provide legitimacy for particular discursive practices that evoke pride in particular ways of thinking, feeling and acting, while evoking shame and humiliation in others. By evoking pride in the organisational representation of a social worker, and shame in failing to live up to such a standard, the sanctioned identity meanings penetrate the identity constructions, revisions and reformations of the social workers exposed to such emotion regulation. This regulation of emotions serves to provide clear messages to employees about what is acceptable and appropriate when practising social work within the organisation. In attempts to avoid being shamed and attract praise, social workers revise, adapt and align their sense of pride and shame accordingly, creating an emotional and social force that regulates what the social workers do, how they do it and what characteristics they use while doing it, and providing the conditions for the creation of an 'appropriate' professional for the context. While these processes may manifest themselves in many different guises, the case example provided demonstrates these in detail for one organisation. While much of these meanings and expectations associated with this organisational representation of a social worker were created to ensure that the Council performed its statutory functions, pride and shame can be seen as at the heart of the processes in which the organisation achieved this aim.

SIX

Theorising social workers' experiences of self-conscious emotions

While we can conceive of the processes that construct and define an organisational representation of a social worker, along with the processes that regulate and police adherence to it, as outlined in Chapter Five, the social workers could not simply be considered as organisational automatons. Even when they engaged in habitualised routines and practices that conformed to all of the meanings and expectations of the organisational representation, they did so with awareness and purpose (see Battilana and D'Aunno, 2009). Furthermore, while a social worker could actively identify with the organisational representation, they could also actively resist it (see Breakwell, 2001; Duveen, 2001), with a range of possibilities in between (see Oliver, 1991). Further still, one social worker could actively identify with it in one context while actively resisting it in another. While emotions and identities have surfaced in the theory and research on social work decision-making (eg Platt, 2005; Taylor and White, 2006; Keddell, 2014, 2017; Platt and Turney, 2014; Saltiel, 2016), the role of self-conscious emotions has not (Gibson, 2016). Furthermore, while there is some literature on social workers' responses to pressures to conform to organisational expectations (eg Wastell et al, 2010; Carey and Foster, 2011; Leigh, 2017), the role of self-conscious emotions in these processes has not been well developed. Indeed, reviewing the literature on social work decision-making in child and family social work, Shlonsky (2015: 154) states that:

> there has been insufficient empirical attention paid to how decisions are made, the nature and extent of influence of individual biases and preferences, and the way in which context influences decisions at various points in the continuum of child welfare services.

This chapter provides a conceptual framework to understand the processes, relevant to self-conscious emotions, through which social workers come to acquiesce or resist organisational attempts at control. It explicates the individual experiences of self-conscious emotions in relation to such institutional processes. This framework is then illustrated with empirical data within Chapters Seven and Eight to demonstrate and detail this framework within the case example. The foundation of this framework is, of course, the experience of self-conscious emotions. As Chapter Two outlined, rather than an emotion being an entity that somehow exists in the mind that can be 'triggered' by events, they were argued to be social concepts, constructed with biological, psychological, social and cultural components and processes by a social group to create a category of experience that can labelled as a specific emotion (Barrett, 2006a; Burkitt, 2014), or, as Barrett et al (2014: 448) put it, they emerge out of 'an ongoing, continually modified constructive process that makes sensory inputs meaningful'. Understanding an experience of pride and shame, therefore, requires an understanding of how people make sense of their experience in the moment. This, of course, includes not only the experience of the internal processes of the person that contribute to their feelings, but also the experience of the external processes intended to regulate their emotions. Drawing on the literature on concepts and categories, Barrett et al (2014) use the idea of situated conceptualisations, introduced in Chapter Two, to analyse the overall experience. This chapter develops this idea by synthesising it with Emirbayer and Mische's (1998) analysis of human agency to outline how social workers come to experience pride, shame and other self-conscious emotions, and how these emotional experiences influence what social workers do and how they do it. These intentions and actions can be seen in relation to organisational attempts to shape, influence and manipulate the individual practice of social work.

This chapter, first, outlines the research on compliance and resistance in social work practice before developing and extending these ideas through the analysis of pride and shame in professional practice. This chapter, therefore, continues by synthesising the idea of situated conceptualisations with human agency to consider the most relevant components in experiencing self-conscious emotions in practice. These components relate to: the level of conflict between how social workers see themselves and their role, and how the organisation conceptualises their role and identities; the level of empathy for the people they are working with; and the level of emotional safety that they experience in the situation. Given a social worker's situated conceptualisation, rather than feel as expected vis-a-vis the organisational representation, they may feel a range of self-conscious emotions. Drawing on Oliver's

(1991) analysis of strategic responses within organisations to wider institutional processes, how the social workers perform professional practice in the context of organisational attempts at control, and the strategies that social workers employ to manage the organisational pressures, expectations and demands, are outlined. While some social workers can actively identify with the organisational representation in the moment, motivating them to enact its meanings and expectations, some reluctantly identify with it as a defensive strategy to avoid being shamed and humiliated, motivating them to comply despite reservation. However, some social workers, in some contexts, resist the organisational representation, feeling unable to comply, and, therefore, seek to compromise what they are expected to do, conceal their acts of resistance or influence the source of organisational attempts at control. This chapter outlines this framework, serving as the theoretical part of the argument, which is then outlined in the following chapters that serve to illustrate these processes.

Compliance and resistance in social work

The issue of compliance with policy aims and initiatives has a long history in organisational theory. Indeed, while Weber (1978) argued that bureaucracies provided the benefit of a set of rules that facilitated efficiency and fairness, they also provided a highly ordered and rigid system that limited individual freedom, creating what he referred to as the 'iron cage'. Yet, while compliance was considered at the heart of the iron cage, Lipsky's (1980) classic book on front-line practice in public service organisations identified the need for practitioners to exercise discretion in implementing bureaucratic rules, procedures and policies. While this facilitated flexibility in the face of complex real-life situations, on the one hand, it enabled variation in practice methods and outcomes, on the other. Such a situation was desirable while those who financed and operated the welfare state believed public servants to be public-spirited altruists as such discretion was considered beneficial to the equitable and efficient process of implementing policy. Le Grand (1997) argues, however, that this view changed within such communities to view public servants as self-interested actors that required greater levels of control over their day-to-day activities and decision-making processes. Indeed, Evans and Harris (2004) argued that professional discretion should be seen as neither 'good' nor 'bad' as it can be a means to positively or abusively use delegated power. Chapter Three outlined a range of policy changes that took place in relation to child and family social work in England in line with such thinking. The changes in institutional structures (see Power, 1997; McLaughlin, 2007; Parton, 2014), the implementation of new information technology (IT) systems and performance management mechanisms, and the standardisation of procedures (see Wastell et al, 2010; White et al, 2010) all sought to reduce the need for discretion and create or force greater levels of compliance in social workers. Furthermore, while such arguments were made for the strengthening of the iron cage for social workers, there are others who argued that the social pressures stemming from politicians, the media and public opinion to conform to certain ways of practising produced more of a panoptic gaze (eg Howe, 1991; Power, 1997; Reed, 1999). Arguably, however, the new 'compliance structures, knowledge systems and surveillance technologies' (Reed, 1999: 17) that have sought to push social work practice towards compliance with external expectations are a result of a merging of the cage and the gaze (see Exworthy, 2015).

Resistance, meanwhile, has long been identified as a component of organisational life, with Oliver's (1991) seminal paper theorising such forms of resistance on an organisational level, and others, such as Ackroyd and Thompson (1999), arguing that employee 'misbehaviour' is relatively widespread. Within the field of social work, Satyamurti (1981) identified subtle forms of resistance in social work practice within the newly formed social service departments, which had introduced new forms of management and bureaucracy. Furthermore, while Wastell et al's (2010) ethnographic study of social workers in England identified conformity in the practice of the social workers to the new imposed mechanisms designed to create compliance, they also identified a range of behaviours that sought to resist such new attempts to control practice (see also Pithouse et al, 2009; Broadhurst et al, 2010b). Carey and Foster's (2011) qualitative study of 14 social workers supported such findings, arguing that small-scale acts of resistance, subterfuge, deception and sabotage were commonplace, yet often hidden, within the unpredictable, demanding, highly regulated and under-resourced profession of social work within England. Also, Leigh's (2017) ethnographic study further identified forms of resistance in English social work, with practitioners seeking to disguise their resistance in attempts to avoid negative organisational consequences. Compliance and resistance are, therefore, long-standing issues in professional practice.

Within such literature, the role that self-conscious emotions have played has been highlighted. Indeed, Carey and Foster's (2011: 585) study identified the pride that some social workers felt as a consequence of "'creative'" and "rewarding" acts of sedition that "duped management"', while Leigh (2017) identified a range of self-presentation strategies used by social workers to avoid being shamed by organisational guardians. Such ideas, however, place the experience of the emotions of pride and shame as products of practice, rather than central to practice. This has, therefore, resulted in disagreement about what, and the reasons why, social workers comply with or resist organisational expectations. Carey and Foster (2011), for example, argue that social workers resist expectations for the benefit of those they are working with. Leigh (2017), meanwhile, argues that resistance is used to cut corners in order to be seen to be meeting expectations, which can be to the detriment of those they work with. Placing pride and shame at the centre of the analysis of practice enables such competing ideas to be unified. Indeed, deviance, as Carey and Foster (2011) refer to it, or recalcitrance, as Leigh (2017) refers to it, may be driven by personal motives, beliefs and identities but all of these ultimately relate to how practitioners feel in any given situation. The literature on compliance and resistance can, therefore, be extended and deepened by considering the process through which social workers come to experience pride and shame and how this process drives practice decisions. Up to this point, this book has considered the processes that have constructed a set of standards and expectations, as well as the processes through which compliance with such standards is encouraged, facilitated or coerced. How social workers come to comply with, or resist, such expectations, however, can now be considered.

Pride and shame in social workers' situated conceptualisations

Chapter Two detailed how personal experiences of self-conscious emotions can be considered to be constructed from the range of biological, physiological, psychological, social and cultural processes that play out in a social interaction. Where a person's bodily sensations, thoughts and actions in the moment, that is, their situated complex (Burkitt, 2014), correspond sufficiently to their understanding of specific emotion concepts, they will report feeling such an emotion, that is, their situated conceptualisation (Barrett, 2006a). An experience of an emotion is, therefore, an enactment of the emotion concept through an embodied experience of a range of processes, embedded within the social situation and cultural context.

The process through which a person experiences a self-conscious emotion incorporates all situational information that holds personal relevance and meaning. Sensory information is, first, related to their store of conceptual and experiential knowledge to categorise the agents, objects, setting, behaviours, events, properties, relations and bodily states in the present (Emirbayer and Mische, 1998; Barsalou, 2009). These situational meanings are then used to imagine alternative possibilities and draw conclusions that go beyond the information given (Emirbayer and Mische, 1998; Barrett et al, 2014). Finally, these *past* and *future* orientations are contextualised within the *present* moment to conceptualise the situation and decide how to act (Emirbayer and Mische, 1998). Thus, novel situated conceptualisations are constructed in the present, which are informed by the past and imagined future (Barsalou, 2009).

The organisational attempts to regulate the social workers' emotions to facilitate conformity influence the social workers' overall experience. By seeking to evoke, eclipse and divert experiences of pride, shame and other self-conscious emotions in social workers as they engage with the rules, regulations, procedures, agendas and relationships within the organisation, leaders and managers can intervene in practice at a much deeper level. Rather than the managerial discourses being the only source of pressure on the social workers' conceptualisation of their role and social group, however, they can be seen as one component of a range of processes by which social workers create meaning in the moment. In some situations and contexts, social workers may identify with the organisational representation of a social worker (see Reicher, 2004) and feel proud of what they are doing, whereas in others, they may dis-identify with it (see Pratt, 1998) and feel ashamed, along with a wide range of other emotional experiences in between.

The experience of self-conscious emotions in child and family social work, particularly in the context of pressures to conform to organisational expectations and demands, is the result of three important processes that contribute to social workers' situated conceptualisations. The first is the level of conflict between the person's identity meanings and those within the organisational representation; the second is the level of empathy that the social worker feels for the family they were working with; and the third is the level of emotional safety that they feel in the situation. While these three components can be considered distinct components of a social worker's situated conceptualisation for the purposes of analysis, they are interdependent and interrelated, and contribute to their overall unified emotional experience in the moment by influencing their situated conceptualisation. As Chapter Two outlined, it is this unified experience that can be either classified as pride, shame or other established emotion categories, or described in other terms.

The level of conflict between identity meanings and the organisational representation

Within identity theory (Burke and Stets, 2009), an identity is a set of meanings associated with the person as a unique individual (such as being a moral person), the societal roles that they perform (such as being a mother) or the characteristics of the group that they belong to (such as being British). An identity is considered to become activated when situational meanings are perceived to be relevant to specific identity meanings (Stryker, 1980; Carter, 2013). Being at work, for example, will activate the person's employee identity. Once activated, the identity provides the means to make behavioural choices and decisions (Burke and Stets, 2009). Of course, each situation holds a range of different meanings, activating multiple identities in the same situation. A social worker may have their identity as a woman, a moral person, a social worker and an employee all activated at the same time. With multiple identities activated, there are many possibilities for how these identities interact with one another, influencing how one thinks, acts and feels. For example, there may be conflicts between what a person believes they should do as a moral person and what they believe they should do as an employee. Furthermore, there are many possibilities for how these identities interact with other people. For example, a person acting as a social worker in the moment may interact with a parent very differently to how they might if they met them in a different role or social situation. One's representation of the self in the moment, therefore, stems from a process of relating the situational meanings *back* to their store of identities (their self-concept), towards the imagined *future*, while addressing the *presenting* issue.

In becoming a social worker, people engage in identity work to form, maintain, strengthen and revise the meanings they hold for their identity as a social worker (Alvesson and Willmott, 2002). Many have considered the influences, forces and pressures in the process of professional socialisation, which results in the internalisation of the values, aims, goals and attitudes of the profession (eg Bogo et al, 1993; Miehls and Moffatt, 2000; Miller, 2010; Leigh, 2013; Wiles, 2013; Webb, 2017). This internalisation of shared understandings about what it means to be a social worker creates and shapes the meanings in a person's social worker identity, on the one hand, while providing a sense of connection and belonging with others who share that identity, on the other (Yuval-Davis, 2006). Social workers do not, therefore, engage with their organisation and concomitant managerial discourses as a blank slate, ready to accept cultural norms, values and expectations without question. Indeed, given the personal relevance and social location that such identity meanings provide, they can be resistant to change (Burke and Stets, 2009).

In some contexts, the organisational conception of social work, and the meanings and expectations provided for social workers, will be inconsistent with their already-established identity standard, that is, the set of meanings for that identity. This sets the scene for negatively valenced experiences of self-conscious emotions. Social workers may perceive, or indeed 'feel', that to conform to the expectations would be a failure to live up to their own idea of what it means to be a social worker in that situation. This leaves social workers with the prospect of experiencing shame and/or guilt for conforming, or risking being shamed or humiliated by organisational guardians for rebelling. In other contexts, however, there will be no conflict between how a social worker perceives their professional identity and the organisational representation of a social worker. This sets the scene for pride as the social workers can adhere to their own identity standards while undertaking tasks that verify their identity through praise and acceptance.

The level of empathy for the people they work with

For the classical pragmatic philosophers,[1] empathy was considered to be an internal emotional experience resulting from taking the perspective of another. Indeed, Dewey argued that empathy required one 'to put ourselves in the place of others, to see things from the standpoint of their purposes and values' (Dewey and Tufts, 1909: 334). From such a perspective, empathy is an active imaginative process. One's capacity for empathy can, therefore, be considered to be both temporal and contingent upon a range of situational factors that may help or hinder an individual's imaginative engagement with another's social world. Having time and space to proactively consider how another person may be experiencing a specific situation may help a person to empathise. Alternatively, being engaged in a difficult task or rushing to finish a piece of work for a deadline can focus one's attention on these tasks and reduce both the attentive and imaginative capacity that an individual needs for empathising with another. Furthermore, particular discourses may facilitate or impede a person's empathic capacity for someone else.

Leith and Baumeister's (1998) study indicated that feeling shame can refocus one's attention onto the self, reducing their capacity for empathy. Tangney and Tracy (2012), meanwhile, argue that experiencing pride as a result of focusing on one's self rather than one's behaviour can also lead to a reduction in one's capacity for empathy. Accepting that the context affects social workers' attentive and imaginative capacity, the ability of a social worker to empathise with children and their family members could be considered to vary depending on the context. This variability can be thought of as a continuum, with high empathy at one end and low empathy at the other (Baron-Cohen, 2011).[2] Feeling empathy for another and their situation influences a social worker's situated conceptualisation by altering what is considered relevant from their *past*, how they imagine the *future* and, therefore, how they understand the *present*.

The level of emotional safety in a situation

Shame avoidance has long been considered a strong motivation (see Goffman, 1963; Lewis, 1971; Tangney and Dearing, 2002), and knowing the conditions and consequences for being shamed inevitably leads social workers to attempt to avoid it. Of course, there are situations where social workers will feel more vulnerable to being shamed than in others, and there will be other contexts in which social workers feel more able to deviate from organisational prescriptions. While Edmondson (1999) uses the term 'psychological safety' to refer to a shared belief within a team that it is safe for members to speak out and take risks without being criticised, Marx (2001) uses the term 'a just culture' to refer to the belief within an organisation an employee will not be blamed for making honest mistakes or criticised for failures in the system beyond their control. Both concepts indicate that the threat of shame not only guides action to avoid shame, but also silences them in attempts to avoid criticism and shaming. Such ideas have strong parallels with Catherall's (2007) concept of emotional safety, described in Chapter Four. Again, we can conceive of emotional safety in an organisational context as the feeling of being protected from being shamed, both in the present and in the future. Conversely, feeling emotionally unsafe can be seen as a negative experience resulting from feeling vulnerable to being shamed and rejected. How emotionally safe a social worker feels influences the overall situated conceptualisation by altering what is considered relevant from their *past* to the current situation, how they imagine the *future* and, therefore, the perceived possibilities for action in the *present*.

Experiencing self-conscious emotions in practice

While a social worker will have many different considerations when practising, these three components provide the foundation for experiences of self-conscious emotions. A social worker may not explicitly ask how they can stay true to who they are and do a good job in the eyes of those evaluating their practice, yet these can be considered background processes in practice. Practitioners do not want to think that they are doing a bad job, and they do not want to think that other people think they are doing a bad job. A major component of organisational control is to regulate the emotions of employees so that these two considerations are aligned. This is complicated, however, by two elements.

The first is the personal conception of a social worker that an individual practitioner may hold. The meanings, expectations and characteristics that constitute such a conception may contrast with the organisational representation of a social worker. Such a conflict can lead to feeling embarrassed and/or ashamed of doing what they are asked to do, and proud of doing what the organisation seeks to prevent. A mechanism of organisational control is, therefore, to evoke pride in organisationally approved ways of practising while shaming and humiliating deviation from this. Furthermore, the threat of shame and humiliation seeks to eclipse any feelings of pride for organisationally perceived deviant actions, while the promise of praise and acceptance attempts to divert their actions towards practising in an organisationally 'appropriate' manner.

The second element is the level of empathy that the individual practitioner feels for the people they are working with. Greater levels of empathy can lead to a greater desire to resist organisational pressures and expectations if these are perceived to adversely affect them. Indeed, acting in a way that is perceived to harm or disadvantage another can evoke guilt in the practitioner or even shame for doing what they believe is wrong. Where this is the case, therefore, a mechanism of organisational control can be to seek to reduce the level of empathy that a social worker feels for the people they work with by eclipsing such experiences with the threat of shame and the promise of praise, while diverting their attention onto organisationally approved tasks. Keeping caseloads high, timescales tight and social workers self-conscious about being judged can, therefore, be seen as a way to regulate the emotions of the social workers so that they are more susceptible to organisational control. Indeed, the feeling of emotional safety, or how protected they feel from being shamed, is a significant contributing factor to the overall conceptualisation of the situation that influences what a social worker does and how they do it. It is the overall experience of all of these considerations that results in experiences of self-conscious emotions. While social workers may experience pride and shame in practice, providing a direct influence on their practice, the threat and promise of them ensures that they also influence practice indirectly.

A framework for understanding social workers' responses to organisational attempts at control

Organisations are constructed within a particular context that has specific shared understandings as to what is praiseworthy and shameful behaviour (see Chapter Three). Given this context, organisational leaders and managers seek to create and maintain a positive reputation of the organisation through the construction and reconstruction of the organisation's identity, activities and relationships (see Chapter Four). By seeking to regulate the emotions of the employees by evoking, eclipsing and directing their experiences of pride, shame and other self-conscious emotions according to organisational standards and expectations, social workers develop a sense of pride and shame relevant to their organisational context (see Chapter Five). With knowledge and experience of being praised, shamed and humiliated, social workers can assess the likelihood of feeling such emotions in every situation. Indeed, they can consider who they believe themselves to be in relation to who they believe they are expected to be; they can empathise with those they are working with to consider if their actions are helping or not; and they can consider how vulnerable to being shamed and humiliated they are, or will be in the future, given these considerations. Such situational meanings combine and interact in the moment to influence what social workers do and how they do it. In response to their situated conceptualisation, social workers engage in emotion work to feel, avoid or change in degree or quality the experience of pride, shame and other self-conscious emotions. Consequently, social workers can identify with some aspects of the organisational representation while resisting others, creating a complex mix of possible responses. Oliver's (1991) typology of strategic responses to institutional processes provides a useful foundation to theorise the behavioural responses of social workers to organisational attempts at control.

A practitioner may identify with the meanings and expectations of an organisational representation of a social worker by accepting the organisationally constructed and promoted interpretive framework. This provides minimal conflict between their concept of themselves as a social worker and the organisation's concept of them as employees, creating a sense of emotional safety and resulting in purposeful practice in the expected manner. Such action may attract praise and acceptance within the organisation, and evoke pride in the practitioner. There may be, however, conflicts between a social worker's identity meanings and the organisational representation, resulting in the meanings and expectations associated with the organisational representation not being accepted as their own. This provides a greater sense of vulnerability to being shamed and humiliated that can lead to action that prioritises shame avoidance while seeking to alleviate any subsequent feelings of shame and guilt so that they can continue to comply with expectations. There are, however, many situations in which either enacting or complying with the organisational representation are considered unworkable or unpalatable. Nevertheless, being a part of the organisation, being subject to the same systemic forces as everyone else and having knowledge of the conditions for being shamed and praised, social workers cannot simply ignore these pressures and demands. Instead, they are compelled to respond to them. As Jenkins (1996: 73) argued, 'identification is often a matter of imposition and resistance'. Social workers may, therefore, display a range of behaviours that demonstrate increasing levels of resistance, from more minor levels that compromise organisational expectations, to more active forms of resistance that attempt to conceal behaviours that would be unacceptable to organisational guardians, to a highly active form of resistance that seeks to influence organisational sources and processes in order to create an outcome that is more acceptable to the social worker. This view, provided in Figure 6.1, provides an analytical framework to understand the role of self-conscious emotions in social work practice.

Summary

Understanding social workers' experiences of self-conscious emotions requires an understanding of the relationship between the individual practitioner and the context in which they are practising. Given that this context is complex, involving the emotional and identity processes of the individual practitioner, their relationship and interactions with children and families, and their relationship and interactions with their organisation, individual experiences of self-conscious emotions are not straightforward. In any given moment, social workers are engaged in a

Figure 6.1: Conceptual framework for social workers' responses to organisational attempts at control

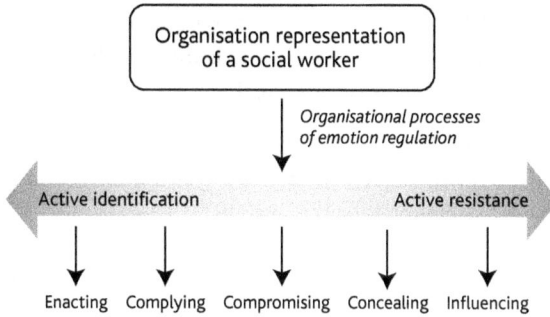

process of making sense of all of the information within the situation and deciding what to do. Who they believe themselves to be, who they believe they are required to be, what they believe to be right, what they have been asked to do and how effective or helpful they believe such actions to be all play a role in the resulting self-conscious emotional experience; however, so, too, does the threat of being shamed, humiliated and rejected, along with the promise of being praised and accepted. Navigating this complex practice environment brings challenges to practising with personal integrity, raises self-doubt and surfaces a troubled conscience.

The attempts to regulate the social workers' emotions prompts the emotion work of the practitioners, who seek to feel proud and avoid or change any feelings of shame, guilt, embarrassment or humiliation. Consequently, some responses can be considered as active identification with the organisational representation of a social worker, seeking to enact its meanings and expectations, and some responses can be seen as a more reluctant identification, simply seeking to comply with it. However, others compromise the expectations placed upon them to satisfy the minimum requirements and avoid being shamed, or disguise their resistance and seek to conceal any acts of resistance. Finally, some forms of resistance are more overt, seeking to influence pressures to bring them into line with personal ideals for practice. This framework, with the strategic responses to organisational attempts at control and the resulting self-conscious emotional experiences, is illustrated by the case example used within this book in Chapters Seven and Eight. First, the forms of identification are considered within the case example in Chapter Seven, followed by the forms of resistance in Chapter Eight.

Notes

1. James, Dewey and Mead often referred to sympathy rather than empathy. However, as the word 'empathy' was not introduced into the English language until 1909 (Greiner, 2015), it was not in use at the time of much of their writing. A review of their discussions can be considered to be closer to what we term today as empathy.

2. Baron-Cohen states that his theory of empathy is grounded in psychology essentialism, which is rejected here; however, his notion of an empathy continuum is a useful one for this analysis.

SEVEN

Forms of identification: a case example

This chapter follows on from Chapter Six to illustrate social workers' experiences of self-conscious emotions within child and family social work. This chapter will use the case example, used throughout this book, to demonstrate how these emotional experiences were constructed in relation to identifying with the organisational representation of a social worker within the Council, that is, the meanings, expectations and characteristics of an ideal form of practice. Identification can be seen as practising in line with the meanings and expectations associated with the organisational representation. By considering the details of how the forms of identification were manifested, the role that pride and shame played in these processes can be analysed. Indeed, those who enacted the organisational representation felt safe from being shamed and humiliated as a result of focusing on meeting the pressures, expectations and demands placed on them. The focus on the organisational needs reduced their capacity for empathy with the family, protecting them from any feelings of shame, guilt or embarrassment as a result of organisationally sanctioned actions. With minimal conflict between the meanings and expectations held within their own social worker identity standard and the externally imposed organisational representation, the social workers felt proud of what they were doing and could share this with others. Those who complied with the organisational representation, meanwhile, did not accept the meanings and expectations associated with it as their own. Indeed, there were greater conflicts between the social workers' identity meanings and the organisational representation, greater levels of empathy for the families, and a greater sense of vulnerability to being shamed. Consequently, social workers felt unsure as to what they should do but prioritised shame avoidance, while, at the same time, seeking to alleviate any subsequent feelings of shame and guilt. This chapter outlines these strategic responses to organisational processes of emotion regulation in attempts to establish control over practice and considers the experience of the parents as a result. Indeed, within the context of a dominant discourse of dangerousness and risk to children, practising in the 'appropriate' manner often resulted in shaming and humiliating experiences for the parents.

Enacting

A social worker could be considered to enact the organisational representation where they actively and willingly sought to practise in a manner consistent with its meanings and expectations. Such situations were founded in accepting the organisational interpretive framework for practice, 'responsibilising' parents, while seeking to create emotional safety, as detailed in the following.

Accepting the organisational interpretive framework

Given the pressures, expectations and demands placed upon the Council, leaders and managers had developed a way of interpreting these for their local context. Such interpretations shaped, guided and influenced how the organisation was reconfigured and the work of the social workers was refashioned. This new interpretive framework promoted and supported the reorganisation and was used to regulate the emotions of the social workers. Where a social worker accepted the organisational interpretive framework, the conditions were set for the enactment of the organisational representation of a social worker.

Despite the stated intentions of the leaders and managers of the Council, the discourses of dangerousness and risk to children (see Webb, 2006; Broadhurst et al, 2010a; Parton, 2011; Featherstone et al, 2014), and accountability and auditability (see Power, 1997; Munro, 2004; Horlick-Jones, 2005; Broadhurst et al, 2010b; Parton, 2014), were imposed on the new child and family social work service through the media, by politicians and by the inspectorate (see Chapter Four). Social work practice was, therefore, conceptualised as working for children, sometimes against their parents and carers, in order to reduce or remove the risk of harm to the child. Furthermore, practitioners were conceptualised as the producers of the evidence that the organisation needed to demonstrate compliance with governmental standards and expectations. The interpretive framework within the Council, therefore, centred on the use of administrative measures to perform a policing function. Being grounded within the wider dominant discourses, this not only served to protect the organisation from criticism, blame and shame for failing to keep children safe, but also served to construct the resulting practice as morally right, as indicated by one team manager's comment:

"I mean, my own personal view on both care and child protection conferences is that these are tools that we shouldn't be afraid to use if we have to.... I've come across social workers who have said 'I don't want to put these parents through the oppressive thing of a case conference' ... well, I don't think it is oppressive for parents actually, certainly not oppressive for children, I view these things as positive tools." (Interview data)

A positive view of professional intervention was provided, which sought to control behaviours perceived as risky or dangerous, evoking pride, and eclipsing feelings of shame or guilt, for the use of such tools. Enacting as a strategic response to the organisational pressures to conform was founded in the acceptance of this interpretation for practice. For example, in explaining the reasons for wilful adherence to organisational expectations, Lucy, a social worker in one of the teams, stated: "'it's procedure. It's what we do when we have an incident. It also sends a message." I ask "What message?" and she says "that it is serious so he won't do it again or he could lose his children'" (fieldnotes).

Being able to achieve behavioural change in the parents provided a foundation for pride as this could then be perceived to have been beneficial, on the whole, for the children, as described by one team manager:

"I do actually feel proud to be a social worker, I'm glad I'm a social worker.... I believe in what we do, I think we do make a difference, we're not perfect sometimes, we make things worse, but, yeah, I'm glad I'm a social worker." (Interview data)

Accepting the interpretive framework provided an important function in the emotion work of the social workers. While the task of removing children from their families evoked negative feelings, the application of the framework diverted such negative feelings, as demonstrated by a conversation within one of the team rooms:

[Amy], [Linda] and [Gill] are sitting at their desks discussing removing children as [Amy] is due to remove a child later that day with [Helen]. [Amy] says that it is not nice but the conversation moves quickly to talk about certain children they know who have thrived in foster care. [Linda] chips in that it is like Miracle Grow for flowers. (Fieldnotes)

Furthermore, such acceptance of the interpretive framework provided meaning to administrative tasks. For example, the social workers were routinely engaged in administrative work on a computer in the office. When asked, they generally stated that they spent about 70–90% of their time doing administrative activities, which was supported by my observations and is consistent with previous research (eg Baginsky et al, 2010; White et al, 2010). The interpretive framework ascribed meaning to such administrative work, however, as Carol explained:

> "Timing is such a right. You've got to have timely assessments. Children and families need to know where they stand. They need to know what is expected of them. They need to know in a timely way. Not just that, but if the family needs support and help, that needs to be put in in a timely manner, it's not delayed. That's the pressure. That's what you're doing it for. You try to get that service in or you're trying to get the risk management plans together because you know that the child's at risk and you should be doing that in a timely way." (Interview data)

This again influenced the emotion work of the social workers, who could then feel proud of such work. Amy, for example, recorded in a diary entry that she felt proud because she had 'completed 2 assessments and closed 2 cases'. Conversely, however, accepting the interpretive framework could influence the emotion work in the opposite direction and evoke shame as a consequence of not being able to adhere to expectations, as Julie described:

> She complained that she had to complete 4 reports for the meeting next Monday but she works part time and has meetings all booked up in the days she is in. She put her head in her hands and said "I don't care" and then said "That's not true, the problem is that I do care". She then said "I tell you what it makes me feel inadequate, like I can't be a good social worker", "I take pride in my reports being robust but it's not good enough" referring to the one she is writing. (Fieldnotes)

Accepting the organisational interpretive framework provided meaning to the social workers for what they did and how they did it, reducing any conflict between the standards they evaluated themselves against and the standards others evaluated them against. Social workers could, therefore, learn to feel proud of undertaking organisationally sanctioned activities that may not be praiseworthy from other perspectives, as Paula demonstrated:

> "I did my first child removal. And although that's not something that an everyday person would be proud of, I felt quite honoured to have experienced it, even though it's not pleasant. So, it almost sounds – well, it does sound wrong. I want to almost say that I enjoyed it, but I didn't enjoy it. I just enjoyed the experience." (Interview data)

Responsibilising parents

Like many cultures, the British sociocultural context provides an expectation that parents have a responsibility towards their children. Being able to provide for their children's basic nutritional and emotional needs is seen as core to the role of being a parent (eg Gadsden et al, 2016). As many have argued, however, it is easier to meet such needs with material and social resources (eg Wilkinson and Pickett, 2009; Featherstone et al, 2014; Morris et al, 2018), placing inequalities and poverty as significant barriers in meeting societal expectations. Indeed, Chapter Two outlined how experiences of shame go hand in hand with such issues as the inability to meet social conventions legitimises actions of disrespect and contempt from others, and internalises feelings of inadequacy and failure. Chapter Three then outlined how neoliberal ideas permeated the politics and management of social work practice (see Gray, 2005; Garrett, 2008), which refashioned the idea of personal responsibility. People are expected to engage in the market economy as autonomous and self-managing individuals, responsible not just for themselves, but also for their family, and not just for their financial, but also for their emotional, well-being (Larner, 2000; Cradock, 2007; Liebenberg et al, 2013). This reconceptualising of personal responsibility is referred to as 'responsibilisation', as help and support that were once considered as collective responsibilities and addressed through the Welfare State are transferred to citizens under the guise of providing greater personal freedom (see Kelly, 2001; Gray, 2005; Liebenberg et al, 2013). Individuals are, therefore, expected to use their personal agency to ensure that they, and their family, are financially secure irrespective of job opportunities, physically safe irrespective of the local situation and emotionally stable irrespective of social circumstances and family history.

Such a process has been considered in the context of public services (eg Clarke et al, 2007; Connell et al, 2009) and social work services in the UK (eg Gray, 2005; Garrett, 2008; Featherstone et al, 2014), and could be seen in simple terms in relation to the Council as being held responsible by the government, the Office for Standards in Education (Ofsted) and the media for their ability to keep children safe. The Council leaders and managers then held the social workers responsible for keeping the children safe. Failure to accept this responsibility, or to fulfil it, risked being shamed. Enacting the organisational representation of a social worker, therefore, involved accepting this responsibility, as demonstrated by Amy's comment that "If something happened to one of my children, I'd probably think, 'Yeah, you know, do one', to myself.... I would feel responsible, and I should feel responsible" (interview data).

Given the conceptualisation of the statutory social work role within the Council, fulfilling this responsibility was inherently tied to identifying the harmful actions of others towards children. Where there was no harm, or there was no person to protect the child from, there was no role for a statutory social worker and referrals were made to family support services. The social workers, however, not only sought to identify the harm that a child had suffered, but more often sought to predict the harm that a child may suffer, which involved interpreting the motivation for such behaviours. As White (2003) argues, social workers are often engaged in moral judgements and issues of blame and responsibility. If a parent was considered to have been responsible for any wrongdoing that contributed to harm, or potential harm, to a child, either through omission or commission, then they were held responsible and action needed to be taken to protect the child, as the following interaction demonstrates:

> [Amy] is talking to [Mandy] while sitting at their desks about the 'starved child' that [Amy] had written the court reports for the other day. She says they got an Interim Care Order and [Mandy] punches the air and says "get in". I ask her why she says that and she then says that she doesn't usually do that when they remove children but this was a particular case. [Amy] says that it was "intentional abuse" and [Mandy] says she didn't like the father, and [Amy] responds, saying "He's a tosser that's why". [Mandy] said that the child was

developmentally small for her age and that the parents must have done some damage to her future development. She said "That is reason I do my job", referring to removing the child from the abusive home. (Fieldnotes)

To Amy and Mandy, the father was clearly responsible for the harm that his daughter had suffered. Having accepted the responsibility for the safety of the child, they were motivated to do something to protect her. Blaming the father evoked anger, reducing their capacity for empathy towards him and the family. Being unhindered by feeling distress for the parents, removing the child did not trouble their conscience and they could enact the organisational expectations and live up to their own identity standards without conflict. It was, therefore, both legitimate and socially acceptable to express pleasure in being involved in removing the child from her family. While not all parents were blamed – indeed, some were considered not to be responsible for wrongdoing and such cases were closed or referred to other services – some social workers commented on the pervasive nature of the cultural trope of individual responsibility in more ambiguous situations, as Melanie demonstrated:

She said the mother was "failing to protect" her children and then that "We blame the mother, because that's what we do", recognising that the father was the person posing the risk but they expect the mother to protect the children. (Fieldnotes)

On the one hand, conceptualising the situation as a parent being responsible for harm to a child evoked anger and disgust in such actions and eclipsed any empathic engagement with the parents, while, on the other, it made the meanings and expectations held within the organisational representation seem reasonable and desirable. This process eased and embedded the neoliberal notion of individual responsibility into the organisational representation. The social workers who identified with it in any given situation could, therefore, enact this representation and feel proud of their work, as the following diary entry showed:

[Situation:] *Last night we were successful in securing an EPO* [Emergency Protection Order] *for Baby C and today he will be placed with carers and be safe.*

[Thinking:] *Relieved the court saw sense and granted EPO last night. Barrister was pompous and disrespectful. This made me annoyed and determined.*
[Bodily sensations:] *Tense all week. More relaxed today. Relieved Baby C does not have to go home as risk immense.*
[Categorised as:] *Pride. Valued. Anger.*
[Influence:] *Will be back on Monday! Getting through a week like this is a challenge but rekindles my determination to protect vulnerable children and those less fortunate.*

Creating emotional safety

By acquiescing to the organisational expectations and demands, the social workers could protect themselves from the possibility of being shamed or humiliated. Indeed, the social workers believed that they would be held responsible not just for the safety of the children in the present, but also for what happens in the future. Consequently, where a situation was considered to explicitly pose a risk to a child's safety, it was also considered to implicitly pose a risk to the social worker, as demonstrated by Donna:

> "I had a day where I was fairly upset about a case before I went away and I was genuinely concerned for the children's safety and I would have – because I always talk about the case, not once did I get given the time of day to ask me about why I was so worried. 'Don't worry. Don't worry about it. It will be fine.' What if it's not fine? It's on my head and I don't feel like anybody's got my back above me." (Interview data)

Strict adherence to the perceived organisational rules, policies and procedures, therefore, increased their sense of emotional safety as they could claim to be beyond blame under scrutiny. A typical situation, for example, was of a social worker prioritising the administrative component of the work at the expense of the relational component, as demonstrated in a session between Donna, a Child and Adolescent Mental Health Service (CAMHS) worker, and a mother:

> As they discuss issues, [Donna] spends most of the time making notes with her head down while the mother and the CAMHS worker talk about her son. The CAMHS worker and the mother laugh at points while [Donna] continues

making notes. [Donna] looks up from her notes and makes a suggestion about her visiting the boy soon with another worker and then puts her head back down to continue making notes while the mother and the CAMHS worker discuss it. When the meeting is over, I ask [Donna] about the notes and she says that if she doesn't do them, you get into the situation, like she had the other week, when [the team manager] accused her of not prioritising her minutes of meetings in front of the parents. (Fieldnotes)

While Donna justifies this practice as necessary to avoid being shamed, it could also be seen to be an active engagement in the process of intentionally selecting and performing particular patterns of behaviour, which enacted the meanings and expectations of the organisational representation. This situation also demonstrates, however, that the primary focus of the work was on the relationship with the organisation, where the greatest risk of being shamed lay. The dominant discourses that framed practice as working for children and preventing harm constructed the experience of parents as irrelevant, as a team manager explained:

> [the team manager] said workers become less sensitive as they progress in their careers but "we get measured on timescales not on not upsetting parents", and described the process as "bruising and horrible" for parents but that they have to go and speak to a head teacher, for example, which may upset a parent. (Fieldnotes)

The sanctions, supports and rewards within the organisation ensured that there was an explicit focus on the priorities as defined by the organisation, which, when adhered to, offered some protection to the social workers from being criticised and shamed. This feeling of protection was experienced as relief from the pressure of potentially being shamed for failing to adhere to expectations, as Melanie's diary entry showed:

> [Situation:] *Completing (typing up and sending to TM [team manager]) an assessment – sat in office.*
> [Thinking:] *I was determined to type and send my assessment to TM. It was overdue in terms of timescale data however I had done it some weeks before and not got around to typing it.*
> [Bodily Sensations:] *Relief.*

[Description:] *Accomplished.*
[Influence:] *After typing this I moved on to another outstanding assessment.*

The sense of emotional safety was not only experienced as a result of alleviating the threat of being shamed, however. Enacting the organisational representation created a stronger sense of emotional safety through praise and acceptance, which served to further support the perception that the organisational interpretive framework was naturally correct. External praising was, therefore, experienced as internal pride as the social workers could conceive of their actions as doing the right thing, as Melanie's diary entry demonstrated:

[Situation:] *I felt good when I was praised and valued for my practice.*
[Thinking:] *Felt accepted like I can do the job.*
[Bodily Sensations:] *Smiled. Warm feelings inside.*
[Categorised as:] *Acceptance. Pride. Embarrassment.*
[Influence:] *Felt confident, self-belief.*

Complying

In contrast to enacting, some social workers did not accept the meanings and expectations associated with the organisational representation as their own, but complied with them anyway. Such compliance stemmed from feeling unsure of what to do in the situation, but in the knowledge that they could be shamed and humiliated for failing to adhere to expectations, they did not see many options but to do as expected or instructed. Such action often resulted in feelings of shame and guilt for their actions, believing what they had done was not helpful, or was, in some cases, harmful, to the people they were working with. Given such feelings, the social workers engaged in emotion work to alleviate their feelings of shame and guilt.

Feeling unsure

Despite the expectation that the social workers should be competent and capable of working with any issue that is referred to them (see Chapter Five), the social workers often felt unsure of what to do, how to do it, what the procedure was, what to say, how to say it and if they had the knowledge and ability to do what they were being asked to do, with Lucy saying on one occasion, "I feel out of my depth with this case" (fieldnotes). Feeling unsure was a result of not knowing if there was potential harm to a child, what the responsibility of the parent was or what the utility of certain procedures would be. This feeling of being unsure, itself, resulted in self-doubt and self-criticism due to not being able to verify their identity as a social worker, as Monica demonstrated on the way back from a home visit: 'She said she doesn't know what to do and "I feel like a bad social worker", like "a shit social worker", if she doesn't know' (fieldnotes).

By accepting that one should live up to the ideal of competence, failing to do so laid the foundations for feeling shame. In seeking to live up to this ideal and avoid feeling shame, however, the social workers became more susceptible to the organisational attempts to regulate their emotions, as Carol demonstrated:

> "you retreat to your colleagues and your manager and say 'Things aren't going well here. Don't know what to do, really. I don't know whether I'm doing this right. Should I be doing a bit more of this? Should I be doing more of the other?'. And then it's like if you see it differently, it's like, 'Well, am I seeing it right? Am I actually seeing it right? Am I being too lenient or are people being risk-averse? Am I not getting it right?'." (Interview data)

The support that the team manager provided served to reinforce the 'appropriateness' of the organisational representation, regulating the emotions of the social workers so that they were able to comply, as Carol explained:

> "[the team manager] certifies that, actually, you're doing okay, you're going along the right lines. Sometimes, when you're frustrated about moving things on and you talk it through in supervision, you can see that the barriers are nothing to do with your practice and you realise that. Yeah, it's just confidence boosting, isn't it, and certifies that you're doing okay and doing what you should." (Interview data)

While the conflict between Carol's identity meanings and the meanings held within the organisational representation was resolved through the regulatory efforts of the team manager, there were many contexts in which the situation was not as simple, as Melanie demonstrated while explaining the impact of her work on one family:

> [Melanie] said that the father had been sacked from his position in the Scouts, was being investigated by his HR [human resources] department at his work and thinks his job is at risk, and the family are now arguing with each other. She said that the children are 16 and 17 and are hard to engage, and are difficult for the parents, too, yet they have put in place a child protection plan, which she said "the plan is destructive and ineffective. It's more damaging than supportive" as she said nothing is going to change and this plan has caused a lot of problems for the family. She said "it's just a tick-box exercise ... stat [statutory] visits ... we have to do it for accountability and show we have tried to engage them when it all goes tits up". She said "I don't know what to do" but she has discussed it with [the team manager], who has told her to continue with what she is doing. She described it as "uncomfortable". (Fieldnotes)

Melanie did not blame the parents and displayed empathy for their situation. Furthermore, the conflicts between her identity standard and the organisational representation created a troubled conscience that questioned the usefulness of the child protection procedures. Yet, while she felt unsure, she also felt that she has no choice but to comply and engage in emotion work to hide her 'uncomfortable' feelings.

Prioritising shame avoidance

While enacting was a result of regulation that embedded the organisational meanings and expectations for social work practice into the social workers' identity standards, thereby constructing experiences for pride, the threat of shame and humiliation enabled the organisation to impose its conceptualisation of what the social workers should be doing by forcing the social workers to comply by prioritising shame avoidance. By adhering to procedure, a sense of emotional safety was created by being seen to be doing the 'appropriate' thing, as a team manager's interaction with Faye demonstrated:

> [the team manager] then enters a conversation with [Faye] about a case and says that "I've decided" it needs to go to child protection conference but that she knows that this "won't effect change but we have to be seen to have tried something" and states that they are children and so they need to do something. (Fieldnotes)

With knowledge of the conditions for being shamed, the social workers routinely adhered to the expectations placed upon them, undertaking tasks that they neither understood nor agreed to, as Helen explained:

> "this week, for example, and it's just a tick-box exercise really, I'm getting information from the families to put on the system. I know it's done so that senior management know it's done. [The team manager] knows it's done. And I'm not actually doing any work with the family, as such. I'm just, kind of, checking everything's going okay … we kind of make judgements of families, but we don't actually spend enough time with them to understand why that may be a problem. Although we ask the question and we, kind of, go away don't we? And we leave them. 'Okay, so you've given us all this information, I'll type it up and then I won't see you for four weeks.'… It just doesn't quite feel right." (Interview data)

Compliance enabled the social workers to perform the administrative tasks that the organisation required for a positive inspection grading without fear of being shamed or humiliated. While the strategy of compliance satisfied the needs of the organisation, it was perceived to be an imposed constraint on the professionals, preventing them from performing social work as they understood it, as illustrated by a conversation I overheard in the team room:

> [Christine] turns to [Jane] and says "They've taken what God gave us: free will".… [Jane] says they are just "highly paid admin workers" and [Christine] says that what they are doing is not social work and "they've taken what was attractive to the job". (Fieldnotes)

While feeling unsure about the right course of action made the social workers more susceptible to emotion regulation, prioritising shame avoidance to create a sense of emotional safety became the main strategy in acts of compliance. This was illustrated by Melanie's experience:

> "I've really struggled with this case of removing a baby, I've just, I've really struggled with it [crying]. And I just, I question whether it's the right decision and then further discussions that I have with social workers about further

assessments, and they, they, they just predict that, they've already made their mind up that this family are not going to be successful, do you, now that's just disheartening that this child could potentially not go back to live with its biological family and I just, that just has, that just really challenges me 'cos I just don't think that's right, do you know what I mean? And I've been a part of that journey and that process and I've gone to court and been cross-examined, and it just made me question everything about my role." (Interview data)

While Melanie was unsure about how unsafe the situation was for the baby and whether she/he should be removed from her/his parents, Melanie still provided written statements as evidence to the court and was cross-examined for over three hours, arguing why the baby needed to be removed. An Interim Care Order was granted and the baby was placed in foster care. By engaging in compliance, Melanie was not only able to avoid being shamed, but was also praised by the senior social worker who attended court with her, by her team manager and by a newly qualified social worker who told her she was jealous of her giving evidence in court.

Feeling shame and guilt

While compliance provided a feeling of emotional safety, it also laid the foundations for feeling shame and guilt. By focusing on performing the tasks as set by the organisation, the attention of the social workers was not on the experience of the people they were working with. Consequently, the performance of such tasks could evoke feelings of guilt in the social workers for harming others when they reflected on their actions, as Jemma's diary entry showed:

> [Situation:] *Making mother cry in a meeting whilst discussing her father who has recently passed away – I was focused on him being a PPRC [person who poses a risk to children] and safeguarding children.*
> [Thinking:] *Insensitive to mother's situation and grief. Others probably thought I was insensitive too. Other professionals remained quiet.*
> [Bodily Sensations:] *I felt hot and tense, sweating, fidgety.*
> [Description:] *Felt guilty – not for what I said but how I said it. Lacked empathy.*

[Influence:] *I rushed into meeting, little preparation, due to other commitments. Came across to mother as very 'matter of fact' with little regard to her feelings. I must show more consideration for families' lived experiences in future.*

The social workers could, however, focus their attention on the impact of any required task on the people they were working with prior to undertaking the task. With the belief that there was no other option but to comply with organisational demands, the social workers could feel ashamed of undertaking tasks that they believed were immoral, as demonstrated by Linda's experience:

> They discussed the situation and [the team manager] began writing down the specifics of the working agreement. [Linda] asked if it could be written in less authoritarian language and [the team manager] said it could not because the mother has to agree with it otherwise they would remove the children. [Linda] said that she was not sure about all of the allegations that have been made about the family.... We left [the team manager]'s office and ... she said she feels she is battling against [the team manager] and the other professionals who have already made their minds up about this family.... She said she feels she has to take out the working agreement, which is worded in a way which is oppressive and so she is an "ally to oppression". (Fieldnotes)

As the social workers evaluated the difference between their values, ideals and beliefs for action as a social worker and that which they had performed as a result of complying with organisational pressures, demands and expectations, these feelings of shame and guilt could be an intense and distressing experience, as Amy described:

> "Makes you feel sick sometimes. Very stressful. When I went off sick, I just felt shit. I felt awful. It does make, it makes you feel really guilty. You feel guilt, and then you feel tired, and then you feel low, and then you just feel, I mean, I got to a point where I was just, like, 'I'm not, I'm not doing anything'.... Like, I got to a point where I didn't feel like me. I felt like I was, like, you know, just a shell, and my personality was elsewhere, because it does, it drains you, it sucks it out of you, when you can't do it properly." (Interview data)

By refashioning practice through administration, constraining what the social workers felt able to do, they were left with limited time to do any direct work with the children and families, leaving social workers with a belief that they were not making a difference. This constructed experiences of shame as the social workers felt responsible for not being able to effect change and improve the situation, as Faye explained:

> "I'm still sitting there crying, thinking, 'Well, actually, no, you're crap social worker' [*sic*].... I will say, 'Oh, oh, what change have I actually made out of hundreds of cases I've had?' ... and I can like think of two cases ... so to me, that's a really small percentage of good stuff that I set out to do. So, sometimes, I will have that conversation and still doubt myself because the majority of your cases aren't, that have nice outcomes, they're not positive, so then I think, 'Well, really, no, you haven't made change in many cases as you possibly could have'." (Interview data)

Rather than blame the constraints within the practice environment, or the parents and carers, as Faye's experience showed, some social workers blamed themselves, resulting in very personal feelings of inadequacy and incompetence. The social workers imagined that the managers would impose the organisational interpretive framework on such personal experiences in attempts to regulate their emotions so that they no longer felt shame and guilt from fulfilling organisationally sanctioned tasks. Such an imagined outcome simply left social workers feeling such emotions in isolation and considering what it takes to be a social worker, as Melanie demonstrated:

> "you're either in agreement with them [managers] or you're not, and can I show that I'm not in agreement with them? I don't feel like I can. I don't know, maybe I could? I don't know. I could speak to [the team manager] about this and say how I'm feeling and how it's challenged me, but she's going to reassure me that what, the decision that I've made has been right, she's not going to say it's wrong is she? Otherwise, we wouldn't have, we wouldn't be here now, she has to believe that the decision we're making is the right one, so if I was to open up to [the team manager] and talk about how upset I feel, I wouldn't get the response I needed ... maybe I just have to push it all to one side so

that I can continue to do the job rather than knowing that what I've done is wrong." (Interview data)

Alleviating feelings of shame and guilt

By engaging in purposeful emotion work, the social workers could alter how they felt to make the task of complying easier. One method of achieving this was to alter any unpleasant feelings by focusing on what they liked about the job, or at least reminding themselves that they liked the job, as demonstrated by Amy:

> "it's like a pressure cooker. You've got it from your families, pressure, 'Bleeding do this', because they're always in crisis and they need you. And then you've got management and your policies, and you're, like, rammed in between. And then you've got your own pressure that you put on yourself … you see shit all day. Just negative, negative, negative. And even when it gets to a positive, and you close a case, you still think, 'I bet that'll come back in', because you're constantly critical of yourself. And then you've got others being critical of yourself. So, it's, actually, you get very little positive. But then, at the same time, you love your, like, I love my job." (Interview data)

The relationships within the teams provided further opportunities to alleviate negative emotions by creating a space in which they felt free from the threat of being shamed, as Jemma stated, "the office is our safe place" (fieldnotes). With all of the social workers occupying a similar social location, subject to the same organisational pressures and demands, and having very similar work experiences, it was easier to empathise with each other, creating a sense of solidarity within the teams, as Donna explained:

> "We support each other. We're always there for each other. We've always got each other's backs and if somebody's down and crying, then there's always someone there with an arm round the shoulder. And I think we just talk cases. We don't suffer in silence." (Interview data)

The creation of a culture of acceptance, empathy and support within the teams served to minimise any feelings of shame and guilt as a result of complying with organisational expectations. This, however, developed an expectation within the teams that they would not criticise or blame each other, as Monica explained: "my intention is not to upset anybody, even on day-to-day running of the team, if I thought I'd offended anybody or excluded anybody, I'd be really upset if I thought that because that isn't how teams work" (interview data). This expectation was upheld even if it meant having to hide feelings if they believed that this would evoke shame or guilt in a colleague, as a conversation with Lucy and Donna demonstrated: '[Lucy] says some people's assessments in this team "I would be ashamed to put my name on" … [Donna] joins in and says it is difficult challenging someone because of a case that was open in the team before' (fieldnotes).

Further attempts at eclipsing and diverting difficult emotional experiences were provided within the team through the use of humour, which was considered essential to being able to cope with the stresses of the job, as Donna explained:

> INTERVIEWER: "The worst part of your job. How do you cope with it?"
> DONNA: "Humour. Humour, food, exercise and just having bloody good teammates." (Interview data)

Mulkay (1988) argues that applied humour can be used for a hidden or veiled purpose and so has a serious point to it. Indeed, the inconsistency between what the social workers believed they should be doing and what they were being asked to do provided many opportunities for humour about their shared predicament, as I observed in one team room: '[Linda] turns around from her desk and jokes to [Amy], in reference to phone calls she has been receiving today from parents, "It's getting in the way of my paperwork!"' (fieldnotes). While humorous, the serious point was that such action sought to alter the quality, intensity or duration of negative self-conscious emotional experiences resulting from conflicts between their actions and their identity meanings. When shared within the teams, such personal emotion work served to regulate the emotions of others by eclipsing and diverting their emotional attention elsewhere. This contributed to the social workers' ability to continue practising despite their troubled conscience, reservations and feelings of shame and guilt, as Monica explained:

> INTERVIEWER: "What's the best part of your work?"
> MONICA: "The team."
> INTERVIEWER: "What about the team?"

Monica : "I dunno. I'm getting upset again [starts to cry], the working together, because I think social work practice is a very lonely job, isn't it really, and I suppose the team just makes it more bearable [crying]." (Interview data)

Parental experience in the context of identification

Given the structure of the new child and family social work service, the social workers were thrown into a context in which they were required to investigate some concern for a child. Their presence, therefore, invariably heightened a parent's self-consciousness. Indeed, it was usually seen either as an unnecessary intrusion into their lives or as unwanted scrutiny of their parenting. Nevertheless, shame could be seen to be a core element of parental experiences. It was not that a social worker necessarily intended to evoke shame in the parents, but by adhering to the organisational expectations and demands, they were placed in a position where they had to discuss concerns raised by others. The context was, therefore, set for experiences of shame and embarrassment, as I observed in the following home visit:

[Jane] read out the referral and the father said none of it was true and that the school had "decided that they are bad people". The mother said that she feels the school are checking up on her and she looked upset and seemed to be fighting back the tears. (Fieldnotes)

In this case, the concerns were not substantiated and the case was closed. The social worker did not seek to shame the parents, and the parents did not blame the social worker, yet the nature of the referral questioned the parents' care of their own child, leading the parents to feel judged as bad parents. Some investigations of concerns, however, further increased the possibility of experiences of shame and embarrassment. In some contexts, for example, the social workers were required to check the cleanliness of the children's bedrooms and the amount of food in the kitchen, as demonstrated in a conversation I had with one social worker about the visit she had undertaken the night before:

[Paula] told me that the mother had got upset when she had asked to see the child's bedroom and look in the cupboards and fridge. She said the mother burst into tears and said "I can't believe you're doing this to me".... She told me the mother said it was really embarrassing. (Fieldnotes)

Again, it was the context of the mandated work that placed the social workers at the centre of a situation in which the parents felt judged as failing to be good-enough parents. Such situations were, however, a demonstration of state power, with the social workers acting as the mechanism for the state surveillance of its citizens. While, of course, such action was necessary to identify parenting that was not considered good enough and to identify what needed to be done to safeguard and protect the child's welfare, it could, nevertheless, be seen as shaming to those on the receiving end. Irrespective of the intentions of social workers, therefore, shame could again be considered to be a core element of parental experiences in such situations. This was illustrated in a child protection core group meeting that I observed, that is, meetings with the parents and professionals to oversee the plans put in place to keep children safe. The mother had served a prison sentence for dealing drugs and was now released. Her children had been placed with their father during this time and she wanted them placed back with her. The very nature of discussing the concerns and issues inevitably brought back memories to the mother of that time, leading her to evaluate herself and her actions:

> The professionals discuss the history of neglect of the children when they lived with the mother before she went into prison. The mother says in the meeting she is ashamed of what she was like and how she treated the children and she has learnt now. She says she wants the children back with her. (Fieldnotes)

While the first parental experience illustrated parents who did not think that they had done anything wrong, but experienced negative self-conscious emotions as a result of the evaluations of others, this parent's experience demonstrates that some felt ashamed of their past, and the organisational process to address such actions served to remind her of her shame. By stating that she had learnt, she engages in emotion work to distance herself from the feeling of being ashamed. While it may not have been possible for the social workers to shape or alter such parental experiences of shame, how a social worker engaged with the parent could affect their overall experience.

By adhering to the organisational expectations and demands, whether by enacting or complying, the social workers could evoke further feelings of shame and even move such experiences to humiliation. Indeed, and as outlined throughout this book, the organisational representation was grounded in the dominant discourse of dangerousness and risk to children's safety. Adhering to the organisational representation, therefore, attracted praise from organisational guardians for any action that was perceived to achieve this aim. While such action evoked pride in compliance with organisational expectations, the dominant discourse not only separated the child from the family as the focus of the work, but also dismissed contextual issues such as class, inequality or poverty as legitimate contributing factors to any risk or harm to children. Indeed, the dominant discourse included the idea that harm to children crossed social boundaries, on the one hand, and notions of individual responsibility, on the other. Consequently, the social workers' empathic attention was diverted away from the parents' wider situation to focus more on their disposition, what is referred to in social psychology as the fundamental attribution error (Ross, 1977). This led to a process of 'othering', which facilitated the context for greater parental experiences of shame and humiliation. Furthermore, for those that identified with the organisational representation, the threat of being shamed and humiliated themselves eclipsed any feelings that they may have had towards the parent that may lead the practitioner to act against organisational expectations in favour of focusing on their own emotional safety. The social workers, therefore, did little to mitigate the shame and humiliation experienced by the parents as a consequence of organisational risk management practices.

Othering

With the focus of the social workers on creating emotional safety by adhering to the organisational expectations, the conditions were set for an institutionally supported perception of 'us' versus 'them' (Sumner, 1906; Tew, 2006; Featherstone et al, 2014), as Monica illustrated: "I think they [parents] think negatively of us anyway, don't they just, because of who we are and what we stand for" (interview data). Such 'othering' had two consequences. The first was that the issues and needs of the parents were not always seen as a legitimate focus of their work, as Lucy showed: '[Donna] stands near [Lucy's] desk and they talk about a case which [Donna] describes as the professionals parenting the parents and [Lucy] says "They suck you in don't they? And make you focus on their issues"' (fieldnotes).

Second, the social workers could perceive the parents as an obstacle to achieving the aims of their work, as Amy described:

> [Amy] says that she knows it is the right decision [to have removed the children] and doesn't think the children should ever go back to their mother because it is easy to make changes without the children. She said that this mother has been so frustrating and I ask why? She says because "I want to effect change" but that "mum got in the way of that". (Fieldnotes)

The failure of the mother to achieve the level of change required posed a threat to Amy's claim to be an effective and competent social worker that could create safety for the children. She placed the responsibility for this failure on the mother, supporting the notion that 'social workers' protect children from 'them'. Given the consequences for the child and practitioner if a child is harmed, the social workers often felt vulnerable and emotionally unsafe, and would often say 'I don't trust him/her'. Such distrust could, at times, be observed to play a role in their situated conceptualisation through imagining the worst-case scenario, as demonstrated in a meeting between the area manager, a solicitor, the team manager and Carla where the issue was of violence in the father's previous relationship:

> The area manager says that there have been no violent incidents between the father and the mother.... [Carla] says that they are saying they will work with children's services.... They discuss the seriousness of the situation and, at one point, the area manager says they can't stop the father throwing the baby against the wall if they are living together. They agree this would not be safe and the area manager states the father has to leave the family home once the baby is born. (Fieldnotes)

Their imagined future provided justification for evoking the need for policing measures. The resulting decision could be considered to be as much an act of emotion work intended to create a feeling of emotional safety for the managers and social worker as it could an act intended to create safety for the child. As the focus of the work was on creating safety, with a lack of focus on the experience of the parents or carers, many parents complained that they were being treated unfairly or not getting what they needed, or that the social workers were making things worse, as Carla's experience demonstrated:

> "he blamed me for splitting the family apart and for me aiding him to drink more because I was stressing him out because he couldn't be with his family but, I, all my focus was for the kids and protecting them and keeping them safe, you know, but, of course, he didn't see it like that so he put several complaints in about that." (Interview data)

Such situations recast the parents as 'shamers' in the eyes of social workers seeking to enact or comply with the organisational representation, as Paula demonstrated on the drive to a meeting with a mother in a school:

> she told me that she had had little sleep last night and when she was eating breakfast, she felt sick.... She said she is scared of the mother and I asked her why and she said that she is aggressive and verbally attacks her. She said the mother is "out to wreck my career before it's begun" and said she undermines her confidence and began to get teary as she drove. We arrived at the school and [Paula] seemed nervous as she got her bag out of the boot of the car and she said she felt like crying and she looked like she was about to cry. (Fieldnotes)

As this scenario showed, at times, seeking to protect oneself from shame and humiliation within the organisation by acquiescing to the external expectations created the conditions for feeling shamed by the reactions of the parents. The social workers could then be seen to protect themselves from this by reducing the possibility of being criticised/shamed by 'them', as Melanie explained:

> "I'm not gonna go to a service user's house and say 'Can you comment on my practice', 'What do you, do you think I'm doing a good job or not?'. Because you're opening yourself up then, aren't you, for criticism." (Interview data)

Shaming and humiliating practice

Given the context of responsibilising parents, complex situations involving social and economic issues were stripped from the analysis of the problem, leaving a dominant narrative of personal inadequacy. Parents were often, therefore, presented as the problem, or as a threat to the child. The document that was produced at the end of an assessment to outline the analysis and professional judgement of the social worker and their team manager demonstrated this process, as one comment by a team manager at the end of a social worker's assessment report illustrated:

> The social worker asserts that [the mother] loves her children and wants the best for them. I would question whether or not this is true as the parenting portrayed here is not that of a mother who wants the best for her son.... [The child] is suffering from episodic punitive parenting and living in an environment that features high criticism and low warmth.... [The child] receives inconsistent care and must be in a state of high arousal never knowing whether his mother is going to be kind or cruel. (Assessment document)

While the concerns about the child's welfare could be identified in many different ways, and most would agree that the mother does have certain responsibilities towards her child, without the context in which the family was living, a simple picture of the situation was provided that could be considered as shaming of the mother. While the mother's actions were adversely affecting the children's development, and it is, of course, possible that the mother did not love her children, by identifying with the organisational representation, the aim of the assessment process, and the resulting document, could be seen not to be about developing a positive and supportive relationship with the mother that could address the underlying issues, but to be about identifying and presenting the risk to the children to an audience, an audience that would verify and legitimise the organisation's identity claims. This focus on organisational expectations and demands could also be seen to direct the social workers' practice in direct work with parents. One example was observed in a home visit where the social worker had been working with the family for a few weeks. The issue was one of neglect and we walked around the home and looked at the children's bedrooms, which the social worker felt were not to an acceptable standard:

> [Helen] asked the mother to help the children clean their rooms. The mother complained that they know how to do it and she is sick of doing it all the time. The mother

sat slumped on the sofa looking away from [Helen], saying very little to [Helen's] questions. [Helen] pushed the issue by saying she needs to see the rooms tidier than they are and that she should show the children "as their mother" how to do it. (Fieldnotes)

The social worker provided a clear message to the mother that she was not fulfilling her duties as a 'mother' and that she was expected to do this without being provided help, advice or support in doing it. At times, such othering and responsibilisation led to very personal feelings towards the parents. For example, some parents were defined by the way they were perceived to have treated their children, as demonstrated by Lucy: '[Lucy] referred to the uncle saying "I hate them" and explained to me that the uncle and his partner had taken the girl in to get back at the mother and to get a bigger house' (fieldnotes). Some were defined by the way the parent was perceived to have treated the social worker:

[Jemma] is sitting at her desk talking to [Jane], who is at her desk, and [Jemma] is talking about a father, saying that he was being hostile to her and [Jane] said he was "vile" and [Jemma] said "a vile man". (Fieldnotes)

Some were defined by more general moral transgressions, such as parental behaviour that was perceived to be dangerous to others or simply strange, as shown in the following meeting:

[The team manager] said the mother has been found in bed with her cousin and answered the door with a parrot on her head one day, all this was said with an element of amusement. The area manager gives some directions and suggests that the mother needs a "different way of living life". (Fieldnotes)

The result was a context for practice that created the conditions for very negative emotions to be sustained throughout the process. As identified earlier, the parents may have felt ashamed of their actions, and as outlined in Chapter Two, they may have felt ashamed of their circumstances, such as living in poverty. The messages that the parents received were, however, often experienced as overly negative and unfairly critical, experiencing practice as shaming and potentially humiliating. Indeed, this was demonstrated in one meeting I observed between a mother, who was complaining about the assessment that the social worker had completed, and the team manager. While humiliation was not a word used by the mother, her actions were consistent with such an experience:

> the mother says that none of the social work report is backed up with evidence and says that she has no mental health problem, does not drink, has not abused her child, and so there is no concern and so should be able to see her child.... The mother is clearly angry, speaking firmly and loudly, and says that the report is lazy and offensive and that she will be spending every penny she has on legal costs then walked out. (Fieldnotes)

Shaming as part of organisational risk management

The negative experience for the parents was exacerbated by the administrative processes put in place to manage the perceived risk. In a child protection conference, for example, the formal arena where concerns about a child's welfare were discussed, parents sat around a table with other professionals and an independent chairperson who managed the process. The foundation of the discussions within the conference was a report provided by the social worker, which made the concerns explicit. Following discussion of the concerns, all the professionals were invited by the chairperson to vote on whether there needed to be a child protection plan, while the parents were not, as demonstrated in the following conference:

> The chair asks the professionals if they think there needs to be a child protection plan and one by one they all say they do under the category of neglect.... The mother asks what neglect means and starts to cry and takes a tissue from the box on the table. This is then explained by the police officer who says, "You are not protecting yourself, therefore you are not protecting the children".(Fieldnotes)

By placing the responsibility for harm, or likelihood of harm, on the parent, a very public negative evaluation was institutionalised. Following the child protection conference, a formal report was provided to all who attended, which was used in subsequent core group meetings to define the problem and provide a foundation for the child protection plan. Within the Council, the first core group meeting was chaired by the team manager, who was required by the organisation to be explicit about the possibility of a child being removed, as the following core group meeting showed:

> The team manager starts the meeting by explaining the purpose of the child protection plan and says that a plan is not put in place lightly as it means people are worried about the safety and welfare of the child. He explains this will mean there will be unannounced visits, that the category for the plan is emotional abuse and that if she doesn't "follow the plan, then we would go to court to get an order which would give us the authority to remove your child". The mother says "What do you mean?", and starts to cry.... The mother stops crying and the team manager says "We need to spell this out". (Fieldnotes)

A number of parents reported that such experiences made it a very difficult process and potentially decreased their belief that they had the ability to change, as demonstrated by a mother's comments to me prior to observing a meeting between her and the social worker:

> She told me that she thought all social workers should be sacked and that it is a horrible experience for parents as they make you feel "stupid", that you have "no voice" and that she had begun to "doubt myself" as a parent. (Fieldnotes)

Summary

Given the re-conceptualisation of child and family social work services in England through the neoliberal discourse, new expectations, pressures and demands were placed upon the Council in fulfilling its societally sanctioned function. Through the political and media shaming and praising of social work organisations, the neoliberal agenda was embedded into the construction of social work services. Consequently, the Council created, defined and promoted particular meanings and expectations for its employees, embedding the neoliberal agenda into the organisational construction of a professional. By ensuring that the social workers knew the conditions and consequences for the adherence to and transgression of these boundaries, they developed a sense of pride and shame in line with these organisational prescriptions, embedding the neoliberal professional conceptualisation into personal identity constructions of what it means to be a professional. The possibility of being shamed for failing to adhere to the organisational representation of a social worker was, therefore, a prominent feature in any situated conceptualisation. In some contexts and situations, the meanings and expectations contained within the organisational representation were perceived to be desirable and aspirational, and social workers sought to embody such a social representation, as demonstrated by Amy in one of her diary entries:

> [Situation:] *I have completed all paperwork in relation to a particular case ready for court. This has been a case I have worked on for 8 years and solidly for the last 2 weeks completing this.*
> [Thinking:] *Relief. Thank god I've finished! Proud of the quality of work that I have produced. Relieved that we will be able to get the children to a place of safety.*
> [Bodily sensations:] *Relaxed, smiled, did a little dance. Less pressure on brain.*
> [Description:] *Relief. Pride. Professional. Happy.*
> [Categorised as:] *Pride.*

By accepting the organisational interpretive framework for practice that gave meaning to administrative tasks and valorised the social policing function of social work, Amy could feel proud of the paperwork she had completed that would be used to get a court order to remove the children. Furthermore, by adhering to expectations and seeking to place the children in a place of safety, she felt 'relieved' as the threat of being shamed or humiliated was lifted. Consequently, she felt 'professional' for living up to the organisational representation. For others, however, the pressures, expectations and demands provided constraints that challenged and conflicted with their established ideals, values and standards for practice. To avoid being shamed and humiliated, however, they sought to adhere to them anyway. Such acts of enactment and compliance were successful mechanisms of organisational reproduction, ensuring that the Council produced what it needed, in the way that it needed, for a positive inspection grading.

From the social workers' perspective, enacting was the most beneficial to their well-being. By living up to organisational meanings and expectations, social workers attracted praise and social acceptance within the organisation and evoked personal feelings of pride. While compliance also avoided being shamed and attracted praise and social acceptance, the conflict with personal identity meanings evoked feelings of shame and guilt as a result of performing tasks that the social workers believed to be wrong. As Culpitt (1999) argues, quite simply, self-protection overrides the ethical concern for others. In such instances, the social workers engaged in emotion work to alter how they felt, and the empathy they experienced for each other moved them to try to regulate each other's feelings so that they alleviated such negative self-conscious emotional experiences. Furthermore, the organisational interpretive framework sought to regulate the emotions of the social workers by eclipsing and diverting negative self-conscious emotions to more organisationally acceptable feelings. Sometimes, this was successful and social workers could move from regret, shame and guilt to pride, while, at other times, this was not so, leaving social workers distressed, hopeless and feeling isolated.

The strategies of enactment and compliance can be located in Satyamurti's (1981) concept of occupational survival, in which social workers' identities and practices are shaped by features of their situation by engaging in activities to increase the tolerability of their work. Whether through enactment or compliance, however, the experience for the parents was often a feeling of being shamed and, at times, humiliated as such strategies ensured that the neoliberal re-conceptualisation of individual responsibility was pushed down from the organisation, to the professionals and, ultimately, to the parents. While parents always have options and choices in relation to their parenting, within the context of social work organisations integrating neoliberal principles and social workers identifying with the resulting organisational representation, they were expected to be able to address complex social and systemic issues that were contributing to the problem. A lack of resources, for example, was not considered a legitimate factor in relation to issues of harm to children. The social workers may not have intended to have caused pain and suffering to the people they worked with, but the processes through which they came to identify with the organisational representation facilitated such a situation. Indeed, there are some who have argued that neoliberal governmentality intends to instil a culture of control to push people towards adherence to neoliberal ideals (eg Garland, 2001) and others who have argued that neoliberal states create systems to punish those who fail to live up to such ideals (eg Wacquant, 2009). While the focus of such writers has been the penal system, the role that social work plays in disciplining and punishing the poor for failing to adhere to these new societal standards has been considered by some (eg Soss et al, 2011; Warner, 2015; Crossley, 2016). The analysis provided in this book extends such ideas to show how social work systems can use shame and humiliation, intentionally or otherwise, in this process. It was not inevitable, however, that the social workers accepted the meanings and expectations associated with the organisational representation. Indeed, some, in some contexts, rejected them and resisted the processes that sought to regulate their emotions so that they complied. It is these situations and conditions to which we can now turn.

EIGHT

Forms of resistance: a case example

This chapter continues the illustration of the theory outlined in Chapter Six and follows the discussion in Chapter Seven to outline the role that pride, shame and guilt played in social workers' situated conceptualisations that supported resistance to the organisational attempts to control professional practice. It focuses on the details of the social workers' experiences within the case-study site used throughout this book to illustrate the forms of resistance. A social worker began to resist the expectations placed upon them where they felt that they conflicted with the meanings held within their own professional identity standard. Such conflicts were fuelled by a perception that what they were expected to do was not in the best interests of the children and families they were working with. On the one hand, they knew that they could be shamed or humiliated for not complying with such expectations, while, on the other, they could feel ashamed for doing what they believed was wrong or guilty for being involved in harming another. With the consequences for being shamed and rejected within the organisation being considered to be too great to risk, the dominant actions of the social workers complied with organisational expectations. In some situations, however, the consequences for feeling ashamed and guilty of one's actions outweighed the consequences for potentially being shamed by organisational guardians. Not being able to cope with what one had done led social workers to resist the pressures and expectations designed to direct their actions in a particular manner. In some situations, this required action that compromised the organisational expectations, forgoing any desire for praise and acceptance, yet still complied with the minimum standards to avoid being shamed. In other situations, the social workers sought to conceal actions that they felt were right but defied the organisational expectations. In still other situations, it was considered necessary to challenge the pressures and expectations to influence, alter or prevent action that they considered inappropriate or immoral and avoid feeling ashamed of their actions. Such acts of resistance provided greater opportunities for relational engagement, recognising both social workers and parents as human, with individual strengths and struggles. This chapter outlines these three forms of resistance in the following before considering the experience of the parents as a consequence.

Compromising organisational expectations

In contexts where the meanings held within a social worker's professional identity conflicted with the meanings held within the organisational representation, a social worker could compromise what they were expected to do while also seeking to avoid being shamed by only partially complying with expectations. Such action could be considered to be either an act of necessity, as what they were being asked to do was considered impossible, or an act of choice, to provide sufficient space to be able to focus on work that they could feel proud of. The foundation to both, however, was adherence to the minimum standards, which did not fully satisfy the organisational requirements, but ensured that they avoided criticism (see also Wastell et al, 2010; White et al, 2010; Leigh, 2017), as Jemma demonstrated:

> [Jemma] told me that they now get a weekly report and showed me hers, which lists all their cases which are out of timescales and by how long they are out…. She said some in the team think this report is helpful while others are not happy about it. I asked "What's the consequence of doing this?" and [Jane] said "We don't do visits" and [Jemma] quickly responded to her, saying "I do my stat visits, I just don't write them up. I just put 'child seen'". (Fieldnotes)

While Jemma's actions were not considered good practice within the Council, having recorded that the visits had been done and the child had been seen, her statistics, and therefore those of the team and the Council, improved. Compromising became an act of necessity where the social workers' situated conceptualisation contained irresolvable competing and conflicting demands. In such situations, the social workers felt that they could not comply with these expectations even if they wanted to, creating a feeling of vulnerability to being shamed. In such cases, the social worker compromised both the organisational standards and their own identity standards, as Amy described:

> "I've gone through a time when I've had 50 cases. I can't dedicate an hour to them per week, you know. You can't … because you've got 6,000 things, as I keep saying. So, it's, you're unable to. So, it impacts on your practice as a whole.

I think it depends on your character because to me, because of the time, sometimes, you're doing a child social work assessment after doing two visits. A 40-day assessment in two visits. That's not 40 days is it? That's not knowing the family for that, to do that assessment justice, or to do the children justice, because that's what it's about." (Interview data)

The expectations as laid out in the Council's procedures were that a 40-day assessment should be an in-depth assessment of the child's needs and circumstances. Amy was aware that two visits over 40 days did not meet this expectation, but she felt that she had no option but to reduce the quality of her work in order to pacify the institution and protect herself from being shamed by not adhering to the competing expectation for timeliness. Furthermore, this reduction in the quality of her work also conflicted with her own social worker identity standard. Amy, and other social workers, could therefore be observed to engage in emotion work to protect themselves from feeling shame by denying any responsibility for failing to live up to these meanings (Scott and Lyman, 1968), as she explained: "I think although my assessments sometimes, the quality can be really good, sometimes, it can be very slapdash for the sake of getting it in for the duty tracker" (interview data).

In some contexts, however, the social workers felt that they had more choice over their actions. In such situations, compromising could be considered a strategy to create some space in which the social worker could do work that they felt proud of while avoiding the likelihood of being shamed or humiliated. By minimally complying with the organisational expectations on some cases, sufficient time could be freed up to focus on a small number of cases in which the social workers could verify their identities. Greater levels of empathy for a child or family provided the foundation to want to focus on a particular case. Such empathic identification created a desire to do more for them than was expected by the organisation. This was illustrated by Helen, who was working with a child she had known previously:

"he woke up, took an overdose in the family home and was left in his bedroom for 36 hours, unconscious. And when he woke up, he had these burns to his body, like, down his back and his bum and his hair. So, he had hair loss and all sorts, blisters everywhere, and he couldn't understand what happened ... he was one of the cases where I did lots of direct work with him, and I put the time in, and I made sure I saw him every week. But that was a massive commitment in my diary, but I made sure that, to do a good job for him, you make sacrifices." (Interview data)

The child was placed in foster care and the expectation was to see the child for 'statutory visits' every six weeks. It was unusual to visit more regularly than that. However, by making sacrifices elsewhere, Helen was able to go above and beyond the expectations with this particular child, which verified her identity as a good social worker, as she demonstrated in her retelling of the account to me:

"I think the foster carer and [the child], at the time, I took time to build a relationship with them both. To get to know if it was the right placement for him, you have to get to know them. And, again, it's about making your stat visits, doing your visits on time and above and beyond what the, you know, the guidance, sort of, says. I think they would see, well, I know they thought I was a good social worker because he was gutted when I left. And the foster carer said that they were disappointed that I was leaving because I had invested a lot of time into [the child]. And there are cases where you do spend more time with than others." (Interview data)

As this case illustrates, compromising tactics could be considered as a minor level of resistance, whereby some of the organisational pressures, expectations and demands were adhered to while others were not. Consequently, the social workers could create a sufficient level of emotional safety and attract a sufficient level of social acceptance, while in some situations, being more active in seeking to verify their own identity meanings. This provided the opportunity to feel satisfied with what they had done, as Helen showed in her concluding comments about her work with the aforementioned child: "that's, like, the best bit. That's why I want to do this job" (interview data).

Concealing acts of resistance

Concealing acts of resistance were founded in the rejection of the meanings and expectations of the organisational representation. A practitioner could not escape the institutional pressures without leaving the organisation, however. The social workers could be seen to comply with the organisational expectations and demands in situations where their actions would be detected by organisational guardians in attempts to avoid being shamed, while resisting them in situations where they would not in order to practise in a manner they could feel proud of. This strategy of disguised resistance (see Oliver, 1991; Hébert, 2006; Carey and Foster, 2011; Leigh, 2017) could be used by both individuals and teams. By rejecting the organisational meanings and expectations for practice, social workers judged the practice of others negatively yet concealed such judgements, as Monica demonstrated:

> "they're very authorative, authorative [*sic*] and very, I'd say, borderline rude and, I dunno, I'm just completely different I think and I know that we're social workers and that we are, you know, it's a career and we're professionals but I don't think you need to be in people's houses making them feel belittled in their own home, you know, and we are there to criticise and also to say the good points about people's parenting and I think sometimes some members of the team are very, you know, belittling of people and quite oppressive." (Interview data)

Given that the social workers shared an identity as professionals, such a negative evaluation of another's practice evoked shame vicariously (see Lickel et al, 2005) as the actions of others could be perceived to reflect badly on the social work profession, and consequently on them as a member of that group, as Linda explained:

> "they conform, they fall in and they don't challenge what the organisation, they just sort of slot in.... Ashamed to see, and that's why I said I wouldn't be a, I wouldn't go through all that blood, sweat and tears with a student again.... But I, why are they in, the anger, the, the, why, why, why, why? What is it that people become so compliant?... [I'm] embarrassed and ashamed. Disappointed, disappointed in what we're churning out." (Interview data)

While the levels of surveillance and monitoring of the social workers were considered constant within the office, there was a distinct lack of monitoring of the social workers' direct work with the children and families. The dominant form of practice could be considered to be enacting or complying, yet the lack of oversight of their direct work provided opportunities to resist the organisational norms, values and expectations, as Monica demonstrated to me as we sat in the car following a home visit:

> [Monica] tells me she is worried she is too soft. She tells me that the 12-year-old boy disappeared yesterday with a nine-year-old boy from next door and that [Julie] is working with that family. She said that [Julie] told her before she went out that she was going to call the mother of the nine-year-old boy and "give her a bollocking". [Monica] said to me "I didn't give her [the mother] a bollocking" but then says she doesn't think it is her job to tell people off. (Fieldnotes)

While Monica expressed self-doubt that her practice did not conform to the organisational expectations, it could be seen as an act of resistance by practising in a manner contrary to them. Such acts of resistance were, however, sporadic and concealed by practice that conformed to the institutional norms and practices in contexts where their practice was exposed to the surveillance and monitoring of the organisation. While some acts of resistance outside of the organisation's sphere of observation could be concealed relatively easily, such as what and how they said things to people, acts of resistance were also reported to be concealed within its sphere of observation through a more active form of deception, such as saying that they had performed certain tasks when they had not done them, as one team manager experienced:

> TEAM MANAGER: "I'd much rather them tell me they can't do something or they need extra help than lie to me and say they've done it and I find out they haven't because I can't cope with that."
> INTERVIEWER: "Does that happen?"
> TEAM MANAGER: "Sometimes, and then that does upset me. If people say to me, 'We've done de, de, de', you have a degree of trust, don't you? You have to trust people and then if I find out that actually, no, that's not been done or, that does upset me. I mean, I don't get cross, but I deal with it and say, 'Right, you haven't done it. I want it done by such and such a date and I will be monitoring more'." (Interview data)

Such resistance enabled the social workers to avoid the demands and expectations placed upon them. Disguising it was a form of emotion work to avoid being shamed. As the team manager demonstrated, however, it was usually only a matter of time before such pretence was identified and action taken to regulate their behaviour by threatening or evoking shame in that individual. To be able to achieve a more enduring form of concealment, action needed to be taken on a collective level.

The team could create sufficient emotional safety to take the risk of deviating from the norm by collectively disguising their resistance. The team managers, who felt proud of their teams, presented a positive image of the team and the individuals within the teams to senior management, as Amy explained: "[the team manager] is very protective of the team, so she probably, she'll say that, you know, we're all wonderful to our area managers" (interview data). The team managers could then take further action to reduce the scrutiny of the team by the senior management, such as by ensuring that the data for the team were acceptable for organisational requirements:

> [The team manager] then said she wanted to look at the "dirty data" and took some printed spreadsheets and said that the "data is doing us a disservice" and that it is "not making us look as good as we are". (Fieldnotes)

The term 'dirty data' was used for any monitored information that presented the team in a bad light, such as having statutory visits out of timescales. Once identified, the team manager would ensure that this was rectified immediately, thus ensuring a positive image was presented to senior management for as much of the time as possible. The team managers then attempted to protect the social workers from being shamed by senior managers, as one team manager explained:

> "I would watch their back, that's probably the best way of putting it. If anything goes wrong in there, I'll defend them. You can come in and bollock me, I say, 'Don't pull that on my social workers', so I will deal with it." (Interview data)

By presenting a positive image of the team and ensuring that acceptable data are provided to senior management, together with preventing episodic shaming of the social workers from the senior managers as best they could, the team managers created the space for resistance within the team, as Linda explained:

"she's given me what I want out of the job and I'm giving
her what she wants, it's a working relationship, I've got the
knowledge and the experience that she can trust me and I
can write credible reports and she's given me the freedom
to practise social work as I was taught, as she was taught
and as [Carol] was taught." (Interview data)

Having rejected the organisational representation, Linda felt that she
was able to verify the meanings of her professional identity free from the
more constraining forces of the organisation because the team manager
was able to present a 'symbolic acceptance of institutional norms,
rules, or requirements' (Oliver, 1991: 155) to senior management.
Such concealment of the team's resistance, however, only lasted for as
long as the disguised resistance remained disguised. Once identified,
the organisational processes of regulation, control and policing were
seen to be legitimate.

Influencing institutional sources and processes

For those who rejected the organisational representation but found
themselves under pressure to act in a manner contrary to their identity
standard, concealing their acts of resistance was not always sufficient
to placate their conscience. In such situations, social workers could
seek to influence the source of the organisational pressures, norms and
expectations either through challenging the source or controlling the
processes that reinforced the cultural norms and practices (see Carey
and Foster, 2011). While this risked being shamed by organisational
guardians, it ensured that they did not feel ashamed of their actions.
The foundation for the strategy of influencing was an attitude of
resistance, as demonstrated by Linda: "I see myself as a proper social
worker, I see myself as a 'social social worker', I don't see myself as an
'agent of the state social worker'" (interview data).

Such attitudes could compel some social workers in some contexts
to challenge what they considered to be inappropriate or even immoral
actions. Indeed, challenging the rules, norms and practices could be
distinguished from other forms of resistance by the lack of desire to
conform or feign conformity. Minor acts of challenge could be seen in
single interactions, such as Monica's actions in a legal gateway meeting
(LGM):

"one particular family of mine, I took it to LGM and they
were sitting there saying, talking about adoption for the

youngest two, I was like 'Are you kidding me? Absolutely no way ... that isn't what I'm asking for, that isn't what I think is proportionate'." (Interview data)

Acts of challenge were necessary, however, across multiple interactions in order to sustain resistance to the pressures to conform to institutional norms and successfully influence the outcome of a situation, as demonstrated by Donna's resistance to the expectation to remove a child from his mother:

"I had already removed two kids off the mum and then the mum got pregnant again but with a different partner and we completely reassessed it, we didn't judge it by, I pushed for that and it was a hard fight. It was a fight with the guardian. It was a fight with management but people did listen to me and it worked. And she's at home now with that baby, well, he's two, not a baby. Number two on the way, child thriving, thriving as an adult herself ... instead of removing at birth, which would have been the natural thing to do because the girl had only just gone.... But it was the fact I fought for her to keep that baby because it was the right decision." (Interview data)

Donna challenged the 'natural' thing to do because she did not think that it was 'right', which compelled her to fight the multiple layers of institutional arrangements that were reinforcing the pressures to remove the child. Such influencing tactics, supported by empathy for the people they were working with, created the conditions for feeling pride, as demonstrated by Jemma's diary entry:

[Situation:] *Achieving a visit to see a disengaged teenager who has moved out of area. I had to persuade TM* [team manager] *to keep case open to me, as it is in child's best interests.*
[Thinking:] *Happy, pleased that I had been persistent and patient. Visit went well, despite young person being very late.*
[Bodily sensations:] *Relaxed, lots of smiles. Informal chat, information gathering (young person is usually closed to conversation).*
[Description:] *Felt like I had achieved what others had been unable to – proud, patient.*
[Categorised as:] *Pride.*

[Influence:] *I have learnt that with some service users, it is important to adopt different approaches, also to challenge decisions I don't think are in child's best interests.*

It is important to note, however, that it was not a simple process of the social workers resisting the senior managers. Systemic shame and pride operated outside of any individual and, at times, it was the social workers who could be considered the source of pressure while the senior managers resisted it. In one example, a social worker brought a case of a boy who had been beaten with a belt by his mother to an LGM asking to enter the pre-proceedings process as a warning to the family, expecting this to be a straightforward agreement, yet this was not the case:

> They discussed the son refusing to have a bath and a few days before he had posted pictures of the mother, who was pregnant, in her underwear on Facebook for the second time. The area manager stated "He's being fucking arsey", and then apologised for swearing while laughing. She explained that she has had teenage boys so "I've lived it"....
> There is a discussion about the benefit of going into pre-proceedings and the senior manager refers to the Facebook photos, saying that "All women could understand" how the mother felt about the pictures going on there while laughing at the thought of it. (Fieldnotes)

Being a woman and a mother, and having parented teenage boys, the area manager had a high capacity for empathy with the mother in this situation and could find reason to excuse her actions. Being in a position of greater power than the social worker and team manager, she had access to greater resources to influence the outcome of the situation. Such instances were infrequent, however, as the senior managers' social location and corresponding responsibilities made it more likely that their situated conceptualisations would be in line with the dominant organisational expectations, creating actions that reinforced them. As one team manager told me, "there must be something in the further back you are, the harsher you are" (fieldnotes).

There were some instances where the social workers sought to gain a greater level of influence than by simply challenging organisational sources. Indeed, in some contexts, social workers felt that they had to more directly control the organisational processes in order to avoid an outcome they could not accept. One example of such action was demonstrated in a conversation between two social workers, where one stated that she felt compelled to act in a manner that provided the maximum amount of influence she could exert:

> The social worker said that she had put her job on the line as her managers were saying they had to separate some siblings, with the younger one to be placed for adoption, but she couldn't agree to this and said she would resign if that happened. She said, in the end, senior managers had to agree to a further sibling assessment, which concluded they shouldn't be split up. She said her name was mud for three or four months. (Fieldnotes)

Oliver (1991) argues that influencing tactics differ from all other forms of action as they do not treat the organisational pressures and expectations as a constraint to be obeyed or defied. Instead, influencing the organisational processes sought to alter or control these pressures to change the outcome of a situation. It was, therefore, a highly active form of emotion work, designed to avoid feeling shame for perceived immoral actions. Influencing tactics, however, could only be effective in relation to influencing another's situated conceptualisation. It was not possible to influence the organisational expectations relating to administration. These were impermeable to influence at an individual level and were, indeed, a constraint to be obeyed or defied. Even defiance of these requirements, however, could only exist by avoiding scrutiny through concealing such behaviour, and once identified, it was subject to episodic shaming and used as an example to deter others from taking such action.

Parental experiences in the context of resistance

Pain and distress could regularly be observed in both the social workers and the parents and carers. The social workers could often be observed to struggle with the actions they had to take and to produce work to a standard that they were satisfied with, and I often observed social workers in tears. The experience of the system for the social workers was summed up by one team manager:

> "this job takes it out of you, it takes it out of everybody, it's hard and the nature of the job, the whole thing about child abuse, child neglect, it's unpleasant, it's not nice … it's emotionally draining. And then on top of it, you've got

too much of it and then on top of that you're being told 'We know it's unpleasant, we know you've got too much but where's that assessment, why is that assessment six months overdue, if you don't improve your performance, well'. So, it's pressure upon pressure upon pressure. In those circumstances, maybe it's a wonder that people aren't crying more often." (Interview data)

Equally, I observed or heard about the parents and carers regularly complaining, becoming angry and feeling distressed. In applying Axel Honneth's (1995) theory of recognition, Houston (2016) and Frost (2016) argue that such experiences can be considered as cases of misrecognition, whereby they are not considered worthy of respect and equal rights unless they conform to externally imposed ideals. For the team managers, resistance provided a mechanism by which they could recognise the social workers as being human. So, while one team manager explained the new context as "the nurturing and the compassion is no longer there, I would say. It's pure business and that's a bit of a conflict for me because I care about people" (interview data), they went on to explain how they used strategies of resistance to provide a more empathic environment:

> "I do what I have to do. I'm not a big fan of timescales. I'm much more bothered about quality and understanding what's going on for that child but we do it. We're a performing team but then I will find time for my staff to do more work with the children and I find other ways of getting it how I want it really. My nurturing is not approved of really, but I'm not going to stop doing it because I'm like that out of work … so I comply to allow me to then be flexible and creative." (Interview data)

This process was paralleled between the social workers and parents as social workers sought to practise in a more compassionate manner. By resisting the organisational pressures, the social workers were able to acknowledge and respond to the pain and distress they saw in the parents and carers, affording them degrees of recognition. Such acts of resistance, however, conflicted with the organisational forces, as demonstrated by Monica's conversation with a mother who was in a relationship with a man who had been violent in the past. Her children were subject to child protection plans due to the concerns about abuse in the relationship and issues of neglect. There was, therefore, pressure to ensure that the children were safe and place the responsibility for this on the mother:

> [Monica] says to the mother that the children's father has said she is scared of her new partner. The mother says she is not. [Monica] says "I want to make sure you're safe". [Monica] asks about child benefit and the mother says she is still receiving it and [Monica] says she doesn't want the mother to end up with a fine and they discuss the issue. [Monica] then asks the mother if she is ok with being in the same room for the core group meeting with the father and she says she is. [Monica] then checks that the mother feels able to end the relationship if she wanted to and they discuss this and how she might do it if she wanted to. (Fieldnotes)

While Monica's actions did not alter the child protection process, she was able to discuss the concerns and listen to the mother, showing concern for her well-being. Where greater degrees of resistance were possible, greater degrees of recognition could be seen, as shown by Linda's experience:

> "he [the father] used to ring me up and I used to give him feedback on his child and I think the bodies around me [the social workers] struggled and I said 'Listen, this little child, when he gets older will see that a social worker tried to promote a positive relationship with his father', albeit a couple of hours contact a week, but at least he'll have that sense of belonging, he'll know who his father was, because the previous social worker had just cut the father out the picture. Well, you know, I don't see that as good practice, I don't care what they've done, the child still has, you know, still has a right to know." (Interview data)

Recognising others as worthy individuals, with rights and needs common to all human beings, was difficult because these were eclipsed by organisational priorities and concerns within their situated conceptualisations. For some, however, such action provided the foundations for feeling proud of their work and being recognised by the parents and carers, providing a more satisfying experience, as Linda, reflecting on her time in the team before she left, explained:

"I took over from another social worker and I took a totally, I took the approach that I was taught to take and, yeah, I mean they're ringing [the team manager] up, they're sending flowers, they're buying cakes, one of them wanted to come to my leaving do, you know, they've been stunned." (Interview data)

Summary

Self-conscious emotions can be considered to have played an important role in the situated conceptualisations of the social workers, which led them to reject the organisational representation and resist the processes involved in regulating their emotions. While perhaps not a simple process, shame and pride could clearly be seen in how the social workers related the situation to their past experiences, imagined what would happen in the future and decided on what they should do and how they should do it in the present. Resistance occurred because the social workers did not want to feel ashamed or guilty of what they had done or who they were. While shame and pride may have been a driving force for action that resisted the organisational pressures and expectations, it was the meanings that the social workers had associated with their identities that conflicted with the organisational representation that drove the feelings of shame and pride. Those who felt compelled to resist invariably felt constrained by the systemic pressures and episodic actions of the organisational guardians. Such constraints served to weaken the attraction of the profession to the social workers, as Amy told me, "I love social work for what it should be" (fieldnotes), and the team managers, as one commented, "I'm just worried it's [social work is] going, or changing its guise, for the worse" (interview data). Indeed, while the recent changes in the profession and the Council provided an "opportunity to move to a more human system", as one team manager commented, she concluded, "it hasn't, it's got worse" (fieldnotes).

NINE

Conclusions

Scheff (2003) argues that shame, or its anticipation, is virtually ubiquitous, yet usually invisible, in modern societies. If this is, indeed, the case, then it is inevitable that social workers will also experience pride and shame in some way. The dearth of empirical studies on the subject (Gibson, 2016), however, limits our capacity both to see these experiences in practice and to understand them within the specific context of social work. Such experiences, therefore, slip from perception (Kaufman, 1989). Consequently, we have had limited answers to the questions of: how and why social workers, and children and families, experience pride and shame; who they are praised and shamed by, and for what reasons; or what consequence there may be from such experiences. The study of pride and shame is, however, the study of the human face of culture, power and belonging. It is through such processes that we can understand the emotional experience of identity, feeling safe and being authentic. This book has shown that these facets are central to the study and practice of social work, placing pride and shame as central concepts for research and practice.

This chapter will review and summarise the theory proposed throughout this book. It will consider this theory within the context of the case-study site used as an example throughout. While all child and family social work organisations will interpret the wider systemic pressures individually and have their own regional needs and local idiosyncrasies, the case example provides an illustration of how pride and shame can be used as technologies of power (Foucault, 1990; Creed et al, 2014) in political attempts to shape, direct and control public services. In addition, it also demonstrates the complexity of the decision-making process, where experiences, or the anticipation, of pride, shame and other self-conscious emotions drive practitioners to comply with, or resist, such pressures. These processes are not reserved specifically for child and family social work, however. Indeed, the whole welfare state and governmental apparatus has been going through a transformation as neoliberal ideas, agendas and values have become embedded into political, media and public discourse. These ideas, therefore, relate to other disciplines and practices. This chapter will begin to sketch out the conditions needed for authenticity and pride in social work practice before concluding with possible future directions in the theory and practice of pride and shame in professional practice.

Towards a theory of pride and shame in professional practice

While there are many debates about how to define practice (see Bourdieu and Wacquant, 1992; Schatzki, 2001; Britzman, 2003; Polkinghorne, 2004; Green, 2009), Kemmis (2009) concludes that professional practice entails the thinking, feeling, acting and relating that has been socially and historically constituted, and reconstituted, by human agency and social action. Given the social and historical foundations of the profession, social work can be considered a social representation (Moscovici, 1961, 1981, 2001), providing a stock of values, ideas, metaphors, beliefs and practices for the social work community. Being embedded within such a context, practitioners form, maintain and alter their constructions of what it means to be a professional in that context (Alvesson and Willmott, 2002; Miller, 2010). This internalised professional identity provides them with personal meanings and expectations for being a social worker that serve to reproduce the institution of social work.

As professional practice is constructed, it is open to influence, adaptation and change. Rather than directly manipulate, alter and disrupt the identity work of individuals to change their actions (eg Alvesson and Willmott, 2002), however, emotions provide a much easier target for behavioural and attitudinal change (see Gross, 2013). Indeed, across many disciplines, pride and shame have been identified as *the* personal referents in relation to identity processes (eg Cooley, 1902; Lynd, 1958; Goffman, 1959; Nathanson, 1994; Britt and Heise, 2000; Stets, 2005; Tangney and Tracy, 2012). Regulating a person's experiences of pride, shame and other self-conscious emotions by evoking, altering and diverting such experiences not only offers the possibility of immediate change in the person's thoughts, feelings and actions, but also influences how the person forms, repairs, maintains, strengthens and revises their identity meanings (Alvesson and Willmott, 2002). Pride and shame are, therefore, effective targets in any attempts to affect or control how a person practises.

Gross (1998) outlines the main areas for emotion regulation as influencing which situation a person is exposed to, changing aspects of that situation, influencing what is perceived in the situation, altering how the situation is cognitively represented and modifying the person's actions in the situation. What is considered in need of regulation is political, however (Warner, 2015). The social representation of social work is interpreted and reinterpreted through different political, social and cultural agendas, constructing and promoting different perspectives, supported by different historical and current events, stories and ideas. This institutional work results in cognitive, emotional and/or moral commitments to particular ways of thinking, feeling, doing and relating by some within the group (Creed et al, 2014). Given sufficient support, broad agreement is reached about what constitutes praiseworthy and shameful behaviour for members of that group. This systemic pride and shame influences professional practice directly, on the one hand, and informs the actions of others in their attempts to regulate and police professional practice, on the other (Creed et al, 2014). The discursive strategies of evoking, eclipsing and diverting pride, shame and other self-conscious emotions can, therefore, be seen as significant strategies in attempts to regulate the emotions of others to create, maintain and disrupt practice (Moisander et al, 2016).

Despite attempts to construct, promote and embed particular interpretive frameworks, however, there remain many alternative views and perspectives across the span of communities and constituencies interested in social work practice. Such possibilities for professional practice continue to influence the identity constructions and reconstructions of individual social workers and social work organisations. Attempts to regulate the emotions of others may, therefore, not always result in the intended response or outcome. Indeed, rather than feel pride and shame as expected, such an imposition of pressures, expectations and demands may conflict with established identity meanings, resulting in feeling shame, guilt, humiliation or embarrassment for acquiescing to external prescriptions. Such attempts at emotion regulation may, therefore, prompt emotion work in individual practitioners, managers, leaders and organisations.

Many have developed Hochschild's (1979) notion of emotion work (see Turner and Stets, 2006) and these can be synthesised specifically for this analysis to define it as purposive action aimed at feeling, avoiding or changing in degree or quality the experience of pride, shame and other self-conscious emotions. Individuals may, therefore, be seen to undertake a wide range of internal and external activities in attempts to respond to the ongoing and unfolding social interactions that influence, affect and disrupt how they feel. People want to feel proud of their own practice, the group they belong to and the profession they represent, and, conversely, do not want to be shamed, feel ashamed or, indeed, feel the vicarious shame of others. There is, therefore, an ongoing and unfolding social interaction in which individuals are evaluating and conceptualising the situation for personal relevance and meaning in order to decide how to respond to how they feel, on the one hand, and the potential for feeling pride, shame and other self-conscious emotions, on the other. By adapting the work of Alvesson and Willmott (2002), my findings suggest that the ongoing recursive relationship between the three areas of emotion regulation, emotion work and professional practice can be represented as in Figure 9.1.

The model depicted in Figure 9.1 outlines the overarching processes behind the experiences of pride and shame within child and family social work outlined within this book. While the details of the case example used to illustrate these processes are specific to the case–study site, the model, and the overarching processes, can be considered in the context of other organisations, disciplines and practices. As Hughes argued back in 1958, such specific accounts of processes in one context can be useful to understanding the processes in others (Hughes, 1958).

Figure 9.1: Emotion regulation, emotion work and professional practice

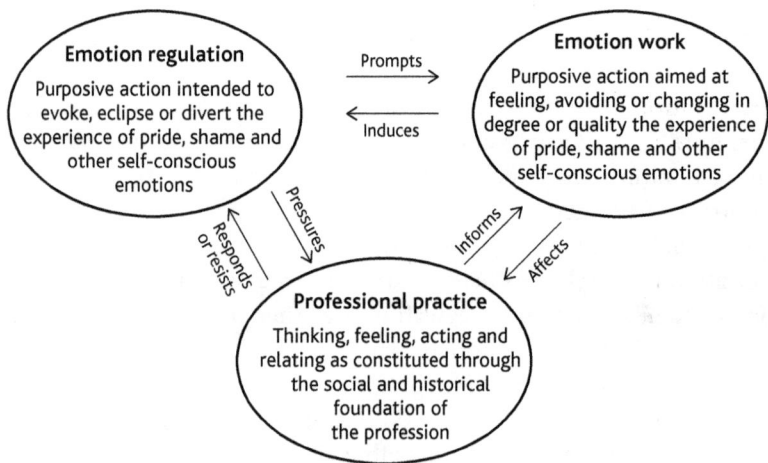

A case illustration of the theory of pride and shame in professional practice

The case study used within this book provides a detailed account of how one organisation sought to navigate the competing and conflicting pressures, demands and expectations placed upon social work organisations and social workers in England in modern times. Warner (2015) demonstrates how the intentional actions of politicians and journalists sought to evoke shame in child and family social work as a profession, social work services more generally, and social workers specifically for politically defined failures. The death of Peter Connelly, combined with the financial crash of 2007/08, provided a political opportunity for particular discourses to be imposed by eclipsing the concerns, ideals and values of the profession with politically constructed, promoted and supported ones (Jones, 2014). With the discourse of neoliberalism forming the basis for such a framework, many accepted as naturally correct the need to reduce spending on social work services, increase commissioning and redesign services in attempts to better protect children from harm. Given these objectives, particular forms of social work practice with historical roots were promoted and supported to achieve present-day aims.

A component of neoliberal discourse, and therefore a foundation in the reconfiguration of public services, is a refashioning of the professionals who provide the public services and those who use the services. The neoliberal subject, that is, how a citizen is conceptualised within the neoliberal discourse, can be characterised as responsible, rational and entrepreneurial, engaging in markets to ensure that they, and their family, are financially secure and physically safe (Read, 2009; Wacquant, 2010; Chandler and Reid, 2016). The neoliberal conceptualisation of those who engage with state services has been to reclassify them as 'consumers' or 'customers', rather than 'clients' of a 'professional' (McDonald, 2006; Garrett, 2009; Pollack and Rossiter, 2010). The neoliberal professional, meanwhile, while similar in theme to the neoliberal subject, contains additional responsibilities as an actor of the state, not least a particular set of values that can conflict with professional social work values. Professionals are expected to support and promote the idea of individual responsibility, perform within and improve the efficiency of markets, and provide public order and safety (Archer, 2008; Wacquant, 2010; Hall and McGinity, 2015; Hyslop, 2018). Social workers are, therefore, conceptualised as 'care managers', on the one hand – assessing need, referring to services within the marketplace and managing packages of care – and as a form of social control, on the other – using the law, controlling dangerous behaviour and ensuring the safety of innocent people (McDonald, 2006; Garrett, 2009; Pollack and Rossiter, 2010; Featherstone et al, 2014; Parton, 2014; Spolander et al, 2014). These conceptualisations provide standards for the roles, actions and characteristics of those engaged in child and family social work that draw on the social administration and social policing representations of practice. Such standards are accepted within new public management ideology, imposed through a system of auditing (Power, 1997; Munro, 2004), providing a systemic force for the praiseworthy and shameful behaviour of social workers and the children and families they work with.

The case example demonstrates the complexity of competing and conflicting attempts to shape professional practice through emotion regulation. One set of constituencies, such as academia, the professional body and practitioners, promoted and supported the institutional logic of social work as a profession, conceiving social workers as having specialist knowledge and skills, underpinned by a specific set of values. This evoked pride and shame in certain forms of action and particular types of practice. Another set of constituencies, however, such as the media, politicians and the inspectorate, promoted and supported an alternative institutional logic, conceiving social work as an adjunct to the neoliberal state, evoking pride and shame in different forms of action and different types of practice. With experiences of being shamed, and sensing the possibility for further shaming and humiliation, the leaders and managers of the Council engaged in emotion work to create an organisational identity that satisfied both. With greater support, and more serious consequences for failing to comply with the institutional logic of public services as businesses, the emphasis within the organisation was placed on meeting the needs, aims and objectives of those constituencies. The child and family social work service was reorganised, creating specific functions for particular groups of social workers, and changing which situations they were exposed to and what they were expected to do within those situations. This organisational emotion work served to regulate the emotions of the social workers so that they performed social work in the way in which the organisation needed to avoid being shamed and attract praise.

The new organisationally supported interpretive framework for practice altered the representation of a social worker within the Council, providing new meanings and expectations for the professional identity. This was embedded within the Council by evoking pride in certain actions and shame in others, eclipsing alternative ways of thinking, feeling and acting, with unacceptable levels of deviance from expectations being policed through humiliation. Given such emotion regulation, the social workers learnt how to practise social work and how to be a social worker within the Council. This organisational representation then featured in every action and interaction of the social workers. By considering all of the information to hand, relating this to their past experience and knowledge, and imagining what may occur in the future, the social workers could sense the possibility of being praised or shamed for living up to the meanings and expectations contained within the organisational representation or not. At the same time, however, the social workers also sensed whether they would feel pride, shame, guilt or embarrassment for a particular action. Given the resulting situated conceptualisation, the social workers identified with, or resisted, the pressures, expectations and demands placed upon them.

While Power (1997) argues that the mechanisms of auditing control organisations by pushing the priorities of the auditors into the organisation, my research illustrates how emotion regulation can serve as the mechanism by which this is achieved. By knowing the conditions of being shamed and praised, the priorities of the auditors were pushed into the identity of the organisation, which were pushed into the identities of the social workers. This process was often unforgiving and the social workers were shamed and/or humiliated for not meeting expectations, even when this was not possible. They, therefore, often felt that they were not good enough, never being able to prove themselves as worthy of acceptance and belonging within the organisation. Consequently, some social workers tried harder to gain acceptance by practising in a manner that attracted praise, increasing their susceptibility to the emotion work strategy of compliance. The social workers could, therefore, often be seen starting work early, finishing late and working at the weekends. This has, perhaps, always been an issue for social workers as there has always been too much work and too little time. What was clear, however, was that much of the work that the social workers were doing outside of work time related to audit and administration, rather than anything they thought would make a difference to the families they were working with.

The practical effect of evoking, eclipsing or diverting certain self-conscious emotions in the social workers was to foreground the needs of the auditors/organisation, irrespective of the needs of the family. Some social workers reported feeling proud of removing children, giving evidence in court, writing reports, meeting timescales and closing cases, not only because they knew that they would be praised for such action, but also because they had come to believe that this was what it means to be a good social worker. Some reported feeling ashamed of making administrative errors, of not completing reports on time or of not having the same opinion as their team manager, not only because they knew they would be shamed for such action, but also because they had come to believe that this was legitimately shameful behaviour for a social worker. Even for those who did not identify with the organisational representation so easily, the processes of emotion regulation were still effective. While some social workers felt ashamed of removing children, upsetting parents or not living up to their own identity standards, they still went against their own reservations because they believed that they would be shamed or humiliated for not doing so. Despite feeling guilty about upsetting the children they worked with, some social workers still cancelled appointments to be able to complete paperwork on time because it was believed that the organisation valued administrative work more than any direct work they could do with the child and family.

Such practice could be considered to contradict the stated aims of professional practice within the Council, which had sought to embed a whole-family approach, using family group conferencing and the Signs of Safety as practice methodologies, all supported by ongoing reflective supervision. Given the context, pressures and expectations, however, it had become difficult for managers and social workers to be able to enact these ideals. Even though the social workers wanted to provide therapeutic support and practical help to families, they not only found it difficult to find the time to do this, but were also often unsure how to. Given the re-conceptualisation of social work through the neoliberal discourse, such work was considered the domain of other agencies or professionals.

The consequence of this was, first, that the focus on administrative tasks ensured that there was a perception of effective management of the risks posed to the children. By organising the service in such a manner, the social workers produced the evidence that the senior managers needed to present to the Office for Standards in Education (Ofsted) during an inspection, which provided organisational legitimacy. Such practice created emotional safety for the organisation by reducing the possibility of being shamed. Second, the focus on administrative tasks reduced the amount of time the social workers had to work with the children and families. Without this time and input, it was difficult to effect any change within the family. Occasionally, the social workers would blame themselves, but as Satyamurti (1981) also found in her ethnographic study of social workers, more usually, they would blame the family for their own painful feelings of inadequacy. Third, therefore, by refocusing the social work role onto administrative tasks, the social workers' capacity for empathy for the parents can be considered to have been reduced. Indeed, Larson argued in 1977 that where there is external pressure to perform non-client-focused tasks, professionals can develop an attitude of indifference towards them, and even that 'external imposition ... may change indifference into unqualified hostility to the client' (Larson, 1977: 188). Furthermore, by refocusing the social work role into one specifically for children, independent of their parents or wider family, it could be considered shameful to be seen to be focusing on the parents' needs, arguably recasting them as undeserving of help and support, and legitimising attempts to control those who were seen as a threat to a child. With the social workers effectively being given personal responsibility for the safety and well-being of the children on their caseload, and knowing that they could be blamed, criticised, shamed and humiliated for any mishaps or tragedies, it was common for a parent or carer to be perceived as a threat to their child. Parents could, therefore, be treated as untrustworthy unless they proved themselves to be worthy of trust by agreeing with the social worker's conceptualisation of the situation and complying with the social worker's requests. Where a parent was seen as responsible for any harm to a child, however, there were many occasions where they were not only blamed, but judged as an immoral person. Such social work practice was, therefore, experienced as shaming and humiliating by many of the parents.

It was not that the social workers wanted to focus on administration, however, or, at times, practise in a derogatory fashion, or that the leaders and managers wanted to design a system where such practice was encouraged. Indeed, to paraphrase Brown (2004), the social workers did not start out with a desire to evoke shame in the people they were trying to help or to go to court wanting to remove a child. They did not start out with a deep anxiety about not being perceived to be competent. They did not start as a social worker with a belief that their worthiness was linked to their ability to meet timescales, on the one hand, and to manage an excessive workload, on the other, all while never being seen to get upset. This situation came about because a set of meanings and expectations were created to evaluate the social workers against, which was imposed through regulating their experiences of pride, shame and other self-conscious emotions. Such attempts at emotion regulation did not erase already-established identity meanings, however, or remove the alternative sources of pressure that regulated their emotions in different ways. In navigating this complex emotional terrain, the social workers could engage in emotion work to feel proud of themselves and their actions and avoid being shamed for actions or characteristics that would be rejected by the dominant perspective within the organisation. Compromising organisational expectations, concealing unsupported actions and influencing organisational sources of emotion regulation were, therefore, common emotion work strategies of resistance.

Despite the rich picture of emotional experiences presented by these data in the case example, much of these embedded, embodied experiences remained hidden from the senior management, the team managers and even each other as they did not often discuss their emotional experiences openly. Yet what is clear is that practice involved a range of self-conscious emotions, sometimes overwhelmingly so, which could be seen as central to the way in which the social workers practised. This is but one case example, however. It is possible that emotional experiences are not as prominent elsewhere as they were within this Council. It may be that other councils are organised differently, resulting in a different experience for the social workers. However, national issues played a large part in setting the context for the emotional experiences of everyone within the Council. So, while the leaders and senior managers provided a vital contextual force for the social workers, they could not be considered to act as heroic leaders, able to set the institutional prescriptions, meanings and expectations as they saw fit. They occupied a particular position within, but were part of, a wider system. The snapshot provided in this case example provides a window into the lives of those who were expected to implement the contextually embedded intentions of these leaders and senior managers. The practical effects of the redesigned service are consistent with the pattern of practice across the UK, where there are increasing requirements for administration (eg Baginsky et al, 2010; Wastell et al, 2010; Munro, 2011), increasing patterns of policing methods to protect children (eg Parton, 2014; Bilson and Martin, 2016; Hood et al, 2016; Bunting et al, 2017) and parental experiences of shame (eg Featherstone and Fraser, 2012; Ghaffar et al, 2012; Gupta and Blumhardt, 2016; Jackson et al, 2017; Smithson and Gibson, 2017). This case study provides the first example of the role that pride and shame play in these developments.

Towards conditions for authenticity and pride in practice

The theory advanced here implies that a major issue for professional practice is responding to emotional experience. Journalists become outraged at children being harmed. The public become angry at the perceived failures of government agencies. Politicians become anxious about being involved in such perceived failures and ultimately losing their jobs. Each person engages in emotion work to respond to their emotional experience, which sees them exercise the power they have to change in degree or quality the negative emotions they feel. Such emotion work regulates the emotions of others, requiring them to respond accordingly. Insufficient attention provided to the emotions of others can lead to even greater outrage, anger and anxiety. Shame, guilt, humiliation and embarrassment are at the heart of many of these experiences. In responding to attempts at emotion regulation, leaders, managers and practitioners move away from the historical ideals, values and objectives of the profession (see Specht and Courtney, 1995). The conflict this creates can lead to practitioners feeling that they are no longer practising social work as they imagined and intended when they entered the profession (Parton, 1996). Divisions can, therefore, arise between those who remain cognitively, emotionally and morally committed to certain historical ideals, values and objectives for the profession and those who acclimatise to, adapt to and integrate new institutional perspectives.

People want to be able to live up to their own ideals and feel proud of what they do and who they are. The settlement within the profession, in terms of its aims, objectives, values and practices, provides individual practitioners with meanings, expectations and personal characteristics for their professional identities. Wilfully and consciously practising in a manner that is consistent with such aims, objectives and values enables practitioners to offer an authentic interaction, which represents the individual and the profession as intended by such ideals (see Lindholm, 2008). It is, however, inevitable that practitioners will make mistakes, get things wrong and fail to live up to their own standards at times. Not only are shame, guilt and embarrassment an inevitability where such concepts are provided by their sociocultural context, but they can be morally warranted experiences (Ferguson et al, 2007), important in the process of learning and improving. It is when such experiences are strategically used to disrupt established practice and impose new ways of practising that social workers are faced with choices about personal integrity and professional authenticity. Many may feel that the new standards and expectations are inconsistent with their long-held beliefs about what should be done and how it should be done. It is, of course, always possible that the new ideals, values and objectives are sufficiently accepted and integrated, eclipsing and replacing old arrangements, to create a new profession, albeit with an old name. At present, however, there are many communities and constituencies interested in the profession of social work who remain committed to certain professional values and ideals, such as within academia (eg Ferguson and Woodward, 2009; Garrett, 2009; Featherstone et al, 2014; Harris, 2014; Jones, 2014), the judiciary[1] and the professional body (BASW, 2014), together with non-governmental organisations and practitioners themselves.

In order to create the conditions for authenticity and pride in practice, the theory proposed here suggests a need to be more specific and explicit about emotions, and being purposeful in the professional response to emotional experience. Such an argument has a long history within the profession for work with individuals and groups (eg Hollis 1964; Yelloly, 1980; Ferguson, 2005; Ruch et al, 2010), and can be further developed for a more strategic institutional response to the collective outrage, anger and anxiety experienced within society (see Warner, 2015). The strength of such collective emotional experiences needs to be acknowledged, space needs to be provided for it to be expressed and such feelings need to be contained through discursive strategies that promote humane responses to leaders, managers, professionals and those who use the services, at the same time as undermining politically defined problems and their concomitant solutions that have little evidence to support their implementation (see Power, 1997; Munro, 2004). Indeed, regulating the emotions of others works both ways but resistance often occurs on an individual basis, be it an individual practitioner, an individual team or an individual organisation. Following a conference I spoke at about this subject, for example, one senior manager of a probation service came up to me to say that the senior leadership team had decided not to attempt to gain the highest inspection grading because to do so would reduce the quality of the service they provided. Such resistance may improve services but is unlikely to be publicised, promoted and praised within or across the professions.

Of course, emotion regulation as a form of resistance requires leadership within the profession to publically engage with difficult and emotive topics, and coordination across multiple organisations and institutions. Indeed, greater links across professional disciplines could be made as the professional struggles in education, health and so on are equally the struggles of social work, and vice versa. Yet rarely are there joint responses and collective action across the professions when one profession has a dispute with the government, for example, as the professional divisions do not engender ownership of the struggle across the divide. Mostly, however, these individual conflicts are about the disruption of professionalism and the imposition of a new set of arrangements informed by the discourse of neoliberalism (Garrett, 2009). It is only through collective action that the power of the regulating capacity of the media and politicians can be challenged, contained and directed. Indeed, the reproduction and continuation of systemic pressures should not be taken for granted as the dominant discourses, beliefs and shared rules require active maintenance over time and are, therefore, always open to reinterpretation.

In attempts to influence the systemic forces that shape and define the shared rules for shameful and praiseworthy behaviour, social work needs to remain engaged in the political process. Social work was born out of political and social struggle, and engaging in politics is an authentic social work activity (see Atlee, 1920); yet, there are many who argue that it is now a neglected component of practice (eg Figueira-Mcdonough, 1993; Ferguson, 2009). It is not only leaders and senior members of the profession that can engage in practice that affects societal change for the benefit of those the profession was set up to serve; organisations can also support social workers to engage in this process by creating a culture of political activity. Social workers can be given time to perform political actions, such as writing to their local councillor or Member of Parliament about issues that are adversely affecting the people they work with, becoming involved in local and national political campaigns, or engaging with the local and national media. It is through such collective groundwork that the context for emotional experience changes. It has not always been the case that social workers were blamed for child deaths or social work organisations were classified as inadequate, for example. Coordinated effort across multiple individuals, organisations and institutions can disassociate the moral foundations and undermine the core assumptions and beliefs that hold such practices in place (see Lawrence and Suddaby, 2006).

In promoting and supporting a particular discourse that fosters policies, practices and structures that creates a more humane system (Taylor and White, 2006; Broadhurst et al, 2010a; Featherstone et al, 2014), greater agreement needs to be reached within the profession regarding definitions, descriptions and categories for practice. Indeed, the debate about what social work practice is (eg Brewer and Lait, 1980; Narey, 2014) has provided political opportunities for some to disrupt one set of ideas for practice and impose and embed new meanings and expectations into the profession and professional identity constructions (Parton, 1996, 2014; Jones, 2014; Shoesmith, 2016). Consequently, the government, the inspectorate and social work organisations expect social workers to engage in activities that are not authentic social work tasks. There are many, for example, who have expressed concerns about social workers' emboldened policing function through the increasing expectation for greater levels of monitoring, surveillance and control, such as by reporting on people's immigration status (Humphries, 1997), assessing their (potential) role in terrorism (McKendrick and Finch, 2017) or seeking to control 'immoral' behaviours (Rogowski, 2011). By creating language that decouples what is shameful and praiseworthy for social work and that which is not, it is possible to create sufficient space for some institutional entrepreneurs to influence or force changes in the systemic shame and pride for their organisation. Indeed, while the values and ethics of the profession continue to be accepted within the social work community, there will always be social work organisations and services that seek to realign their practice to such professional values, ethics and ideals (for recent examples, see Forrester et al, 2017; Mason et al, 2017).

Furthermore, the language of emotions can be an important tool in the construction of a new interpretive framework as emotions can powerfully describe both the actions of the regulators and the experience of those being regulated. Through such powerful descriptions, cultural legitimacy for certain practices can be disrupted and new ones created. The lack of communication about feelings (see Ruch, 2012) enables people to associate meaning with their actions divorced from the experience of those actions, allowing shaming and humiliating practices to continue, embedded in the belief that they are doing the 'right' thing. To perceive oneself as shaming and humiliating another, while painful and uncomfortable, can facilitate sufficient empathy and reflection to motivate change (Gausel and Leach, 2011). Talking about how we feel, and talking about how we imagine others may be feeling, are, therefore, important components of being able to disrupt and create new institutional norms, rules and practices. Speaking up about feeling shame and humiliation is, however, painful and difficult (see Brown, 2004), requiring courage and self-compassion; yet, this may be necessary to exert an episodic force that influences, challenges and manipulates the actions of those involved in the regulation of the profession and the professionals.

Changing the boundaries for shameful and praiseworthy behaviour for the social workers in any council would, inevitably, heighten a sense of shame in the leaders and managers. Arguably, all established arrangements can be considered to be a product of navigating and settling on a set of rules and practices intended to avoid being shamed and attract being praised. Leaders and managers would, therefore, require the courage to make changes to these in the knowledge that something could, at some point, attract unwanted attention to their service, leaving them feeling vulnerable. Honesty about such feelings, with greater communication between individuals and organisations about such vulnerabilities, along with better coordination of practical and political support for leaders and managers that are shamed and humiliated, may provide greater strength to stay true to their original vision (Shoesmith, 2016). Honesty about how we feel and courage to speak up about this can be considered to be a deliberate and crucial form of institutional work. It is through such action that political, and ultimately regulatory, support can be mobilised (Lawrence and Suddaby, 2006) in efforts to create a more authentic social work system that social workers can feel proud of.

Summary and future directions for pride and shame research

There are, of course, many factors that influence how social workers practice, but if pride, shame and other self-conscious emotions are at the heart of all of our interactions (eg Cooley, 1902; Goffman, 1959), then they are at the heart of any form of practice. This book has sought to highlight these as highly significant components of practice, which everyone 'feels' but does not always communicate. Their influence can, therefore, remain unacknowledged. This book has critiqued and synthesised a range of conceptual ideas relating to the nature and experience of these emotions, and offered a new conceptual framework to explain and predict them. The application of the theory of pride and shame to child and family social work practice has constructed, for the first time, a general theory of how these emotions are strategically used and experienced, and influence professional practice. This theory develops our understanding of practice by demonstrating how they were involved in: (1) installing a particular interpretive framework for practice; (2) embedding ideal-typical meanings and characteristics for practitioners; and (3) guiding and shaping the acquiescence or resistance to expectations.

This perspective complements and expands the existing literature on the forces that are created by wider social mechanisms in response to social, political and functional pressures, and their effect on organisations and their actors (Parton, 2014; Warner, 2015). It suggests that, as an embodied experience, self-conscious emotions are an inherent part of social workers' experience and, therefore, guide and constrain the actions and interactions that underpin what they do and how to do it, extending the debates on naturalistic decision-making in social work practice (Platt and Turney, 2014). It also highlights, as an embedded experience, the significant role of those who set the context for their practice and how this context specifically influences what the social workers do and how they do it (Featherstone et al, 2014;

Ferguson, 2016). The perspective provided in this book has provided a language to highlight the use of pride and shame as political tools and cultural-cognitive resources, which can be used to understand and influence these emotional, psychological and social processes.

Furthermore, this view contributes to the debates on what power is and how it is exercised in institutional processes (Lukes, 2005; Lawrence, 2008) and social work practice (Hasenfeld, 1987; Tew, 2006). Considering self-conscious emotions as a component of the micro-foundations of interpersonal dynamics, communication and social and symbolic interaction provides new avenues for theorising and researching how certain actions can be deterred, constrained and shaped, while others are encouraged, maintained and supported (Voronov and Vince, 2012). Indeed, by considering self-conscious emotions as both an effect and source of power, this perspective compliments the literature on how power opens up or closes off certain opportunities not only for the social workers, but also for the managers and the organisation as a whole (Tew, 2006). In the construction of notions of legitimacy and standards to achieve legitimacy, both for organisations and professionals, shame and pride can be considered as the mechanisms for the exercise of power in the legitimising process, with humiliation a standard organisational product (Czarniawska, 2008) in the rituals of verification (Power, 1997). Indeed, self-conscious emotions provide the systemic force that achieves motivation and commitment to certain ways of acting and being within a given institution. This book has also, however, contributed to the debates on resistance; as Hudson et al (2015) argue, notions of legitimacy are always contested, and as the case study demonstrated, self-conscious emotions can be considered an essential component in attitudes and actions of resistance.

As an emerging perspective and field of research within social work, there remains much to be explored, expanded and implemented in relation to pride and shame in practice. While the dominant discourse on shame and pride characterises shame as 'bad' and pride as 'good', this book has highlighted how pride can have a dark side, potentially being used to promote practice that causes distress and pain in others, while shame could be used for good, deterring oppressive practice and nurturing ethical professional identities. It is the social context that provides the meaning and therefore the direction of the constraints. What might the lived experience of such emotions be like when the boundaries for praiseworthy and shameful behaviour are aligned with professional values? Where may the drivers for resistance come from and what might these look like? How might such experiences be managed when they are acknowledged and communicated effectively within practice? What may be the unintended consequences for such a development in practice? What happens when people become aware that their actions shame and humiliate others? What might be the consequence of preventing humiliation as a legitimate organisational action? Such questions may develop and open up new techniques for management and develop a new evidence base for humane policy and practice. Furthermore, this book has focused primarily on the lived experience of pride and shame of professionals, and has only really considered such experiences in the people they work with in relation to their interactions with the professionals. Despite the emerging evidence of experiences of self-conscious emotions (mainly shame) in parents and carers (see Dale, 2004; Dumbrill, 2006; Buckley et al, 2011; Sykes, 2011; Ghaffar et al, 2012; Harris, 2012; Thrana and Fauske, 2014; Gupta, 2015; Gupta and Blumhardt, 2016; Smithson and Gibson, 2017; Gupta et al, 2018), there is still much to be understood about the role that pride and shame play in their experiences, actions and relationships with other members of their social network, as well as with professionals. Further still, as this book has mainly focused on individual experiences of pride and shame, it leaves questions for research to consider the collective feelings of pride and shame and the role of vicarious pride and shame in leadership, management and practice. In our efforts to create a more humane system, pride and shame potentially offer a central organising theme.

Note

[1.] See, for example, Re B-S (Children) [2013] EWCA Civ 1146 (available at: www.bailii.org/ew/cases/EWCA/Civ/2013/1146.html [accessed 14 April 2016]) and Re N (Children) (Adoption: Jurisdiction) [2015] EWCA Civ 1112 (available at: www.bailii.org/ew/cases/EWCA/Civ/2015/1112.html [accessed 28 March 2016]).

Appendix 1: Theoretical foundations of the study

Given that pride, shame, guilt, humiliation and embarrassment have both social and psychological elements to their experiences, the study of pride and shame is usually conducted by social psychologists. Social psychology is, however, not itself a unified field, consisting of psychological and sociological perspectives (House, 1977; DeLamater, 2006). Psychological social psychology starts from the inside out, focusing on the individual to study how they respond to social stimuli, whereas sociological social psychology starts from the outside in, starting with the social and cultural context and studying how this affects individuals. While pride and shame has mainly been studied from the psychological perspective (eg Tangney and Dearing, 2002), there are many who have critiqued such an approach as too narrow and limiting to understand the complexity of experiences of pride and shame (eg Gordon, 1981; Scheff, 2003). The approach taken in the research outlined in this book follows on from such critiques to argue that we cannot understand these experiences without understanding the social, cultural and political pressures that are exerted on social work institutions, organisations and practitioners.

This book, therefore, takes a sociological approach to social psychology, being broadly grounded in a constructionist orientation. The foundation of such a position is that people make sense of their experience through social interaction (Geertz, 1973), principally through language (Wittgenstein, 1967), which is not considered to represent some objective reality, but, rather, constitutes their social worlds. Language, therefore, enables not just knowledge and beliefs to be created, but also social institutions and identities (Berger and Luckmann, 1967). Given the importance of language in the creation of people's worlds, to understand their experience, their beliefs, their identities and their emotions, we need to understand the discourses that construct and maintain such a world. We can consider a discourse as 'a set of meanings, metaphors, representations, images, stories, statements ... that in some way together produce a particular version of events' (Burr, 1995: 48), which not only provides meaning for individuals and communities, but also provides the boundaries and, therefore, the possibilities for acting, thinking and feeling (Foucault, 1990).

A major strand of sociological social psychology within Europe argues that within the marketplace of discourse, certain opinions, images, metaphors and ideologies eventually become collectively adopted, and objects and things in the world are named, equipped with attributes and values, and integrated into a socially meaningful world (Wagner, 1996). These systems of values, ideas and practices can be considered as social representations constructed 'for the purpose of behaving and communicating' (Moscovici, 1961: 251). As Putnam (1988) argues, a representation is the conceptual 'cookie' cut out of the world-'dough' by virtue of discourse, consensus and social behaviour. Social representations are constructed for all social objects, such as for the profession of social work, the role of organisations that deliver social work services, the role of the social worker or the people social workers work with. The emotions of pride and shame are not experienced in isolation, but the product of active engagement within one's social worlds that are filled with standards for thinking, feeling and acting. The use of social representations theory (Moscovici, 1961) provides a theoretical frame through which the creation, communication and integration of such standards, and therefore self-conscious emotional experience, can be analysed.

A social representation is both a process and content (Moscovici, 1961; Abric, 1987). It is the process of, for example, exploring, recognising, categorising and making sense of a particular phenomenon. It is also the content of the resulting 'presentation', or image, of the phenomenon through that process. The result is the practical, everyday knowledge of people within particular communities about particular social objects (Lahlou and Abric, 2011). A social representation can, therefore, be considered to be the body of information, beliefs, opinions and attitudes about a given object, which is discursively constructed over time and, as such, is part of a social group's collective memory. Moscovici (1961) described two main processes in the construction of a social representation. The first is anchoring, in which meaning is given to new phenomena by integrating it into pre-established categories so that the unfamiliar becomes familiar. The second is objectification, in which abstract ideas are turned into concrete objects. People can, therefore, engage with, interact with and respond to social work as a profession and a practice in concrete ways.

A representation can be characterised as the relation between those who carry the representation, the object that is represented and the social context in which the representation makes sense (Bauer and Gaskell, 1999). Social representations are, therefore, not 'things' in the minds of people, but rather the significant structure, or meaning, that orientates a person's or group's interaction in a specific context (Harré and Gillet, 1994). There are, however, always power struggles within and between social groups as to the representation of social objects, and divergent, competing and conflicting representations can evolve and become available within these groups. The structural approach to social representations (Abric, 1976) argues that a representation consists of a central core set of elements that give it its meaning and peripheral elements that, while providing the context, constitute the moving and evolving aspect of the representation. How social objects are represented within and between specific communities is, therefore, not fixed and is under constant revision, change and renewal (Wagner, 1996).

The broad appeal of the social representations approach is that is provides a framework to analyse the social processes that affect individual experience. It is, however, an approach that complements a range of other theoretical ideas. Indeed, Breakwell (1993) has sought to develop both social representations theory and social identity theory by considering how they extend their respective explanatory powers. Also, given that many social representations become institutionalised, Koza and Thoenig (1995) sought to identify how the social representations approach could complement and extend institutional theory. So, while this book is grounded in a social representations approach, it draws on other ideas relating to identity and institutions, both of which are highly relevant to self-consciousness and the emotional experiences that result from it.

Appendix 2: Theoretical codes

Source	Theoretical codes
Glaser (1978, 1998, 2005)	• 'The 6 Cs': causes, contingencies, consequences, contexts, covariance, conditions • The 'type family': ideal-type, constructed type • The 'strategy family': strategies, tactics, mechanisms, techniques, dealing with, handling, arrangements, managed goals, means • The 'identity–self family': self-image, self-concept, self-worth, self-evaluation, identity, social worth, transformations of self, conversions of identity • The 'means–goal family': end, purpose, goal, anticipated consequences, product • The 'cultural family': norms, values, beliefs, sentiments • The 'consensus family': agreement, cooperation, definitions of the situation, opinion, conformity, conflict, perception, non-conformity, mutual expectation • The 'mainline family': social control, socialisation, social organisation, social mobility, stratification, social institutions, social interaction • The 'unit family': collective, group, organisation, situation, context, behavioural pattern, family positional units, that is, status, role, role relationship
Creed et al (2014)	• Systemic shame (and pride) • A sense of shame (and pride) • Episodic shaming (and praising) • The felt experience
Moisander et al (2016)	• Evoking emotions • Eclipsing emotions • Diverting emotions
Lawrence and Suddaby (2006)	• 'Creating institutions': defining, constructing identities, changing normative associations, constructing normative networks, mimicry, theorising, educating • 'Maintaining institutions': enabling work, policing, deterring, valorising and demonising, mythologising, embedding and routinising • 'Disrupting institutions': disconnecting sanctions, disassociating moral foundations, undermining assumptions and beliefs
Oliver (1991)	• Acquiescing: habit, imitate, comply • Compromising: balance, pacify, bargain • Avoiding: conceal, buffer, escape • Defying: dismiss, challenge, attack • Manipulating: co-opt, influence, control
Alvesson and Willmott (2002)	• Defining the person directly • Defining a person by defining others • Providing a specific vocabulary of motives • Explicating morals and values • Knowledge and skills • Group categorisation and affiliation • Hierarchical location • Establishing and clarifying a distinct set of rules of the game • Defining the context

References

Abric, J.-C. (1976) *Jeux, conflicts et représentations sociales*. Thèse d'état, Aix-en-Provence: Université de Provence.

Abric, J.-C. (1987) *Coopération, compétition et représentations sociales*. Cousset-Fribourg: DelVal.

Ackroyd, S. and Thompson, P. (1999) *Organizational misbehaviour*. London: Sage.

Albert, S. and Whetten, D.A. (1985) Organizational identity. *Research in Organizational Behavior*, 7: 263–95.

Alvesson, M. and Willmott, H. (2002) Identity regulation as organizational control: producing the appropriate individual. *Journal of Management Studies*, 39(5): 619–44.

Archer, L. (2008) The new neoliberal subjects? Young/er academics' constructions of professional identity. *Journal of Education Policy*, 23(3): 265–85.

Armon-Jones, C. (1986) The thesis of constructionism. In R. Harré (ed) *The social construction of emotions*. New York, NY: Blackwell, pp 32–56.

Arnold, M.B. (1960) *Emotion and personality*. New York, NY: Columbia University.

Attlee, C.R. (1920) *The social worker*. London: Bell and Sons.

Audit Commission (2002) *Recruitment and retention: A public service workforce for the twenty-first century*. London: Audit Commission.

Austin, J.L. (1975) *How to do things with words*. Oxford: Oxford University Press.

Averill, J.R. (1980) A constructivist view of emotion. In R. Plutchik and H. Kellerman (eds) *Theory, research and experience*. New York, NY: Academic Press, pp 305–39.

Baginsky, M., Moriarty, J., Manthorpe, J., Stevens, M., MacInnes, T. and Nagendran, T. (2010) *Social workers' workload survey: Messages from the frontline*. London: DCSF.

Bailey, F.G. (1977) *Morality and expediency*. Oxford: Blackwell.

Bailey, R. and Brake, M. (1975) *Radical social work*. London: Edward Arnold.

Bancroft, N.P. (2007) Physician shame: an obstacle to disclosing adverse outcomes. *Clinician in Management*, 15: 3–10.

Barbalet, J.M. (2001) *Emotion, social theory, and social structure: A macrosociological approach*. Cambridge: Cambridge University Press.

Barclay Report (1982) *Social workers: Their role and tasks.* London: Bedford Square Press.

Baron-Cohen, S. (2011) *Zero degrees of empathy.* London: Penguin.

Barrett, L.F. (2006a) Solving the emotion paradox: categorization and the experience of emotion. *Personality and Social Psychology Review,* 10: 20–46.

Barrett, L.F. (2006b) Are emotions natural kinds? *Perspectives on Psychological Science,* 1(1): 28–58.

Barrett, L.F. and Russell, J.A. (eds) (2015) *The psychological construction of emotion.* London: Guilford Press.

Barrett, L.F., Lindquist, K.A., Bliss-Moreau, E., Duncan, S., Gendron, M., Mize, J. and Brennan, L. (2007) Of mice and men: natural kinds of emotions in the mammalian brain? A response to Panksepp and Izard. *Perspectives on Psychological Science,* 2(3): 297–312.

Barrett, L.F., Wilson-Mendenhall, C.D. and Barsalou, L.W. (2014) A psychological construction account of emotion regulation and dysregulation: the role of situated conceptualizations. In J.J. Gross (ed) *The handbook of emotion regulation.* New York, NY: Guilford, pp 447–65.

Barsalou, L.W. (1999) Perceptual symbol systems. *Behavioral and Brain Sciences,* 22(4): 637–60.

Barsalou, L.W. (2009) Simulation, situated conceptualization, and prediction. *Philosophical Transactions of the Royal Society of London B: Biological Sciences,* 364(1521): 1281–9.

BASW (British Association of Social Workers) (2014) *The code of ethics for social work.* Birmingham: British Association of Social Workers.

Battilana, J. and D'Aunno, T. (2009) Institutional work and the paradox of embedded agency. In T.B. Lawrence, R. Suddaby and B. Leca (eds) *Institutional work. Actors and agency in institutional studies of organizations.* Cambridge: Cambridge University Press, pp 31–58.

Bauer, M.W. and Gaskell, G. (1999) Towards a paradigm for research on social representations. *Journal for the Theory of Social Behaviour,* 29(2): 163–86.

Baumeister, R.F., Stillwell, A.M. and Heatherton, T.F. (1995) Personal narratives about guilt: role in action control and interpersonal relationships. *Basic and Applied Social Psychology,* 17(1/2): 173–98.

Behrendt, H. and Ben-Ari, R. (2012) The positive side of negative emotion: the role of guilt and shame in coping with interpersonal conflict. *Journal of Conflict Resolution,* 56(6): 1116–38.

Bell, E.M. (1943) *Octavia Hill: A biography.* London: Constable & Co.

Bell, M. (1999) *Child protection: Families and the conference process.* Aldershot: Ashgate.

Berger, P. and Luckmann. T. (1967) *The social construction of reality*. New York, NY: Double and Company.

Berger, T.U. (2012) *War, guilt, and world politics after World War II*. Cambridge: Cambridge University Press.

Beveridge, W.H.B.B. (1942) *Social insurance and allied services*. London: HMSO.

Bewes, T. (2010) *The event of postcolonial shame*. Princeton, NJ: Princeton University Press.

Bilson, A. and Martin, K.E.C. (2016) Referrals and child protection in England: one in five children referred to children's services and one in nineteen investigated before the age of five. *British Journal of Social Work*, bcw054. Available at: http://doi.org/10.1093/bjsw/bcw054

Blumer, H. (1969) *Symbolic interactionism*. Englewood Cliffs, NJ: Prentice-Hall.

Bogo, M., Raphael, D. and Roberts, R. (1993) Interests, activities, and self-identification among social work students: toward a definition of social work identity. *Journal of Social Work Education*, 29(3): 279–92.

Boiger, M., Mesquita, B., Uchida, Y. and Barrett, L.F. (2013) Condoned or condemned: the situational affordance of anger and shame in the United States and Japan. *Personality & Social Psychology Bulletin*, 39(4): 540–53.

Bond, M.E. (2009) Exposing shame and its effect on clinical nursing education. *Journal of Nursing Education*, 48: 132–40.

Booth, C. (1889) *Life and labour of the people in London*. London: Macmillan.

Bourdieu, P. (1994) Rethinking the state: genesis and structure of the bureaucratic field. *Sociological theory*, 12(1): 1–18.

Bourdieu, P. and Wacquant, L.J.D. (1992) *An invitation to reflexive sociology*. Chicago, IL: University of Chicago Press.

Bradley, M.M. and Lang, P.J. (2000) Measuring emotion: behavior, feeling, and physiology. In R.D. Lane and L. Nadel (eds) *Cognitive neuroscience of emotion*. New York, NY: Oxford University Press, pp 242–76.

Brandon, M., Belderson, P., Warren, C., Howe, D., Gardner, R., Dodsworth, J. and Black, J. (2008) *Analysing child deaths and serious injury through abuse and neglect: What can we learn? A biennial analysis of serious case reviews 2003–2005*. London: DCSF.

Branta, H., Jacobson, T. and Alvinius, A. (2017) Professional pride and dignity? A classic grounded theory study among social workers. In A.A. Vilas Boas (ed) *Quality of life and quality of working life*. Rijeka, Croatia: InTech, pp 285–301.

Breakwell, G.M. (1993) Integrating paradigms, methodological implications. In G.M. Breakwell and D.V. Canter (eds) *Empirical approaches to social representations*. Oxford: Oxford University Press, pp 180–201.

Breakwell, G.M. (2001) Social representational constraints upon identity development. In K. Deaux and G. Philogène (eds) *Representations of the social: Bridging theoretical traditions*. Oxford: Blackwell, pp 271–84.

Breuer, J. and Freud, S. (1895) *Studies on hysteria*. New York, NY: Basic Books.

Brewer, C. and Lait, J. (1980) *Can social work survive?* London: Temple Smith.

Brieland, D. (1990) The Hull-House tradition and the contemporary social worker: was Jane Addams really a social worker? *Social Work*, 35(2): 134–8.

Briggs, A. and Macartney, A. (2011) *Toynbee Hall: The first hundred years*. London: Routledge.

Britt, L. and Heise, D. (2000) From shame to pride in identity politics. In S. Stryker, T.J. Owens and R.W. White (eds) *Self, identity, and social movements*. London: University of Minnesota Press.

Britzman, D. (2003) Introduction to the revised edition. In D. Britzman (ed) *Practice makes practice: A critical study of learning to teach*. Albany, NY: State University of New York, pp 1–23.

Broadhurst, K., Hall, C., Wastell, D., White, S. and Pithouse, A. (2010a) Risk, instrumentalism and the humane project in social work: identifying the informal logics of risk management in children's statutory services. *British Journal of Social Work*, 40(4): 1046–64.

Broadhurst, K., Wastell, D., White, S., Hall, C., Peckover, S., Thompson, K., Pithouse, A. and Davey, D. (2010b) Performing 'initial assessment': identifying the latent conditions for error at the front-door of local authority children's services. *British Journal of Social Work*, 40: 352–70.

Brown, B. (2004) *Women and shame*. Austin, TX: 3C Press.

Brown, B. (2006) Shame resilience theory: a grounded theory study on women and shame. *Families in Society*, 87: 43–52.

Buckley, H., Carr, N. and Whelan, S. (2011) 'Like walking on eggshells': service user views and expectations of the child protection system. *Child and Family Social Work*, 16(1): 101–110.

Buckley, S. (2013) *The cruelty man: Child welfare, the NSPCC and the state in Ireland, 1889–1956*. Manchester: Manchester University Press.

Bunting, L., McCartan, C., McGhee, J., Bywaters, P., Daniel, B., Featherstone, B. and Slater, T. (2017) Trends in child protection across the UK: a comparative analysis. *The British Journal of Social Work*. Available at: https://doi.org/10.1093/bjsw/bcx102

Burke, P.J. (1991) Identity processes and social stress. *American Sociological Review*, 56: 836–49.

Burke, P.J. and Stets, J.E. (2009) *Identity theory*. New York, NY: Oxford University Press.

Burkitt, I. (2014) *Emotions and social relations*. London: Sage.

Burr, V. (1995) *An introduction to social constructionism*. London: Routledge.

Buss, A.H. (1980) *Self-consciousness and social anxiety*. San Francisco, CA: Freeman.

Buss, A.H. (2001) *Psychological dimensions of the self*. London: Sage.

Butler-Sloss, E. (1988) *Report of the Inquiry into Child Abuse in Cleveland 1987*. Cm 412. London: HMSO.

Cameron, D. (2016) My promise to every child in care: I will help you build a better life. *The Sunday Times*, 15 May. Available at: www.thetimes.co.uk/article/my-promise-to-every-child-in-care-i-will-help-you-build-a-better-life-q7rwxnvpd (accessed 21 June 2018).

Carey, M. and Foster, V. (2011) Introducing 'deviant' social work: contextualising the limits of radical social work whilst understanding (fragmented) resistance within the social work labour process. *British Journal of Social Work*, 41: 576–93.

Carter, M.J. (2013) Advancing identity theory: examining the relationship between activated identities and behavior in different social contexts. *Social Psychology Quarterly*, 76(3): 203–23.

Catherall, D.R. (2007) *Emotional safety*. New York, NY: Routledge.

Ceunen, E., Vlaeyen, J.W. and Van Diest, I. (2016) On the origin of interoception. *Frontiers in Psychology*, 7: Art 743.

Chambon, A.S. (1999) *Reading Foucault for social work*. New York, NY: Columbia University.

Chandler, D. and Reid, J. (2016) *The neoliberal subject*. London: Rowman and Littlefield.

Chang, M.L. (2009) An appraisal perspective of teacher burnout: examining the emotional work of teachers. *Educational Psychology Review*, 21(3): 193–218.

Charmaz, K. (2006) *Constructing grounded theory*. London: Sage.

Chase, E. and Bantebya-Kyomuhendo, G. (eds) (2014) *Poverty and shame: Global experiences*. Oxford: Oxford University Press.

Chase, E. and Walker, R. (2012) The co-construction of shame in the context of poverty: beyond a threat to the social bond. *Sociology*, 47: 739–54.

Clapton, G. (2008) 'Yesterday's men': the inspectors of the Royal Scottish Society for the Prevention of Cruelty to Children, 1888–1968. *British Journal of Social Work*, 39(6): 1043–62.

Clark, A. and Chalmers, D. (1998) The extended mind. *Analysis*, 58: 10–23.

Clarke, J., Newman, J., Smith, N., Vidler, E. and Westmarland, L. (2007) *Creating citizen-consumers: Changing publics and changing public services*. London: Sage.

Combs, D.J.Y., Campbell, G., Jackson, M. and Smith, R.H. (2010) Exploring the consequences of humiliating a moral transgressor. *Basic and Applied Social Psychology*, 32: 128–43.

Connell, R., Fawcett, B. and Meagher, G. (2009) Neoliberalism, new public management and the human service professions: introduction to the special issue. *Journal of Sociology*, 45(4): 331–8.

Cooley, C.H. (1902) *Human nature and the social order*. New York, NY: Scribner's Sons.

Cotogni, I. (2018) Ofsted praises council's children's services. *Warrington Guardian*, 5 March. Available at: www.warringtonguardian.co.uk/news/16065929.Ofsted_praises_council___s_children___s_services/ (accessed 21 June 2018).

Courtney, M.E., Needell, B. and Wulczyn, F. (2004) Unintended consequences of the push for accountability: the case of national child welfare performance standards. *Children and Youth Services Review*, 26(12): 1141–54.

Cradock, G. (2007) The responsibility dance: creating neoliberal children. *Childhood*, 14: 153–72.

Creed, W.E.D., Hudson, B.A., Okhuysen, G.A. and Smith-Crowe, K. (2014) Swimming in a sea of shame: incorporating emotion into explanations of institutional reproduction and change. *Academy of Management Review*, 39(3): 275–301.

Cronen, V.E., Pearce, W.B. and Harris, L.M. (1982) The coordinated management of meaning: a theory of communication. In F.E.X. Dance (ed) *Human communication theory*. New York, NY: Harper and Row, pp 61–89.

Crossley, S. (2016) 'Realising the (troubled) family', 'crafting the neoliberal state'. *Families, Relationships and Societies*, 5(2): 263–79.

Crowley, J. (1999) The politics of belonging: some theoretical considerations. In A. Geddes and A. Favell (eds) *The politics of belonging: Migrants and minorities in contemporary Europe*. Aldershot: Ashgate, pp 15–41.

Crozier, W.R. (2014) Differentiating shame from embarrassment. *Emotion Review*, 6(3): 269–72.

Csordas, T.J. (ed) (1994) *Embodiment and experience*. Cambridge: Cambridge University Press.

Culpitt, I. (1999) *Social policy and risk*. London: Sage.

Cunningham, W. and Wilson, H. (2011) Complaints, shame and defensive medicine. *BMJ Quality and Safety*, 20: 449–52.

Cutler, T. and Waine, B. (2003) Advancing public accountability? The social services 'Star' ratings. *Public Money and Management*, 23(2): 125–8.

Czarniawska, B. (2008) Humiliation: a standard organizational product? *Critical Perspectives on Accounting*, 19(7): 1034–53.

Dahlqvist, V., Soderberg, A. and Norberg, A. (2009) Facing inadequacy and being good enough: psychiatric care providers' narratives about experiencing and coping with troubled conscience. *Journal of Psychiatric and Mental Health Nursing*, 16: 242–7.

Dale, P, (2004) 'Like a fish in a bowl': parents' perceptions of child protection services. *Child Abuse Review*, 13: 137–57.

Damasio, A. (1994) *Descartes' error: Emotion, reason, and the human brain*. London: Vintage.

D'Andrade, R. (1987) A folk model of the mind. In D. Holland and N. Quinn (eds) *Cultural models in language and thought*. Cambridge: Cambridge University Press.

Danzinger, K. (1997). The varieties of social construction. *Theory and Psychology*, 7(3): 399–416.

Darwin, C. (1872) *The expression of the emotions in man and animals*. London: John Murray.

Davidoff, F. (2002) Shame: the elephant in the room. *Quality and Safety in Health Care*, 11: 2–3.

Davies, M. (1994) *The essential social worker* (3rd edn). Aldershot: Arena.

Dearing, R.L. and Tangney, J.P.E. (2011) *Shame in the therapy hour*. Washington, DC: American Psychological Association.

Deaux, K. and Philogène, G. (eds) (2001) *Representations of the social*. Oxford: Blackwell.

Deetz, S. (1995) *Transforming communication, transforming business: Building responsive and responsible workplaces*. Cresskill, NJ: Hampton Press.

Delamater, J. (ed) (2006) *Handbook of social psychology*. New York, NY: Springer.

Deonna, J.A., Rodogno, R. and Teroni, F. (2012) *In defense of shame: The faces of an emotion*. Oxford: Oxford University Press.

Department for Children, Schools and Families (2010) *Working together to safeguard children: A guide to inter-agency working to safeguard and promote the welfare of children*. London: The Stationery Office.

Dewey, J. (1929) *Experience and nature*. London: George Allen and Unwin.

Dewey, J. and Tufts, J.H. (1909) *Ethics*. New York, NY: Henry Holt and Company.

Dey, I. (1999) *Grounding grounded theory*. San Diego, CA: Academic Press.

Dey, I. (2013) Grounding categories. In A. Bryant and K. Charmaz (eds) *The Sage handbook of grounded theory*. London: Sage, pp 167–90.

Dodsworth, F.M. (2008) The idea of police in eighteenth-century England: discipline, reformation, superintendence, c. 1780–1800. *Journal of the History of Ideas*, 69(4): 583–604.

Dolezal, L. (2015) *The body and shame*. Lanham, MD: Lexington Books.

Dolezal, L. and Lyons, B. (2017) Health-related shame: an affective determinant of health? *Medical Humanities*, 43: 257–63.

Dreier, O. (2007) *Psychotherapy in everyday life*. Cambridge: Cambridge University Press.

Dumbrill, G. (2006) Parental experience of child protection intervention: a qualitative study. *Child Abuse & Neglect*, 30(1): 27–37.

Duveen, G. (2001) Representations, identities, resistance. In K. Deaux and G. Philogène (eds) *Representations of the social: Bridging theoretical traditions*. Oxford: Blackwell, pp 257–70.

Dwyer, J.G. (2010) *Moral status and human life: The case for children's superiority*. Cambridge: Cambridge University Press.

Edmondson, A. (1999) Psychological safety and learning behavior in work teams. *Administrative Science Quarterly*, 44(2): 350–83.

Ekman, P. and Friesen, W.V. (1971) Constants across cultures in the face and emotion. *Journal of Personality and Social Psychology*, 17(2): 124–9.

Elias, N. (1978) *The civilizing process: Vols. 1–3*. New York, NY: Pantheon.

Elison, J. (2005) Shame and guilt: a hundred years of apples and oranges. *New Ideas in Psychology*, 23(1): 5–32.

Elison, J. and Harter, S. (2007) Humiliation: causes, correlates, and consequences. In J.L. Tracy, R.W. Robins and J.P. Tangney (eds) *The self-conscious emotions*. New York, NY: Guilford, pp 310–29.

Elks, M.A. and Kirkhart, K.E. (1993) Evaluating effectiveness from the practitioner perspective. *Social Work*, 38(5): 554–63.

Ellsworth, P.C. (2013) Appraisal theory: old and new questions. *Emotion Review*, 5(2): 125–31.

Elshout, M., Nelissen, R.M.A. and Van Beest, I. (2017) Conceptualising humiliation. *Cognition and Emotion*, 31(8): 1581–94.

Emerson, R.M., Fretz, R.I. and Shaw, L.L. (2011) *Writing ethnographic fieldnotes*. London: University of Chicago Press.

Emirbayer, M. and Mische, A. (1998) What is agency? *The American Journal of Sociology*, 103(4): 962–1023.

Englander, D. (1998) *Poverty and Poor Law reform in nineteenth-century Britain, 1834–1914*. Harlow: Longman.

Evans, T. and Harris, J. (2004) Street-level bureaucracy, social work and the (exaggerated) death of discretion. *The British Journal of Social Work*, 34(6): 871–95.

Exworthy, M. (2015) The iron cage and the gaze: interpreting medical control in the English health system. *Professions and Professionalism*, 5(1). Available at: https://journals.hioa.no/index.php/pp/article/view/944.

Fairweather, E. (2008) I don't dream about murdered Victoria Climbié ... I live with her every day, says social worker who became a scapegoat. *The Daily Mail*, 14 June. Available at: www.dailymail.co.uk/femail/article-1026441/I-dont-dream-murdered-Victoria---I-live-day-says-social-worker-scapegoat.html#ixzz2Dk3ShsJd (accessed 4 December 2015).

Farrell, A.E. (2011) *Fat shame*. New York, NY: New York University.

Featherstone, B. and Fraser, C. (2012) 'I'm just a mother. I'm nothing special, they're all professionals': parental advocacy as an aid to parental engagement. *Child & Family Social Work*, 17(2): 244–53.

Featherstone, B., White, S. and Morris, K. (2014) *Re-imagining child protection: Towards humane social work with families*. Bristol: Policy Press.

Felblinger, D.M. (2008) Incivility and bullying in the workplace and nurses' shame responses. *Journal of Obstetric Gynaecology and Neonatal Nursing*, 37: 234–41.

Ferguson, H. (2005) Working with violence, the emotions and the psycho-social dynamics of child protection: reflections on the Victoria Climbié case. *Social Work Education*, 24(7): 781–95.

Ferguson, H. (2011) *Child protection practice*. Basingstoke: Palgrave Macmillan.

Ferguson, H. (2016) Researching social work practice close up: using ethnographic and mobile methods to understand encounters between social workers, children and families. *The British Journal of Social Work*, 46(1): 153–68.

Ferguson, I. (2009) 'Another social work is possible!' Reclaiming the radical tradition. In V. Leskošek (ed) *Theories and methods of social work: Exploring different perspectives*. Ljubljana: University of Ljubljana, pp 81–98.

Ferguson, I. and Woodward, R. (2009) *Radical social work in practice*. Bristol: Policy Press.

Ferguson, T.J., Brugman, D., White, J. and Eyre, H.L. (2007) Shame and guilt as morally warranted experiences. In J.L. Tracy, R.W. Robins, and J.P. Tangney (eds) *The self-conscious emotions*. New York, NY: Guilford, pp 330–48.

Figueira-Mcdonough, J. (1993) Policy practice: the neglected side of social work intervention. *Social Work*, 38(2): 179–88.

Fischer J. (1976) *The effectiveness of social casework*. Springfield, IL: Charles Thomas.

Flax, J. (1999) *American dream in black and white: The Clarence Thomas hearings*. New York, NY: Cornell University Press.

Flegel, M. (2016) *Conceptualizing cruelty to children in nineteenth-century England: Literature, representation, and the NSPCC*. London: Routledge.

Flyvbjerg, B. (2001) *Making social science matter: Why social inquiry fails and how it can succeed again*. Cambridge: Cambridge University Press.

Flyvbjerg, B. (2006) Five misunderstandings about case-study research. *Qualitative Inquiry*, 12(2): 219–45.

Forrester, D., Lynch, A., Bostock, L., Newlands, F., Preston, B. and Cary, A. (2017) *Family safeguarding Hertfordshire evaluation report*. London: DfE.

Foucault, M. (1977) *Discipline and punish*. Harmondsworth: Penguin.

Foucault, M. (1990) *The history of sexuality*. New York, NY: Vintage.

Foucault, M. (1991) Governmentality (trans R. Braidotti and revised by C. Gordon). In G. Burchell, C. Gordon and P. Miller (eds) *The Foucault effect: Studies in governmentality*. Chicago, IL: University of Chicago, pp 87–104.

Fraser, M.W., Galinsky, M.J. and Richman, J.M. (1999) Risk, protection, and resilience: toward a conceptual framework for social work practice. *Social Work Research*, 23(3): 131–43.

Freidson, E. (1970) *Professional dominance*. Chicago, IL: Aldine.

Freud, S. (1962 [1905]) *Three essays on the theory of sexuality* (trans J. Strachey). New York, NY: Basic Books.

Friedland, R. and Alford, R.R. (1991) Bringing society back in: symbols, practices and institutional contradictions. In W.W. Powel and P.J. DiMaggio (eds) *The new institutionalism in organizational analysis*. Chicago, IL: University of Chicago, pp 232–66.

Frijda, N.H. (1986) *The emotions*. New York, NY: Cambridge University Press.

Frijda, N.H., Manstead, A.S. and Bem, S. (eds) (2000) *Emotions and beliefs: How feelings influence thoughts*. New York, NY: Cambridge University Press.

Frost, L. (2016) Exploring the concepts of recognition and shame for social work. *Journal of Social Work Practice*, 30(4): 431–46.

Fuller, J.B., Marler, L., Hester, K., Frey, L. and Relyea, C. (2006) Construed external image and organizational identification: a test of the moderating influence of the need for self-esteem. *Journal of Social Psychology*, 146(6): 701–16.

Gadsden, V.L., Ford, M. and Breiner, H. (2016) *Parenting matters: Supporting parents of children ages 0–8*. Washington, DC: National Academies Press.

Garland, D. (2001) *The culture of control*. Oxford: Oxford University Press.

Garrett, P.M. (2008) How to be modern: New labour's neoliberal modernity and the Change for Children programme. *British Journal of Social Work*, 38: 270–89.

Garrett, P.M. (2009) *Transforming children's services? Social work, neoliberalism and the 'modern' world*. Maidenhead: McGraw Hill/Open University.

Garrett, P.M. (2010) Examining the 'conservative revolution': neoliberalism and social work education. *Social Work Education*, 29(4): 340–55.

Gausel, N. and Leach, C.W. (2011) Concern for self-image and social-image in the management of moral failure: rethinking shame. *European Journal of Social Psychology*, 41: 468–78.

Gazeley, I. (2003) *Poverty in Britain, 1900–1965*. Basingstoke: Palgrave Macmillan.

Geertz, C. (1973) *The interpretation of cultures*. New York, NY: Basic Books.

Gendron, M. and Barrett, L.F. (2009) Reconstructing the past: a century of ideas about emotion in psychology. *Emotion Review*, 1(4): 316–39.

Gergen, K.J. (1994) *Realities and relationships: Soundings in social construction*. Cambridge, MA: Harvard University Press.

Ghaffar, W., Manby, M. and Race, T. (2012) Exploring the experiences of parents and carers whose children have been subject to child protection plans. *British Journal of Social Work*, 42(5): 887–905.

Gibson, M. (2013) Shame and guilt in child protection social work: new interpretations and opportunities for practice. *Child & Family Social Work*, 4 July. Available at: https://doi.org/10.1111/cfs.12081

Gibson, M. (2014) Social worker shame in child and family social work: inadequacy, failure, and the struggle to practise humanely. *Journal of Social Work Practice*, 28(4): 417–31.

Gibson, M. (2016) Social worker shame: a scoping review. *British Journal of Social Work*, 46: 549–65.

Gilbert, P. (2003) Evolution, social roles, and the differences in shame and guilt. *Social Research*, 70(4): 1205–30.

Gilbert, P. and Andrews, B. (eds) (1998) *Shame: Interpersonal behavior, psychopathology, and culture*. New York, NY: Oxford University Press.

Gilbert, P. and Miles, J. (eds) (2014) *Body shame: Conceptualisation, research and treatment*. London: Routledge.

Gilroy, D. (2004) *The Social Services Inspectorate: A history origins, impact and legacy*. London: Department of Health.

Glaser, B.G. (1978) *Theoretical sensitivity*. Mill Valley, CA: Sociology Press.

Glaser, B.G. (1998) *Doing grounded theory: Issues and discussions*. Mill Valley, CA: Sociology Press.

Glaser, B.G. (2005) *The grounded theory perspective III: Theoretical coding*. Mill Valley, CA: Sociology Press.

Glaser, B.G. and Strauss, A.L. (1967) *The discovery of grounded theory: Strategies for qualitative research*. Chicago, IL: Aldine.

Goffman, E. (1956) Embarrassment and social organisation. *American Journal of Sociology*, 62(3): 264–71.

Goffman, E. (1959) *The presentation of self in everyday life*. New York, NY: Doubleday.

Goffman, E. (1963) *Stigma: Notes on the management of spoiled identity*. Englewood Cliffs, NJ: Prentice-Hall.

Gold, R. (1958) Roles in sociological field observation. *Social Forces*, 36: 217–23.

Goldberg, C. (1991) *Understanding shame*. Northvale, NJ: Aronson.

Golding, K.S. and Hughes, D. (2012) *Creating loving attachments*. London: Jessica Kingsley.

Gordon, S. (1981) The sociology of sentiments and emotion. In M. Rosenberg and R. Turner (eds) *Social psychology: Sociological approaches*. New York, NY: Basic Books, pp 562–92.

Gray, M., Dean, M., Agllias, K., Howard, A. and Schubert, L. (2015) Perspectives on neoliberalism for human service professionals. *Social Service Review*, 89(2): 368–92.

Gray, P. (2005) The politics of risk and young offenders' experiences of social exclusion and restorative justice. *British Journal of Criminology*, 45: 938–57.

Green, B. (ed) (2009) *Understanding and researching professional practice*. Rotterdam: Sense Publishers.

Greenland, C. (1986) Inquiries into child abuse and neglect (C.A.N) deaths in the United Kingdom. *British Journal of Criminology*, 26(2): 164–72.

Greiner, R. (2015) 1909: the introduction of the word 'empathy' into English. Available at: www.branchcollective.org/?ps_articles=rae-greiner-1909-the-introduction-of-the-word-empathy-into-english (accessed 25 August 2015).

Griffiths, P.E. (1997) *What emotions really are: The problem of psychological categories*. Chicago, IL: University of Chicago Press.

Gross, J.J. (1998) The emerging field of emotion regulation: an integrative review. *Review of General Psychology*, 2(3): 271–99.

Gross, J.J. (2008) Emotion regulation. In M. Lewis, J.M. Haviland-Jones and L.F. Barrett (eds) *The handbook of emotions*. New York, NY: Guilford, pp 497–512.

Gross, J.J. (ed) (2013) *Handbook of emotion regulation*. New York, NY: Guilford.

Gubrium, E.K., Pellissery, S. and Lødemel, I. (eds) (2013) *The shame of it: Global perspectives on anti-poverty policies*. Bristol: Policy Press.

Gupta, A. (2015) Poverty and shame – messages for social work. *Critical and Radical Social Work*, 3(1): 131–9.

Gupta, A. and Blumhardt, H. (2016) Giving poverty a voice: families' experiences of social work practice in a risk-averse system. *Families, Relationships & Societies*, 5(1): 163–72.

Gupta, A., Blumhardt, H. and ATD Fourth World (2018) Poverty, exclusion and child protection practice: the contribution of the politics of recognition & respect. *European Journal of Social Work*, 21: 247–59.

Hahn, W.K. (2000) Shame: countertransference identifications in individual psychotherapy. *Psychotherapy*, 37: 10–21.

Hahn, W.K. (2001) The experience of shame in psychotherapy supervision. *Psychotherapy*, 38: 272–82.

Hall, D. and McGinity, R. (2015) Conceptualizing teacher professional identity in neoliberal times: resistance, compliance and reform. *Education Policy Analysis Archives/Archivos Analíticos de Políticas Educativas*, 23(88). Available at: http://dx.doi.org/10.14507/epaa.v23.2092

Halliday, J. (2017) Social workers missed signs to save toddler stamped to death by mother. *The Guardian*, 6 September. Available at: www.theguardian.com/society/2017/sep/05/social-workers-missed-signs-to-save-toddler-stamped-to-death-by-mother (accessed 21 June 2018).

Harré, R. (1990) Embarrassment: a conceptual analysis. In W.R. Crozier (ed) *Shyness and embarrassment: Perspectives from social psychology*. Cambridge: Cambridge University Press, pp 181–204.

Harré, R. and Gillet, G. (1994) *The discursive mind*. Thousand Oaks, CA: Sage.

Harris, J. (2003) *The social work business*. London: Routledge.

Harris, J. (2014) (Against) Neoliberal social work. *Critical and Radical Social Work*, 2(1): 7–22.

Harris, N. (2012) Assessment: when does it help and when does it hinder? *Child & Family Social Work*, 17(2): 180–91.

Harvey, D. (2007) *A brief history of neoliberalism*. New York, NY: Oxford University Press.

Hasenfeld, Y. (1987) Power in social work practice: the neglect of power in practice theory. *Social Service Review*, 61(3): 469–83.

Hearn, B. (1991) Registration or protection? *Community Care*, 13 June, p 21.

Hébert, V. (2006) Disguised resistance? The story of Kurt Gerstein. *Holocaust and Genocide Studies*, 20(1): 1–33.

Heine, S.J., Lehman, D.R., Markus, H.R. and Kitayama, S. (1999) Is there a universal need for positive self-regard? *Psychological Review*, 106: 766–94.

Hellenbrand, S.C. (1972) Freud's influence on social casework. *Bulletin of the Menninger Clinic*, 36(4): 407.

Henkel, M. (1991) *Government, evaluation and change*. London: Jessica Kingsley.

Higgins, E.T. (1987) Self-discrepancy: a theory relating self and affect. *Psychological Review*, 94: 319–40.

Higgins, M. (2015) The struggle for the soul of social work in England. *Social Work Education*, 34(1): 4–16.

Hill, O. (1877) *District visiting*. London: Longmans, Green and Co/Charity Organization Society.

HM Government (2006) *Working together to safeguard children: A guide to inter-agency working to safeguard and promote the welfare of children.* London: The Stationery Office.

HM Government (2013) *Working together to safeguard children: A guide to inter-agency working to safeguard and promote the welfare of children.* London: DfE.

HM Treasury (2010) *Budget 2010.* London: TSO.

Hochschild, A.R. (1979) Emotion work, feeling rules, and social structure. *American Journal of Sociology*, 85(3): 551–75.

Hochschild, A.R. (1983) *The managed heart.* Berkeley, CA: University of California Press.

Hogg, M. and Abrams, D. (1988) *Social identifications: A social psychology of intergroup relations and group processes.* London: Routledge.

Hollis, F. (1964) *Casework, a psychosocial therapy.* New York, NY: Random House.

Honneth, A. (1995) *The struggle for recognition.* Cambridge: Polity.

Hood, R., Goldacre, A., Grant, R. and Jones, R. (2016) Exploring Demand and Provision in English child protection services. *British Journal of Social Work*, 46(4): 923–41.

Horlick-Jones, T. (2005) On 'risk work': professional discourse, accountability and everyday action. *Health, Risk and Society*, 7(3): 293–307.

Horton, L. and Gay, O. (2011) *Public sector reform.* Commons Briefing Papers SN06011. London: House of Commons Library.

House, J.S. (1977) The three faces of social psychology. *Sociometry*, 40(2): 161–77.

Houston, S. (2013) Social work and the politics of recognition. In M. Gray and A.W. Stephen (eds) *The new politics of social work.* Basingstoke: Palgrave, pp 63–75.

Houston, S. (2016) Empowering the 'shamed' self: recognition and critical social work. *Journal of Social Work*, 16(1): 3–21.

Howe, D. (1991) Knowledge, power and the shape of social work practice. In M. Davies (ed) *The sociology of social work.* London: Routledge, pp 202–20.

Hudson, B.A., Okhuysen, G.A. and Creed, W.E.D. (2015) Power and institutions: stones in the road and some yellow bricks. *Journal of Management Inquiry*, 24: 233–8.

Hughes, E.C. (1958) *Men and their work.* Glencoe: The Free Press.

Hughes, J.M. (2007) *Guilt and its vicissitudes.* London: Routledge.

Humphries, B. (1997) Reading social work: competing discourses in the rules and requirements for the Diploma in Social Work. *British Journal of Social Work*, 27(5): 641–58.

Hyslop, I. (2018) Neoliberalism and social work identity. *European Journal of Social Work*, 21(1): 20–31.

Ingram, R. (2013) Emotions, social work practice and supervision: an uneasy alliance? *Journal of Social Work Practice*, 27(1): 5–19.

Izard, C.E. (1971) *The face of emotions*. New York, NY: Appleton-Century-Crofts.

Izard, C.E. (2007) Basic emotions, natural kinds, emotion schemas, and a new paradigm. *Perspectives on Psychological Science*, 2(3): 260–80.

Jackson, M.A. (2000) Distinguishing shame and humiliation. Dissertation Abstracts International, 61(04), 2272 (UMI No. 9968089).

Jackson, S., Kelly, L. and Leslie, B. (2017) Parental participation in statutory child protection intervention in Scotland. *The British Journal of Social Work*, 47(5): 1445–63.

James, W. (1884) What is an emotion? *Mind*, 9: 188–205.

James, W. (1907) *Pragmatism: A new name for some old ways of thinking*. New York, NY: Longmans, Green.

Jaques E. (1955) Social systems as a defence against persecutory and depressive anxiety. In M. Klein, P. Heimann and E. Money-Kyrle (eds) *New directions in psychoanalysis*. London: Tavistock, pp 478–98.

Jenkins, R. (1996) Social identity. New York, NY: Routledge.

Jepperson, R.L. (1991) Institutions, institutional effects, and institutionalism. In W.W. Powell and P.J. DiMaggio (eds) *The new institutionalism in organizational analysis*. Chicago, IL: University of Chicago, pp 143–63.

Jones, A. and Crossley, D. (2008) 'In the mind of another' shame and acute psychiatric inpatient care: an exploratory study. A report on phase one: service users. *Journal of Psychiatric and Mental Health Nursing*, 15: 749–57.

Jones, R. (2014) *The story of Baby P*. Bristol: Policy Press.

Kahn, E.M. (1979) The parallel process in social work treatment and supervision. *Social Casework*, 60: 520–8.

Karlsson, G. and Sjöberg, L.G. (2009) The experiences of guilt and shame: a phenomenological-psychological study. *Human Studies*, 32(3): 335–55.

Kärreman, D. and Alvesson, M. (2004) Cages in tandem: management control, social identity, and identification in a knowledge-intensive firm. *Organization*, 11(1): 149–76.

Kaufman, G. (1989) *The psychology of shame*. New York, NY: Springer.

Kaufmann, P., Kuch, H., Neuhaeuser, C. and Webster, E. (eds) (2010) *Humiliation, degradation, dehumanization: Human dignity violated*. New York, NY: Springer.

Kaya, N., Aştı, T., Turan, N., Karabay, B. and Emir, E. (2012) The feelings of guilt and shame experienced by nursing and midwifery students. *Nurse Education Today*, 32: 630–5.

Keddell, E. (2014) Current debates on variability in child welfare decision-making: a selected literature review. *Social Sciences*, 3: 916–40.

Keddell, E. (2017) Interpreting children's best interests: needs, attachment and decision-making. *Journal of Social Work*, 17(3): 324–42.

Kelchtermans, G. (2005) Teachers' emotions in educational reforms: self-understanding, vulnerable commitment and micropolitical literacy. *Teaching and Teacher Education*, 21(8): 995–1006.

Kemmis, S. (2009) Understanding professional practice: a synoptic framework. In B. Green (ed) *Understanding and researching professional practice*. Rotterdam: Sense, pp 19–38.

Kemper, T.D. (1987) How many emotions are there? Wedding the social and the autonomic components. *American Journal of Sociology*, 93(2): 263–89.

Klein, D.C. (1991) The humiliation dynamic. *Journal of Primary Prevention*, 12(2): 93–121.

Klinger, R.S., Ladany, N. and Kulp, L.E. (2012) It's too late to apologize: therapist embarrassment and shame. *The Counseling Psychologist*, 40: 554–74.

Knowles, G. and Sharpe, M. (2012) The IRO service: still a work in progress? Part 2. *Family Law*, 42: 1377–81.

Kovecses, Z. (1990) *Emotion concepts*. New York, NY: Springer-Verlag.

Koza, M.P. and Thoenig, J.C. (1995) Organizational theory at the crossroads: some reflections on European and United States approaches to organizational research. *Organization Science*, 6(1): 1–8.

Kraatz, M. and Block, E. (2008) Organizational implications of institutional pluralism. In R. Greenwoord, C. Oliver, K. Sahlin-Andresson and R. Suddaby (eds) *Handbook of organizational institutionalism*. London: Sage, pp 243–75.

Kreiner, G.E., Hollensbe, E.C. and Sheep, M.L. (2006) Where is the 'me' among the 'we'? Identity work and the search for optimal balance. *Academy of Management Journal*, 49(5): 1031–57.

Lahlou, S. and Abric, J-C. (2011) What are the 'elements' of a representation? *Papers on Social Representations*, 20: 20–1.

Laming, H. (2003) *The Victoria Climbié Inquiry*. London: The Stationery Office.

Lane, S.R. and Pritzker, S. (2018) *Political social work: Using power to create social change*. New York, NY: Springer.

Lansky, M.R. and Morrison, A.P. (1997) *The widening scope of shame*. Hillsdale, NJ: Analytic.

Larner, W. (2000) Neoliberalism: policy, ideology, governmentality. *Studies in Political Economy*, 63, 5–25.

Larson, M.S. (1977) *The rise of professionalism*. London: University of California Press.

Lave, J. and Wenger, E. (1991) *Situated learning*. Cambridge: Cambridge University Press.

Lawler, E.J. (2001) An affect theory of social exchange. *American Journal of Sociology*, 107: 321–52.

Lawrence, T.B. (2008) Power, institutions and organizations. In R. Greenwoord, C. Oliver, K. Sahlin-Andresson and R. Suddaby (eds) *Handbook of organizational institutionalism*. London: Sage, pp 170–97.

Lawrence, T.B. and Suddaby, R. (2006) Institutions and institutional work. In S.R. Clegg, C. Hardy, T.B. Lawrence and W.R. Nord (eds) *The SAGE handbook of organization studies* (2nd edn). London: Sage, pp 215–54.

Lawrence, T.B., Suddaby, R. and Leca, B. (2009) Introduction: theorising and studying institutional work. In T.B. Lawrence, R. Suddaby and B. Leca (eds) *Institutional work: Actors and agency in institutional studies of organisations*. Cambridge: Cambridge University Press, pp 1–27.

Lazarus, R.S. (1991) *Emotion and adaptation*. New York, NY: Oxford University Press.

Lee, R.G. and Wheeler, G. (eds) (2003) *The voice of shame*. Hillside, NJ: Analytic Press.

Leeming, D. and Boyle, M. (2004) Shame as a social phenomenon: a critical analysis of the concept of dispositional shame. *Psychology and Psychotherapy*, 77: 375–96.

Leeming, D. and Boyle, M. (2013) Managing shame: an interpersonal perspective. *The British Journal of Social Psychology*, 52: 140–60.

Le Grand, J. (1997) Knights, knaves or pawns? Human behaviour and social policy. *Journal of Social Policy*, 26(2): 149–69.

Leigh, J. (2013) The process of professionalisation: exploring the identities of child protection social workers. *Journal of Social Work*, 14(6): 625–44.

Leigh, J. (2017) Recalcitrance, compliance and the presentation of self: exploring the concept of organisational misbehaviour in an English local authority child protection service. *Children and Youth Services Review*, 79: 612–19.

Leith, K.P. and Baumeister, R.F. (1998) Empathy, shame, guilt, and narratives of interpersonal conflicts: guilt-prone people are better at perspective taking. *Journal of Personality*, 66(1): 1–37.

Lemke, T. (2001) The birth of bio-politics: Michael Foucault's lectures at the College de France on neo-liberal governmentality. *Economy and Society*, 30(2): 190–207.

Leonard, P. (1968) The application of sociological analysis to social work training. *The British Journal of Sociology*, 19(4): 375–84.

Levin, I., Haldar, M. and Picot, A. (2015) Social work and sociology: historical separation and current challenges. *Nordic Social Work Research*, 5(sup 1): 1–6.

Lewis, H.B. (1971) *Shame and guilt in neurosis*. New York, NY: International Universities.

Lewis, M. (1992) *Shame: The exposed self*. New York: The Free Press.

Lickel, B., Schmader, T., Curtis, M., Scarnier, M. and Ames, D.R. (2005) Vicarious shame and guilt. *Group Processes and Intergroup Relations*, 8: 145–57.

Liebenberg, L., Ungar, M. and Ikeda, J. (2013) Neo-liberalism and responsibilisation in the discourse of social service workers. *The British Journal of Social Work*, 45(3): 1006–21.

Lindholm, C. (2008) *Culture and authenticity*. Oxford: Blackwell.

Lipsky, M. (1980) *Street-level bureaucracy: dilemmas of the individual in public services*. New York: Russell Sage Foundation.

Lizard, O. and Collett, J.L. (2013) Embarrassment and social organization: a multiple identities model. *Social Forces*, 92(1): 353–75.

Loch, C.S. (1895) *How to help cases of distress: A handy reference book for almoners and others*. London: Charity Organisation Society.

Lombard, D. (2009) Social work failure stories crowd out positive news. *Community Care*, 12 May. Available at: www.communitycare.co.uk/2009/05/12/social-work-failure-stories-crowd-out-positive-news/ (accessed 21 June 2018).

Longhofer, J.L. (2013) Shame in the clinical process with LGBTQ clients. *Clinical Social Work Journal*, 41(3): 297–301.

Lukes, S. (2005) *Power: A radical view* (2nd edn). Basingstoke: Palgrave.

Lutz, C. (1988) *Unnatural emotions: Everyday sentiments on a Micronesian atoll and their challenge to Western theory*. Chicago, IL: University of Chicago.

Lymbery, M. (2005) *Social work with older people: Context, policy and practice*. London: Sage.

Lynd, H. (1958) *On shame and the search for identity*. New York, NY: Harcourt, Brace & World.

Macdonald, K.M. (1995) *The sociology of the professions*. London: Sage.

Maguire, S. and Hardy, C. (2013) Organizing processes and the construction of risk: a discursive approach. *Academy of Management Journal*, 56: 231–55.

Manzoor, A. (2014) A look at efficiency in public administration: past and future. *SAGE Open*, 4(4), 21 December. Available at: https://doi.org/10.1177/2158244014564936

Markus, H.R. and Kitayama, S. (2001) The cultural construction of self and emotion: implications for social behaviour. In W. Gerrod Parrott (ed) *Emotions in social psychology: Essential reading*. Philadelphia, PA: Psychology Press, pp 119–37.

Markus, H.R. and Wurf, E. (1987) The dynamic self-concept: a social psychological perspective. *Annual Review of Psychology*, 38(1): 299–337.

Marx, D. (2001) *Patient safety and the 'just culture': A primer for health care executives*. New York, NY: Columbia University.

Mascolo, M.F. and Fischer, K.W. (1995) Developmental transformation in appraisals for pride, shame, and guilt. In J.P. Tangney and K.W. Fischer (eds) *Self-conscious emotions: The psychology of shame, guilt, embarrassment, and pride*. New York, NY: Guilford, pp 64–113.

Mason, P., Ferguson, H., Morris, K., Munton, T. and Sen, R. (2017) *Leeds Family Valued evaluation report*. London: DfE.

Mayer, J.E. and Timms, N. (1970) *The client speaks: Working class impressions of casework*. London: Routledge.

McCall, G.J. and Simmons, J.L. (1978) *Identities and interactions*. New York, NY: The Free Press.

McCarthy, J. and Prudham, S. (2004) Neoliberal nature and the nature of neoliberalism. *Geoforum*, 35: 275–83.

McDonald, C. (2006) *Challenging social work: The institutional context of practice*. Basingstoke: Palgrave Macmillan.

McDougall, W. (1908) *An introduction to social psychology*. Boston, MA: John W. Luce.

McKendrick, D. (2016) Crafting the society of control: exploring Scottish child welfare policy in a neoliberal context. *Aotearoa New Zealand Social Work*, 28(3): 37–46.

McKendrick, D. and Finch, J. (2017) 'Under heavy manners?': social work, radicalisation, troubled families and non-linear war. *The British Journal of Social Work*, 47(2): 308–24.

McLaughlin, K. (2007) Regulation and risk in social work: the General Social Care Council and the Social Care Register in context. *British Journal of Social Work*, 37(7): 1263–77.

Mead, G.H. (1934) *Mind, self, and society*. Chicago, IL: University of Chicago Press.

Menzies, I.E.P. (1960) A case in the functioning of social systems as a defence against anxiety: a report on a study of the nursing service of a general hospital. *Human Relations*, 13: 95–121.

Mesquita, B., Boiger, M. and De Leersnyder, J. (2016) The cultural construction of emotions. *Current Opinion in Psychology*, 8: 31–6.

Miehls, D. and Moffatt, K. (2000) Constructing social work identity based on the reflexive self. *British Journal of Social Work*, 30: 339–48.

Miller, P. and O'Leary, T. (1987) Accounting and the construction of the governable person. *Accounting, Organizations and Society*, 12(3): 235–65.

Miller, R. (1969) *An experimental study of the observational process in casework. Exemplars of social research*. Itasca, IL: Peacock.

Miller, R.S. and Tangney, J.P. (1994) Differentiating embarrassment and shame. *Journal of Social and Clinical Psychology*, 13(3): 273–87.

Miller, R.S. (1996) *Embarrassment: Poise and peril in everyday life*. New York, NY: Guilford.

Miller, S. (2013) *Shame in context*. London: Routledge.

Miller, S.E. (2010) A conceptual framework for the professional socialization of social workers. *Journal of Human Behavior in the Social Environment*, 20(7): 924–38.

Mills, C.W. (1940) Situated actions and vocabularies of motive. *American Sociological Review*, 5(6): 904–13.

Moisander, J.K., Hirsto, H. and Fahy, K.M. (2016) Emotions in institutional work: a discursive perspective. *Organization Studies*, 8 February. Available at: http://doi.org/10.1177/0170840615613377

Montalvo, F.F. (1982) The third dimension in social casework: Mary E. Richmond's contribution to family treatment. *Clinical Social Work Journal*, 10(2): 103–12.

Moors, A., Ellsworth, P.C., Scherer, K.R. and Frijda, N. (2013) Appraisal theories of emotion: state of the art and future development. *Emotion Review*, 5(2): 119–24.

Morris, K., Mason, W., Bywaters, P., Featherstone, B., Daniel, B., Brady, G., Bunting, L., Hooper, J., Mirza, N., Sourfield, J. and Webb, C. (2018) Social work, poverty, and child welfare interventions. *Child and Family Social Work*, 17 January. Available at: http://onlinelibrary.wiley.com/doi/10.1111/cfs.12423/abstract

Morrison, A.P. (2014) *Shame: The underside of narcissism*. London: Routledge.

Morrison, T. (2007) Emotional intelligence, emotion and social work: context, characteristics, complications and contribution. *The British Journal of Social Work*, 37(2): 245–63.

Moscovici, S. (1961) *La psychoanalyse: Son image et son public*. Paris: Presses Universitaires de France.

Moscovici, S. (1973) Foreword. In C. Herzlich (ed) Health and illness: A social psychological analysis. London and New York, NY: Academic Press, pp ix–xiv.

Moscovici, S. (1981) On social representation. In J. Forgas (ed) Social cognition: Perspectives on everyday understanding. London: Academic Press, pp 181–209.

Moscovici, S. (2001) Why a theory of social representations? In K. Deaux and G. Philogène (eds) Representations of the social. Oxford: Blackwell, pp 8–36.

Mulkay, M. (1988) On humour: Its nature and its place in modern society. Cambridge: Polity.

Munro, E. (2004) The impact of audit on social work practice. British Journal of Social Work, 34(8): 1075–95.

Munro, E. (2011) The Munro review of child protection: Final report a child-centred system. London: DfE.

Munt, S. (2008) Queer attachments: The cultural politics of shame. London: Routledge.

Nair, N. (2010) Identity regulation: towards employee control? International Journal of Organizational Analysis, 18(1): 6–22.

Narey, M. (2014) Making the education of social workers consistently effective: Report of Sir Martin Narey's independent review of the education of children's social workers. London: DfE.

Nathanson, D.L. (1994) Shame and pride: Affect, sex, and the birth of the self. New York, NY: WW Norton.

Nelson, K.R. and Merighi, J.R. (2002) Emotional dissonance in medical social work practice. Social Work in Health Care, 36(3): 63–79.

Newburn, T. (2003) Crime and criminal justice policy. Harlow: Pearson Education.

Newkirk, T. (2017) Embarrassment: And the emotional underlife of learning. Portsmouth, NH: Heinemann.

Nightingale, D.J. and Cromby, J. (2002) Social constructionism as ontology: exposition and example. Theory & Psychology, 12(5): 701–13.

NSPCC (National Society for the Prevention of Cruelty to Children) (1912) The cruelty man: Actual experiences of an inspector of the N.S.P.C.C. graphically told by himself. London: NSPCC.

Nussbaum, M.C. (2009) Hiding from humanity: Disgust, shame, and the law. Oxford: Princeton University Press.

Ofsted (Office for Standards in Education) (2012) Framework for the inspection of local authority arrangements for the protection of children. London: Ofsted.

Ofsted (2015) *Inspection handbook: Inspections of services for children in need of help and protection, children looked after and care leavers.* London: Ofsted.

Oliver, C. (1991) Strategic responses to institutional processes. *Academy of Management Review,* 16(1): 145–79.

Ortony, A. and Turner, T.J. (1990) What's basic about basic emotions? *Psychological Review,* 97: 315–31.

Pajaczkowska, C. and Ward, I. (2014) *Shame and sexuality: Psychoanalysis and visual culture.* London: Routledge.

Panksepp, J. (2007) Neurologizing the psychology of affects: how appraisal-based constructivism and basic emotion theory can coexist. *Perspectives on Psychological Science,* 2(3): 281–96.

Parkinson, B. and Manstead, A.S.R.R. (2015) Current emotion research in social psychology: thinking about emotions and other people. *Emotion Review,* 7(4): 371–80.

Parton, N. (1991) *Governing the family: Child care, child protection and the state.* Basingstoke: Macmillan.

Parton, N. (1996) Social theory, social change and social work: an introduction. In N. Parton (ed) *Social theory, social change and social work.* London: Routledge, pp 4–18.

Parton, N. (2011) Child protection and safeguarding in England: changing and competing conceptions of risk and their implications for social work. *British Journal of Social Work,* 41(5): 854–75.

Parton, N. (2014) *The politics of child protection: Contemporary developments and future directions.* London: Palgrave.

Pattison, S. (2014) *Saving face: Enfacement, shame, theology.* London: Routledge.

Payne, M. (2005) *The origins of social work: Continuities and change.* Basingstoke: Palgrave Macmillan.

Payne, M. (2015) *Modern social work theory.* Oxford: Oxford University Press.

Pearce, W.B. and Cronen, V.E. (1980) Communication, action and meaning: The creation of social realities. New York, NY: Praeger.

Peirce, C.S. (1903) Pragmatism as the logic of abduction. *Harvard Lectures on Pragmatism,* 7: 180–212.

Perryman, J. (2007) Inspection and emotion. *Cambridge Journal of Education,* 37(2): 173–90.

Pezé, S. (2013) Controlling managers' 'becoming': the practice of identity regulation. *Materiality and Space: Organizations, Artefacts and Practices.* London: Palgrave Macmillan, pp 240–60.

Piaser, A. and Bataille, M. (2012) Of contextualised use of 'social' and 'profession'. In M. Chaib, B. Danermark and S. Selander (eds) *Education, professionalization and social representations: On the transformation of social knowledge*. London: Routledge, pp 44–54.

Pithouse, A., Hall, C., Peckover, S. and White, S. (2009) A tale of two CAFs: the impact of the electronic common assessment framework. *British Journal of Social Work*, 39(4): 599–612.

Platt, D. (2005) Social workers' decision-making following initial assessments of children in need in the UK. *International Journal of Child and Family Welfare*, 8: 177–90.

Platt, D. and Turney, D. (2014) Making threshold decisions in child protection: a conceptual analysis. *British Journal of Social Work*, 44(6): 1472–90.

Plehwe, D., Walpen, B.J. and Neunhöffer, G. (eds) (2007) *Neoliberal hegemony: A global critique*. London: Routledge.

Polkinghorne, D.E. (2004) *Practice and the human sciences: The case for a judgement-based practice of care*. Albany, NY: State University of New York Press.

Pollack, S. and Rossiter, A. (2010) Neoliberalism and the entrepreneurial subject: implications for feminism and social work. *Canadian Social Work Review/Revue Canadienne de Service Social*, 27(2): 155–69.

Powell, F.W. (2001) *The politics of social work*. London: Sage.

Power, M. (1997) *The audit society: Rituals of verification*. Oxford: Oxford University Press.

Pratt, M.G. (1998) To be or not to be: central questions in organizational identification. In D.A. Whetten and P.C. Godfrey (eds) *Identity in organisations*. London: Sage, pp 171–208.

Pray, K.L.M. (1945) Social work and social action. In H.R. Knight (ed) *The proceedings of the national conference of social work: Selected papers seventy-second annual meeting*. New York, NY: Colombia Press, pp 348–59.

Putnam, H. (1988) *Representations and reality*. Cambridge: MIT Press.

Read, J. (2009) A genealogy of homo-economicus: neoliberalism and the production of subjectivity. *Foucault Studies*, (6): 25–36.

Reamer, F.G. (1998) The evolution of social work ethics. Social Work, 43(6): 488–500.

Reddy, W.M. (1997) Against constructionism: the historical ethnography of emotions. *Current Anthropology*, 38(3): 327–51.

Reed, M. (1999) From the cage to the gaze? The dynamics of organizational control in late modernity. In G. Morgan and L. Engwall (eds) *Regulation and organizations: International perspectives*. London: Routledge, pp 17–49.

Reich, J.A. (2008) The child welfare system and state intervention in families: from historical patterns to future questions. *Sociology Compass*, 2(3): 888–909.

Reicher, S.D. (2004) The context of social identity: domination, resistance, and change. *Political Psychology*, 25(6): 921–45.

Reynolds, B.C. (1934) Between client and community: a study of responsibility in social case work. *Smith College Studies in Social Work*, 5(1): 1–128.

Richmond, M.E. (1922) *What is social case work?* New York, NY: Russell Sage Foundation.

Ridgeway, C.L. (2006) Linking social structure and interpersonal behaviour. *Social Psychology Quarterly*, 69(1): 5–16.

Roberts, L.M. (2005) Changing faces: professional image construction in diverse organizational settings. *Academy of Management Review*, 30(4): 685–711.

Rogowski, S. (2011) Social work with children and families: challenges and possibilities in the neo-liberal world. *British Journal of Social Work*, 42(5): 921–40.

Romney, A.K., Moore, C.C. and Rusch, C.D. (1997) Cultural universals: measuring the semantic structure of emotion terms in English and Japanese. *Proceedings of the National Academy of Sciences of the United States of America*, 94: 5489–94.

Rorty, R. (1979) *Philosophy and the mirror of nature*. Princeton, NJ: Princeton University Press.

Rorty, R. (1989) *Contingency, irony, and solidarity*. New York, NY: Cambridge University Press.

Rosaldo, M.Z. (1984) Toward an anthropology of self and feeling. In R.A. Shweder and R.A. LeVine (eds) *Culture theory: Essays on mind, self, and emotion*. Cambridge: Cambridge University Press, pp 137–57.

Roseman, I.J. (1991) Appraisal determinants of discrete emotions. *Cognition & Emotion*, 5: 161–200.

Rosenberg, M. (1979) *Conceiving the self*. New York, NY: Basic Books.

Rosenberg, M. (1991) Self processes and emotional experiences. In J.A. Howard and P.L. Callero (eds) *The self–society interface: Cognition, emotion and action*. New York, NY: Cambridge University Press, pp 123–42.

Ross, L. (1977) The intuitive psychologist and his shortcomings: distortions in the attribution process. In L. Berkowitz (ed) *Advances in experimental social psychology*. New York, NY: Academic Press, pp 173–220.

Rowlands, M. (2010) *The new science of the mind: From extended mind to embodied phenomenology*. Cambridge, MA: MIT Press.

Rowntree, B.S. (1901) *Poverty: A study of town life*. London: Macmillan.

Ruch, G. (2012) Where have all the feelings gone? Developing reflective and relationship-based management in child-care social work. *British Journal of Social Work*, 42(7): 1315–32.

Ruch, G., Turney, D. and Ward, A. (eds) (2010) *Relationship-based social work: Getting to the heart of practice*. London: Jessica Kingsley.

Russell, J.A. (1991) In defense of a prototype approach to emotion concepts. *Journal of Personality and Social Psychology*, 60(1): 37–47.

Russell, J.A. (2003) Core affect and the psychological construction of emotion. *Psychological Review*, 110: 145–72.

Russell, J.A. and Barrett, L.F. (1999) Core affect, prototypical emotional episodes, and other things called emotion: dissecting the elephant. *Journal of Personality and Social Psychology*, 76(5): 805–19.

Russell, J.A. and Mehrabian, A. (1977) Evidence for a three-factor theory of emotions. *Journal of Research in Personality*, 11: 273–94.

Sabini, J. and Silver, M. (1997) In defense of shame: shame in the context of guilt and embarrassment. *Journal for the Theory of Social Behaviour*, 27(1): 1–15.

Saltiel, D. (2016) Observing front line decision making in child protection. *British Journal of Social Work*, 46(7): 2104–19.

Sanders, K., Pattison, S. and Hurwitz, B. (2011) Tracking shame and humiliation in accident and emergency. *Nursing Philosophy*, 12: 83–93.

Satyamurti, C. (1981) *Occupational survival: The case of the local authority social worker*. Oxford: Blackwell.

Sayer, A. (2005) Class, moral worth and recognition. *Sociology*, 39(5): 947–63.

Schachter, S. and Singer, J.E. (1962) Cognitive, social, and physiological determinants of emotional state. *Psychological Review*, 69: 379–99.

Schatzki, T.R. (2001) Introduction: practice theory. In T.R. Schatzki, K.K. Cetina and E. Von Savigny (eds) *The practice turn in contemporary theory*. London: Routledge, pp 10–23.

Scheff, T.J. (1988) Shame and conformity: the deference–emotion system. *American Sociological Review*, 53(3): 395–406.

Scheff, T.J. (1997) *Emotions, the social bond, and human reality: Part/whole analysis*. Cambridge: Cambridge University Press.

Scheff, T.J. (2000) Shame and the social bond: a sociological theory. *Sociological Theory*, 18(1): 84–99.

Scheff, T.J. (2003) Shame in self and society. *Symbolic Interaction*, 26(2): 239–62.

Scheff, T.J. (2014) Goffman on emotions: the pride–shame system. *Symbolic Interaction*, 37(1): 108–21.

Scheff, T.J. and Retzinger, S.M. (2001) *Emotions and violence: Shame and rage in destructive conflicts*. Lincoln, NE: iUniverse.

Scheper-Hughes, N. (1993) Death without weeping: The violence of everyday *life* in Brazil. London: University of California Press.

Scherer, K.R. (1984) Emotion as a multicomponent process: a model and some cross-cultural data. In P. Shaver (ed) *Review of personality and social psychology* (vol 5). Beverly Hills, CA: Sage, pp 37–63.

Scherer, K.R. (1992) On social representation of emotional experience: stereotypes, prototypes, or archetypes? In M. von Cranach, W. Doise and G. Mugny (eds) *Social representations and the social bases of knowledge*. Bern, Germany: Huber, pp 30–6.

Scherer, K.R. (2005) What are emotions? And how can they be measured? *Social Science Information*, 44(4): 695–729.

Scott, M. and Lyman, S. (1968) Accounts. *American Sociological Review*, 33: 46–62.

Scott, W.R. (2014) *Institutions and organisations: Ideas, interests, and identities* (4th edn). London: Sage.

Secretary of State (1993) *A report by the Secretary of State for Health and for Wales on the Children Act 1989 in pursuance of their duties under section 83(6) of the Act*. London: HMSO.

Seebohm Report (1968) *Report of the Committee on Local Authority and Allied Personal Social Services*. London: HMSO.

Selznick, P. (1957) *Leadership in administration*. New York, NY: Harper & Row.

Sen, A. (1984) *Resources, values and development*. Cambridge, MA: Harvard University Press.

Sennett, R. and Cobb, C. (1973) *The hidden injuries of class*. New York, NY: Vintage Books.

Shlonsky, A. (2015) Current status and prospects for improving decision making research in child protection: a commentary. *Child Abuse and Neglect*, 49: 154–62.

Shoesmith, S. (2016) *Learning from Baby P: The politics of blame, fear and denial*. London: Jessica Kingsley.

Shweder, A. (1994) 'You're not sick, you're just in love': emotion as an interpretive system. In P. Ekman and R.J. Davidson (eds) *The nature of emotion: Fundamental questions*. New York, NY: Oxford University Press, pp 32–44.

Sieber, S.D. (1981) *Fatal remedies: The ironies of social intervention*. New York, NY: Plenum Press.

Silfver, M. (2007) Coping with guilt and shame: a narrative approach. *Journal of Moral Education*, 36(2): 169–83.

Sluss, D.M. and Ashforth, B.E. (2007) Relational identity and identification: defining ourselves through work relationships. *Academy of Management Review*, 32(1): 9–32.

Smith, A. (1776) *An inquiry into the nature and causes of the wealth of nations*. London: Strahan and Cadell.

Smith, A.K., Fisher, J., Schonberg, M.A., Pallin, D.J., Block, S.D., Forrow, L., Phillips, R.S. and McCarthy, E.P. (2009) Am I doing the right thing? Provider perspectives on improving palliative care in the emergency department. *Annals of Emergency Medicine*, 54(1): 86–93.

Smith, R.H., Webster, J.M., Parrott, W.G. and Eyre, H.L. (2002) The role of public exposure in moral and nonmoral shame and guilt. *Journal of Personality and Social Psychology*, 83: 138–59.

Smithson, R. and Gibson, M. (2017) Less than human: a qualitative study into the experience of parents involved in the child protection system. *Child & Family Social Work*, 22(2): 565–74.

Social Work Task Force (2009) *Building a safe, confident future*. London: DCSF.

Solms, M. and Zellner, M.R. (2012) Freudian affect theory today. In A. Fotopoulou, D. Pfaff and M.A. Conway (eds) *From the couch to the lab*. Oxford: Oxford University Press, pp 133–44.

Soss, J., Fording, R.C. and Schram, S. (2011) *Disciplining the poor: Neoliberal paternalism and the persistent power of race*. London: University of Chicago Press.

Specht, H. and Courtney, M.E. (1995) *Unfaithful angels: How social work has abandoned its mission*. New York, NY: Simon and Schuster.

Spicker, P. (1984) *Stigma and social welfare*. London: Croom Helm.

Spolander, G., Engelbrecht, L., Martin, L., Strydom, M., Pervova, I., Marjanen, P., Tani, P., Sicora, A. and Adaikalam, F. (2014) The implications of neoliberalism for social work: reflections from a six-country international research collaboration. *International Social Work*, 57(4): 301–12.

Springer, S. (2012) Neoliberalism as discourse: between Foucauldian political economy and Marxian poststructuralism. *Critical Discourse Studies*, 9(2): 133–47.

Stake, R.E. (1995) *The art of case study research*. Thousand Oaks, CA: Sage.

Stanford, S. (2010) 'Speaking back' to fear: responding to the moral dilemmas of risk in social work practice. *British Journal of Social Work*, 40(4): 1065–80.

Stanley, J., Goddard, C. and Sanders, R. (2002) In the firing line: violence and power in child protection work. *Child & Family Social Work*, 7(4): 323–4.

Stets, J.E. (2005) Examining emotions in identity theory. *Social Psychology Quarterly*, 68(1): 39–56.

Stets, J.E. and Burke, P.J. (2003) A sociological approach to self and identity. In M. Leary and J.P. Tangney (eds) *Handbook of self and identity*. New York, NY: Guilford, pp 128–52.

Stets, J.E. and Turner, J.H. (eds) (2006) *Handbook of the sociology of emotions*. New York, NY: Springer.

Stets, J.E. and Turner, J.H. (eds) (2014) *Handbook of the sociology of emotions. Volume 2*. New York, NY: Springer.

Stevenson, O. (2013) *Reflections on a life in social work: A personal & professional memoir*. Buckingham: Hinton House.

Stryker, S. (1980) *Symbolic interactionism: A social structural version*. Menlo Park: Benjamin Cummings.

Stryker, S. (2004) Integrating emotion into identity theory. *Advances in Group Processes*, 21: 1–23.

Sullivan, G.B. (ed) (2014) *Understanding collective pride and group identity: New directions in emotion theory, research and practice*. London: Routledge.

Sullivan, H.S. (1953) *The interpersonal theory of psychiatry*. New York, NY: Norton.

Sumner, W.G. (1906) *Folkways: A study of the sociological importance of usages, manners, customs, mores, and morals*. Boston, MA: The Athenæum Press.

Sveningsson, S. and Alvesson, M. (2003) Managing managerial identities: organizational fragmentation, discourse and identity struggle. *Human Relations*, 56: 1163–93.

Sykes, J. (2011) Negotiating stigma: understanding mothers' responses to accusations of child neglect. *Children and Youth Services Review*, 33(3): 448–56.

Tajfel, H. (1981) *Human groups and social categories: Studies in social psychology*. Cambridge: Cambridge University Press.

Tangney, J.P. and Dearing, R. (2002) *Shame and guilt*. New York, NY: Guilford.

Tangney, J.P. and Tracy, J.L. (2012) Self-conscious emotions. In M.R. Leary and J.P. Tangney (eds) *Handbook of self and identity* (2nd edn). London: Guilford, pp 446–80.

Tangney, J.P., Miller, R.S., Flicker, L. and Barlow, D.H. (1996) Are shame, guilt, and embarrassment distinct emotions? *Journal of Personality and Social Psychology*, 70: 1256–69.

Tangney, J.P., Niedenthal, P.M., Covert, M.V. and Barlow, D.H. (1998) Are shame and guilt related to distinct self-discrepancies? A test of Higgins's (1987) hypotheses. *Journal of Personality and Social Psychology*, 75(1): 256–68.

Tangney, J.P., Stuewig, J. and Mashek, D.J. (2007) Moral emotions and moral behavior. *Annual Review of Psychology*, 58: 345–72.

Taylor, C. and White, S. (2006) Knowledge and reasoning in social work: educating for humane judgement. *British Journal of Social Work*, 36(6): 937–54.

Taylor, F.W. (1911) *Principles of scientific management*. London: Harper Brothers.

Tew, J. (2006) Understanding power and powerlessness: towards a framework for emancipatory practice in social work. *Journal of Social Work*, 6(1): 33–51.

Thoits, P.A. (1989) The sociology of emotions. *Annual Review of Sociology*, 15(1): 317–42.

Thoits, P.A. (1990) Emotional deviance: research agendas. In T.D. Kemper (ed) *Research agendas in the sociology of emotions*. Albany, NY: State University of New York Press, pp 180–203.

Thoits, P.A. and Virshup, L.K. (1997) Me's and we's: forms and functions of social identities. In R.D. Ashmore and L.J. Jussim (eds) *Self and identity: Fundamental issues. Rutgers series on self and social identity* (vol 1). New York, NY: Oxford University Press, pp 106–33.

Thomaes, S., Stegge, H., Olthof, T., Bushman, B.J. and Nezlek, J.B. (2011) Turning shame inside-out: 'humiliated fury' in young adolescents. *Emotion*, 11: 786–93.

Thomas, G. (2010) Doing case study: abduction not induction, phronesis not theory. *Qualitative Inquiry*, 16(7): 575–82.

Thomas, G. (2016) *How to do your case study* (2nd edn). London: Sage.

Thomas, J. (2017) Five years of shame: how Wirral Council failed its most vulnerable. *Liverpool Echo*, 29 November. Available at: www.liverpoolecho.co.uk/news/liverpool-news/five-years-shame-how-wirral-13045435 (accessed 21 June 2018).

Thomas, T. (1988) The police and social workers: creativity or conflict? *Practice*, 2(2): 120–9.

Thornton, P.H. and Ocasio, W. (1999) Institutional logics and the historical contingency of power in organizations: executive succession in the higher education publishing industry, 1958–1990. *American Journal of Sociology*, 105(3): 801–43.

Thornton, P.H. and Ocasio, W. (2005) Institutional logics. In R. Greenwood, C. Oliver, R. Suddaby and K. Sahlin (eds) *The SAGE handbook of organizational institutionalism*. London: Sage, pp 99–129.

Thrana, H.M. and Fauske, H. (2014) The emotional encounter with child welfare services: the importance of incorporating the emotional perspective in parents' encounters with child welfare workers. *European Journal of Social Work*, 17(2): 221–36.

Ting, L., Sanders, S., Jacobson, J.M. and Power, J.R. (2006) Dealing with the aftermath: a qualitative analysis of mental health social workers' reactions after a client suicide. *Social Work*, 51(4): 329–41.

Titmuss, R.M. (1951) Social administration in a changing society. *The British Journal of Sociology*, 2(3): 183–97.

Titmuss, R.M. (1958) *Essays on the welfare state*. London: Allen and Unwin.

Todd, S. (2014) Family welfare and social work in post-war England, c. 1948–c. 1970. *The English Historical Review*, 129(537): 362–87.

Tomkins, S.S. (1962) *Affect imagery consciousness: Volume I, the positive affects*. London: Tavistock.

Tomkins, S.S. (1963) *Affect imagery consciousness: Volume II, the negative affects*. London: Tavistock.

Torres, W.J. and Bergner, R.M. (2010) Humiliation: its nature and consequences. *The Journal of the American Academy of Psychiatry and the Law*, 38(2): 195–204.

Tracy, J. (2016) *Take pride: Why the deadliest sin holds the secret to human success*. Boston, MA: Houghton Mifflin Harcourt.

Tracy, J.L. and Robins, R.W. (2004) Putting the self into self-conscious emotions: a theoretical model. *Psychological Inquiry*, 15(2): 103–25.

Tracy, J.L. and Robins, R.W. (2007) The psychological structure of pride: a tale of two facets. *Journal of Personality and Social Psychology*, 92(3): 506–25.

Tracy, J.L., Robins, R.W. and Tangney, J.P. (eds) (2007) *The self-conscious emotions: Theory and research*. London: Guilford.

Troman, G. and Woods, P. (2001) *Primary teachers' stress*. London: RoutledgeFalmer.

Tsakalotos , E. (2004) Social norms and endogenous preferences: the political economy of market expansion. In P. Arestis and M.C. Sawyer (eds) *The rise of the market: Critical essays on the political economy of neo-liberalism*. Cheltenham: Edward Elgar, pp 5–37.

Turnell, A. and Edwards, S. (1999) *Signs of safety: A solution and safety oriented approach to child protection*. London: W.W. Norton.

Turner, F.J. (2017) *Social work treatment: Interlocking theoretical approaches*. Oxford: Oxford University Press.

Turner, J.E. and Husman, J. (2008) Emotional and cognitive self-regulation following academic shame. *Journal of Advanced Academics*, 20: 138–73.

Turner, J.H. (2000) *On the origins of human emotions: A sociological inquiry into the evolution of human affect*. Stanford, CA: Stanford University Press.

Turner, J.H. (2002) *Face-to-face: Toward a sociological theory of interpersonal behavior.* Stanford, CA: Stanford University Press.

Turner, J.H. (2009) The sociology of emotions: basic theoretical arguments. *Emotion Review*, 1(4): 340–54.

Turner, J.H. and Stets, J.E. (2005) *The sociology of emotions.* New York, NY: Cambridge University Press.

Turner, J.H. and Stets, J.E. (2006) Sociological theories of human emotions. *Annual Review of Sociology*, 32(1): 25–52.

Van Heugten, K. (2010) Bullying of social workers: outcomes of a grounded study into impacts and interventions. *British Journal of Social Work*, 40(2): 638–55.

Voronov, M. and Vince, R. (2012) Integrating emotions into the analysis of institutional work. *Academy of Management Review*, 37(1): 58–81.

Wacquant, L. (2009) *Punishing the poor: The neoliberal government of social insecurity.* Durham, NC: Duke University Press.

Wacquant, L. (2010) Crafting the neoliberal state. *Sociological Forum*, 25(2): 197–220.

Wagner, W. (1996) Queries about social representation and construction. *Journal for the Theory of Social Behaviour*, 26(2): 95–120.

Walker, J. (2011) The relevance of shame in child protection work. *Journal of Social Work Practice*, 25: 451–63.

Walker, R. (2014) *The shame of poverty.* Oxford: Oxford University Press.

Wallace, M. (1993) Discourse of derision: the role of the mass media within the education policy process. *Journal of Education Policy*, 8(4): 321–37.

Warner, J. (2015) *The emotional politics of child protection.* Bristol: Policy Press.

Wastell, D., White, S., Broadhurst, K., Peckover, S. and Pithouse, A. (2010) Children's services in the iron cage of performance management: street-level bureaucracy and the spectre of Švejkism. *International Journal of Social Welfare*, 19(3): 310–20.

Watkins-Hayes, C.M. and Kovalsky, E. (2016) The discourse of deservingness: morality and the dilemmas of poverty relief in debate and practice. In D. Brady and L.M. Burton (eds) *The Oxford handbook of the social science of poverty.* Oxford: Oxford University Press, pp 193–220.

Webb, D. (1996) Regulation for radicals: the state, CCETSW and the academy. In N. Parton (ed) *Social theory, social change and social work.* London: Routledge, pp 172–89.

Webb, S. (2000) The politics of social work: power and subjectivity. *Critical Social Work*, 1(2): 1–2.

Webb, S. (2006) *Social work in a risk society: Social and political perspectives.* London: Palgrave Macmillan.

Webb, S. (ed) (2017) Professional identity and social work. Abingdon: Routledge.

Weber, M. (1978) *Economy and society: An outline of interpretive sociology.* London: University of California Press.

Weuste, M.B. (2005) *Critical incident stress and debriefing of child welfare workers.* PhD thesis. Chicago, IL: Institute of Clinical Social Work.

Whetten, D.A. and Mackey, A. (2002) A social actor conception of organizational identity and its implications for the study of organizational reputation. *Business & Society*, 41(4): 393–414.

White, S. (2003) Social worker as moral judge: blame, responsibility and case formulation. In C. Hall, K. Juhila, N. Parton and T. Pösö (eds) *Constructing clienthood in social work and human services: Interaction, identities and practices.* London, Jessica Kingsley, pp 177–92.

White, S., Wastell, D., Broadhurst, K. and Hall, C. (2010) When policy o'erleaps itself: the 'tragic tale' of the Integrated Children's System. *Critical Social Policy*, 30(3): 405–29.

Wierzbicka, A. (1992) Defining emotion concepts. *Cognitive Science*, 16: 539–81.

Wiles, F. (2013) 'Not easily put into a box': constructing professional identity. *Social Work Education*, 32(7): 854–66.

Wilkinson, R. and Pickett, K. (2009) *The spirit level: Why more equal societies always do better.* London: Penguin.

Williams, B. (2008) *Shame and necessity.* Berkeley, CA: University of California Press.

Wilson, W. (1887) The study of administration. *Political Science Quarterly*, 2(2): 197–222.

Winter, K. and Connolly, P. (2005) 'Keeping it in the family': Thatcherism and the Children Act 1989. In J. Pilcher and S. Wagg (eds) *Thatcher's children? Politics, childhood and society in the 1980s and 1990s.* London: Routledge, pp 30–43.

Wittgenstein, L. (1967) *Philosophical investigations.* Oxford: Basil Blackwell.

Woodroofe, K. (1962) *From charity to social work in England and the United States.* Toronto: University of Toronto.

Woolford, A. and Nelund, A. (2013) The responsibilities of the poor: performing neoliberal citizenship within the bureaucratic field. *Social Service Review*, 87(2): 292–318.

Wootton, B. (1959) *Social science and social pathology.* London: Routledge.

Yelloly, M. (1980) *Social work theory and psychoanalysis.* London: Van Nostrand Reinhold.

Young, A.F. and Ashton, E.T. (1967) *British social work in the nineteenth century* (3rd edn). London: Butler and Tanner.

Younghusband, E. (1981) *The newest profession: A short history of social work.* Sutton: Community Care/IPC Business Press.

Yuval-Davis, N. (2006) Belonging and the politics of belonging. *Patterns of Prejudice,* 40(3): 197–214.

Zelizer, V.A.R. (1985) *Pricing the priceless child: The changing social value of children.* Princeton, NJ: Princeton University Press.

Zwaan, R.A. (2004) The immersed experiencer: toward an embodied theory of language comprehension. *Psychology of Learning and Motivation,* 44: 35–62.

Index

Note: Page numbers in *italics* indicate figures. Page numbers followed by n indicate end-of-chapter notes.

A

abduction 15
Abrams, D. 105
Abric, J.-C. 206, 207
accountability 71
Ackroyd, S. 132
activism 58–59, 61–62
administration 54–56, 92–95, 97, 108–110, 146, 194
affects 25
Albert, S. 79
Alford, R.R. 78, 79
Alvesson, M. 104, 105, 106, 107, 111, 116, 135, 188
theoretical codes 209
appraisal theories 26–27, 43
Archer, L. 191
Arnold, M.B. 26
Arthurworrey, Lisa 5
Ashton, E.T. 54, 55, 57, 58, 60, 62
Attlee, Clement 59, 199
Audit Commission 71–72, 74
austerity 86
Austin, J.L. 39
authenticity 196–201
Averill, J.R. 27, 28, 47

B

babies 29
Baginsky, M. 146, 196
Bailey, F.G. 66
Bailey, R. 63
Barbalet, J.M. 47
Barclay Report 73, 85
Barnett, Samuel 58
Baron-Cohen, S. 137, 142n
Barrett, L.F. 3, 23–24, 25, 26, 28, 29, 30–31, 37, 38, 40, 41, 46, 47, 130, 133, 134
Barsalou, L.W. 37, 38, 134
basic emotions argument 24–26
Battiliana, J. 129
Bauer, M.W. 206

Baumeister, R.F. 36, 137
Behrendt, H. 36
Bell, E.M. 61
Bell, M. 58
belonging, politics of 95–96
Ben-Ari, R. 36
Berger, P. 205
Bergner, R.M. 37, 46
Beveridge, William 59
Bilson, A. 196
Block, E. 79
Blumer, H. 15
Blumhardt, H. 196, 203
bodily states 30–31
embarrassment 36
guilt 35
humiliation 36–37
pride 34
shame 35
see also embodied experiences of self-conscious emotions
body language 39
Boiger, M. 43
boundary maintenance 95–96
Bourdieu, P. 53, 125
Brake, M. 63
Brandon, M. 93
Branta, H. 2, 9
Breakwell, G.M. 103, 105, 129, 207
Brewer, C. 62, 67
Brieland, D. 61
Briggs, A. 58
Brown, B. 46, 194–195, 200
Buckley, S. 56, 203
Bunting, L. 196
bureaucracies 131
bureaucratic field 53, 62–64
Burke, P.J. 32, 33, 52, 103, 105, 135, 136
Burkitt, I. 3, 24, 29, 37, 38, 40, 46, 47, 130, 133
Burr, V. 205
Buss, A.H. 36
Butler-Sloss, E. 69

C

Cameron, David 4–5
Can social work survive? (Brewer and Lait) 67
Carey, M. 129, 132, 133, 180
Carter, M.J. 135
case study approach 10
Catherall, D.R. 6, 81, 137
Central Council for Education and Training in Social Work (CCETSW) 67, 68, 70
Ceunen, E. 30
challenge, acts of 180–183
Chalmers, D. 37
Chandler, D. 191
Charity Organisation Society (COS) 55, 61
Charmaz, K. 11, 15, 16, 17
child and family social work
   contemporary 64–74
      discourse of derision 66–72
      discourse of neoliberalism 64–66, 73–74
   professional representations 53–64
      activism 58–59, 61–62
      within the bureaucratic field 62–64
      practical helper 61–62
      social administration 54–56
      social policing 56–58
      therapy 59–61
   professionalisation 49–53
   see also professional practice; social work role; social workers
child and family social work services
   creation, maintenance and disruption 78–82
      new service identity 87–88, 99–100
      organisational emotional safety 89–99
      organisational identity 83–85
      professional identity 85–86
      public administration identity 86–87
child-centredness 116–119
Children Act 1989 73, 90, 101n, 117
Children Act 2004 70
civilizing process, The (Elias, 1978) 44
Clapton, G. 58
Clark, A. 37
Climbié, Victoria 5, 69, 70
Colwell, Maria 68, 69
Combs, D.J.Y. 37
communication *see* language; speech acts
competence 122–123
compliance 114–116, 131–132, 152–161, 170–171

competence 152–154
   shame and guilt 156–161
   shame avoidance 154–156
   see also resistance
conformity 132
Connelly, Peter 69, 89–90, 110, 191
Connolly, P. 73
Conservative Party 65
constant comparative method 15
constructionism 27–30
   comparison with other theories 41–48
   embodied experiences of self-conscious emotions 37–38
   framework for a conception of self-conscious emotions 38–41, *42*
   interoception 30–31
      core affect *31*
   self-concept 32–33
   social representations of self-conscious emotions 33–37
   sociocultural context 31–32
constructivist grounded theory 11, 15–17
Cooley, C.H. 32, 33, 34, 201
core affect *31*
Cotogni, I. 5
Courtney, M.E. 79, 197
Cradock, G. 147
Creed, W.E.D. 32, 33, 51, 52, 62, 187, 189
   theoretical codes 209
Cromby, J. 28
Cronen, V.E. 39, 40
Crowley, J. 95
Crozier, W.R. 11
Csordas, T.J. 37
Culpitt, I. 170
cultural differences 43
Czarniawska, B. 202

D

Dahlqvist, V. 118
Dale, P. 203
D'Andrade, R. 23
Danzinger, K. 28
data analysis 15–17
data collection 10–11, 12–15
D'Aunno, T. 129
Davies, M. 56
Dearing, R. 26, 34, 41, 43
Deaux, K. 105
decision-making 129
Deetz, S. 106
DeLamater, J. 205
derision, discourse of 66–72
deviation 123–125
   see also resistance

Dewey, J. 18, 32, 37, 136
Dey, I. 16
dirty data 179
disciplinary procedures 125
discretion 131–132
disguised resistance 176–180
Dodsworth, F.M. 56
Dreier, O. 59
Dumbrill, G. 203
duty trackers 97–99
Duveen, G. 103, 105, 129
Dwyer, J.G. 116

E

Edmondson, A. 137
education 66, 67, 68
Edwards, S. 86
efficiency 54, 55
Ekman, P. 24
Elias, N. 44
Elison, J. 35, 36, 37
Elks, M.A. 1
Ellsworth, P.C. 26
Elshout, M. 29
embarrassment 27, 36
embodied experiences of self-conscious
    emotions 37–38
Emerson, R.M. 13
Emirbayer, M. 130, 134
emotion constructionism *see*
    constructionism
emotion regulation 52, 53, 188–189,
    190, 193
emotion theory 23–48
  appraisal theories 26–27
  basic emotions argument 24–26
  constructionism 27–30
    comparison with other theories
      41–48
    embodied experiences of self-
      conscious emotions 37–38
    framework for a conception of self-
      conscious emotions 38–41, *42*
    interoception 30–31, *31*
    self-concept 32–33
    social representations of self-
      conscious emotions 33–37
    sociocultural context 31–32
emotion work 51–52, 189–190, *190*
  casework relationship 60
  compliance 152, 154, 159–160
  organisational 192
  organisational control 139, 141
  organisational interpretive framework
    145–147
  parents 162
  resilience 121
  resistance 175, 183

shame avoidance 53, 55, 114
  see also organisational emotional safety
emotional resilience 120–122
emotional safety 6, 81, 137
  see also organisational emotional safety
emotions
  basic emotions argument 24–26
  see also self-conscious emotions
empathy 136–137, 142n, 175–176,
    182, 184
enactment 144–152, 170–171
  emotional safety 150–152
  organisational interpretive framework
    144–147
  responsibilisation 147–150
Englander, D. 57
English language 25, 38
episodes of social interaction 39
episodic shaming 52, 57, 69, 88
ethical practice 92–93
Evans, T. 131

F

Fairweather, E. 5, 69
Fauske, H. 203
Featherstone, B. 117, 147, 163, 191,
    196, 201
Ferguson, H. 10, 57, 58, 62, 69, 74,
    117, 202
Ferguson, I. 59, 61, 63, 199
Ferguson, T.J. 4, 197
Figueira-Mcdonough, J. 199
financial savings 86–87
Finch, J. 200
Fischer, J. 67
Fischer, K.W. 34
Flax, J. 54
Flegel, M. 57
Flyvbjerg, B. 10
focused coding 15
Forrester, D. 200
Foster, V. 129, 132, 133, 180
Foucault, M. 32, 65, 187, 205
Fraser, C. 196
Freidson, E. 49, 50
French language 38
Freud, S. 25
Friedland, R. 78, 79
Friesen, W.V. 24
Frijda, N.H. 26
Frost, L. 9, 184
fundamental attribution error 163

G

Gadsden, V.L. 147
Garland, D. 171
Garrett, P.M. 147, 191, 198
Gaskell, G. 206

Gausel, N. 4, 26, 35, 200
Gay, O. 87
Gazeley, I. 59
Geertz, C. 205
Gendron, M. 23–24, 26, 28
General Social Care Council (GSCC)
    68, 70
Gergen, K.J. 37
Ghaffar, W. 196, 203
Gibson, M. 2, 8, 9, 129, 187, 196, 203
Gilbert, P. 25
Gillet, G. 207
Gilroy, D. 71, 72
Glaser, B.G. 15, 16
  theoretical codes 209
Goffman, E. 1, 36, 38, 45, 51, 88, 125,
    201
Gold, R. 18
Golding, K.S. 8
Gordon, S. 29, 205
governmentality 65, 171
Gray, M. 147
Greenland, C. 68
Griffiths, P.E. 47
Gross, J.J. 52, 188
Guardian 4
guilt 35–36, 156–161
Gupta, A. 8, 196, 203

H

Hall, D. 191
Halliday, J. 4
Hardy, C. 51
Harré, R. 29, 207
Harris, J. 131, 203
Harter, S. 36, 37
Harvey, D. 64
Hasenfeld, Y. 202
Hearn, B. 93
Heine, S.J. 43
Hellenbrand, S.C. 60
Henkel, M. 65
Higgins, E.T. 32, 33
Higgins, M. 68
Hill, Octavia 61
Hochschild, A.R. 25, 51, 189
Hogg, M. 105
Hollis, F. 61
Honneth, Axel 184
Hood, R. 196
Horton, L. 87
House, J.S. 205
Houston, S. 9, 184
Hudson, B.A. 202
Hughes, D. 8
Hughes, E.C. 190
humiliation 27, 29–30, 36–37,
    124–125, 165–168

humour 160
Humphries, B. 67, 200
Hyslop, I. 191

I

ideal-type 126
identification 143
  compliance 152–161, 170–171
    competence 152–154
    shame and guilt 156–161
    shame avoidance 154–156
  enactment 144–152, 170–171
    emotional safety 150–152
    organisational interpretive
      framework 144–147
    responsibilisation 147–150
  parental experience in the context of
    161–169, 171
    othering 163–165
    risk management 168–169
    shaming and humiliating practice
    165–168
identity meanings 135–136
identity regulation 106
identity theory 103, 105, 135
identity work 52, 105, 135
Ifaluk language 25
illocutionary utterances 39
independent reviewing officers (IROs)
    109
infant mortality 29
influence 4
influencing tactics 180–183
inspections 72
institutional guardians 32, 52–53
institutional logics 78, 79
institutional sources and processes
    180–183
institutional work 50–51, 52–53
institutionalisation 50
interoception 30–31
  core affect *31*
interpretive framework 144–147
Izard, C.E. 24, 28

J

Jackson, M.A. 36, 37, 46
Jackson, S. 196
James, W. 18, 31
Jenkins, R. 140
Jepperson, R.L. 50
Jones, R. 69, 85, 110, 191
just culture 137
  see also emotional safety

K

Karlsson, G. 36
Kaufman, G. 187

Kemmis, S. 188
Kemper, T.D. 25
Kirkhart, K.E. 1
Kitayama, S. 28
Klein, D.C. 27, 36, 37, 46
knowledge 28
Knowles, G. 109
Kovalsky, E. 54
Kovecses, Z. 34, 35
Kraatz, M. 79

L

Labour government 67, 72
Lahlou, S. 206
Lait, J. 62, 67
Laming, H. 74
Lane, S.R. 59
language 25, 28, 30, 38, 205
   body language 39
Larner, W. 147
Larson, M.S. 49, 50, 67, 117, 194–195
Lave, J. 37
Lawler, E.J. 34
Lawrence, T.B. 50, 66, 89, 123, 201, 202
   theoretical codes 209
Le Grand, J. 131
Leach, C.W. 4, 26, 35, 200
leaders *see* organisational leaders
Leadership in administration (Selznick) 79
Leigh, J. 129, 132, 133, 174
Leith, K.P. 36, 137
Lemke, T. 65
Leonard, P. 60
Levin, I. 60
Lewis, H.B. 1, 26, 36, 46
Lewis, M. 25
Lickel, B. 177
Liebenberg, L. 147
Lindholm, C. 197
Lipsky, M. 131
literature 7–9
Loch, Charles Stewart 55
Lombard, D. 4
Longhofer, J.L. 8
Luckmann, T. 205
Lukes, S. 202
Lutz, C. 25, 28
Lyman, S. 175
Lymbery, M. 55, 56

M

Macartney, A. 58
Macdonald, K.M. 50
Mackey, A. 80
Maguire, S. 51
Manstead, A.S.R.R. 10–11

Manzoor, A. 54, 55
Markus, H.R. 28, 32, 33
Martin, K.E.C. 196
Marx, D. 137
Mascolo, M.F. 34
Mason, P. 200
Mayer, J.E. 67
McCall, G.J. 52, 105, 108
McDonald, C. 118, 191
McDougall, W. 24
McGinity, R. 191
McKendrick, D. 200
McLaughlin, K. 70
Mead, G.H. 18, 32, 33, 105
media 4, 5, 7
Mehrabian, A. 25–26
Merighi, J.R. 1
Miller, P. 54
Miller, R.S. 36
Miller, S.E. 106, 188
Mills, C.W. 118
Mische, A. 130, 134
misrecognition 184
Moisander, J.K. 51, 52, 189
   theoretical codes 209
Montalvo, F.F. 60
Moors, A. 26
moral community 116–119
Morris, K. 147
Moscovici, S. 33–34, 37, 49, 78, 103, 105, 188, 206
Mulkay, M. 160
Munro, E. 63, 71, 72, 74, 85, 192, 196, 198
myths 66

N

Narey, M. 68
Nathanson, D.L. 25
National Society for the Prevention of Cruelty to Children (NSPCC) 57–58
natural kind theories 41, 43, 45–46
Nelson, K.R. 1
Nelund, A. 65
neoliberal discourse 64–66, 73–74, 79, 147, 171, 191
Newburn, T. 67
Nightingale, D.J. 28

O

observer-as-participant 18
Ocasio, W. 78, 79
occupational survival 171
Office for Standards in Education (Ofsted) 5, 10, 72, 84, 87–88, 92, 94, 100
O'Leary, T. 54

Oliver, C. 81, 130–131, 132, 139, 180, 183
  theoretical codes 209
organisational control 104
  pride and shame as mechanisms of 104–107, 134 (*see also* organisational representation)
    case example 107–127
    social workers' responses to 139–140, *141*
organisational emotional safety 77, 81, 89–99, 137, 150–152, 154–156
  administration 92–95, 97
  boundaries of membership 95–97
  social policing 89–91
  status hierarchy 97–99
organisational identity 79–80, 82, 83–85
organisational identity management project 80, *80*
organisational interpretive framework 144–147
organisational leaders 79, 81
organisational representation 125–126
  community characteristics 116–123
    competent community 122–123
    moral community 116–119
    resilient community 120–122
  compliance 114–116, 131–132, 170–171
    competence 152–154
    shame and guilt 156–161
    shame avoidance 154–156
  deviation/resistance 123–125, 132–133, 173–183
    compromising expectations 174–176
    concealing acts of 176–180
    influencing institutional sources and processes 180–183
  enactment 144–152, 170–171
    emotional safety 150–152
    organisational interpretive framework 144–147
    responsibilisation 147–150
  parental experience 161–169, 183–186
    othering 163–165
    risk management 168–169
    shaming and humiliating practice 165–168
  self-conscious emotions 133–139, 140–141
  social work role 108–116
    administration 108–110
    compliance 114–116
    responsibility 112–114
    social policing 110–112
  othering 163–165

P

Panksepp, J. 24, 28
paper work *see* administration
parents 147–150, 161–169, 171, 183–186, 195
Parkinson, B. 10–11
Parton, N. 57, 58, 64, 68, 69, 70, 71, 73, 89, 110, 117, 191, 196, 197, 201
Payne, M. 56, 59, 60, 61, 62, 70, 117
Pearce, W.B. 39
Peirce, C.S. 15
performance 93–95
performance management 70, 71, 72, 132
Perryman, J. 72
Philogène, G. 105
Pickett, K. 147
Platt, D. 201
police 56
politics of belonging 95–96
Pollack, S. 191
Poor Laws 54
poverty 45
Powell, F.W. 57
power 4, 28, 45, 50
Power, M. 65, 70, 71–72, 74, 79, 192, 193, 198, 202
practical helper 61–62
Pratt, M.G. 134
Pray, K.L.M. 59
pride
  appraisals as a foundation for theories of 26–27, 43
  basic emotions as foundation for theories of 24–26
  constructions as a foundation for theories of 27–30
  in the creation, maintenance and disruption of child and family social work services 78–82
    case example 83–100
  future research 201–203
  as mechanism of organisational control 104–107, 134
    case example 107–127
  in professional practice 3–10, 188–190, 196–201
    case illustration 190–196
  construction of professional representations of practice 53–64
  contemporary practice 64–74
  in the professionalisation of social work 49–53
  social representation of 34–35

in social workers' situated
conceptualisations 133–139
systemic 32, 33, 51, 52
Pritzker, S. 59
professional discretion 131–132
professional identity 85–86, 125
professional practice
contemporary 64–74
discourse of derision 66–72
discourse of neoliberalism 64–66,
73–74
pride and shame in 3–10, 188–190,
190, 196–201
case illustration 190–196
see also child and family social work
professional project 50
professional representations of social
work 53–64
activism 58–59, 61–62
within the bureaucratic field 62–64
practical helper 61–62
social administration 54–56
social policing 56–58
therapy 59–61
professionalisation of social work
49–53
psychological safety 137
see also emotional safety
psychology 205–206
psychosocial therapy 61
psychotherapy 60
public administration identity 86–87
Putnam, H. 206

R

Read, J. 191
Reamer, F.G. 63
recognition 184
recording *see* administration
Reddy, W.M. 28
Reed, M. 132
Reich, J.A. 57
Reicher, S.D. 134
Reid, J. 191
relationships 40, 81, 111–112
report cards 97–99
research study 10–12
data analysis 15–17
data collection 10–11, 12–15
limitations 17–18
theoretical foundations 203
resilience 120–122
resistance 6–7, 132–133, 173–183
compromising expectations 174–176
concealing acts of 176–180
influencing institutional sources and
processes 180–183

parental experience in the context of
183–186
responsibilisation 147–150
responsibility 112–114, 185
Richmond, Mary 60
Ridgeway, C.L. 32
risk management 168–169
Robins, R.W. 27, 34, 35, 36
Rogowski, S. 200
role identity 105, 108
Romney, A.K. 43
Rorty, R. 18, 31, 62, 78
Rosaldo, M.Z. 37
Rosenberg, M. 32
Ross, L. 163
Rossiter, A. 191
Rowlands, M. 37
Royal Society for the Prevention of
Cruelty to Animals 56
Russell, J.A. 3, 25–26, 30–31, 37, 38,
47

S

Sabini, J. 36
sacralisation 57
Saltiel, D. 129
Satyamurti, C. 70, 132, 171, 194
Sayer, A. 44, 45, 46
Scheff, T.J. 25, 34, 35, 38, 41, 43, 187,
205
Scheper-Hughes, N. 29
Scherer, K.R. 14, 34
Scott, M. 175
Scott, W.R. 114
self-concept 32–33
self-conscious emotions 1–2, 41–48
embodied experiences of 37–38
framework for a constructionist
conception of 38–41, *42*
social representations of 33–37,
43–44, 47
social workers' experience of 133–
139, 140–141
see also embarrassment; emotion
theory; guilt; humiliation; pride;
shame
Selznick, P. 79
Sen, A. 45
sense of shame 38
sensitising concepts 15
serious case reviews (SCRs) 72
settlement movement 58, 59
shame
appraisals as a foundation for theories
of 26–27, 43
basic emotions as foundation for
theories of 24–26
and compliance 156–161

constructions as a foundation for
theories of 27–30
in the creation, maintenance and
disruption of child and family social
work services 78–82
case example 83–100
definition 29
future research 201–203
as mechanism of organisational
control 104–107, 134
case example 107–127
natural kind theories 41, 43, 45–46
in professional practice 2, 3–10,
188–190
case illustration 190–196
construction of professional
representations of practice 53–64
contemporary practice 64–74
in the professionalisation of social
work 49–53
sense of 38
situated conceptualisations 40,
133–139
social construction of 44
social representations of 35
and stigma 45
systemic 32, 33, 51, 52
shame avoidance 53, 55, 114, 154–156
shaming 165–169
Sharpe, M. 109
Shlonsky, A. 129
Shoesmith, S. 69, 85, 110, 201
Sieber, S.D. 74
Silfver, M. 36
Silver, M. 36
Simmons, J.L. 52, 105, 108
situated complex 40
situated conceptualisations 40,
133–139, 191–193
Sjöberg, L.G. 36
Smith, Adam 45
Smith, A.K. 1
Smithson, R. 196, 203
social administration 54–56
social class 44, 45
social identity 105, 116
Social insurance and allied services
(Beveridge) 59
social interactions 38–40
social policing 56–58, 89–91, 110–112
social psychology 205–206
social representations 206–207
of self-conscious emotions 33–37, 40,
43–44, 47
of social workers 49, 105, 170,
188–189
social work see child and family social
work

social work role 108–116
administration 108–110
compliance 114–116
responsibility 112–114
social policing 110–112
social work services see child and family
social work services
Social Work Task Force 74, 85
social workers
mutual support 159–161
organisational control 104–107,
139–140, 141
organisational representation 125–
127, 139–140, 169–172
competence 122–123
compliance 131–132, 152–161,
170–171
deviation/resistance 123–125,
132–133, 173–183
enactment 144–152, 170–171
morality 116–119
parental experience 161–169,
183–186
resilience 120–122
self-conscious emotions 133–139,
140–141
situated conceptualisations 133–139,
191–193
social representations 49, 105, 170,
188–189
sociocultural context 31–32, 40
sociology 55
Solms, M. 25
Specht, H. 197
speech acts 39
Spicker, P. 55
Spolander, G. 191
Springer, S. 64, 65, 66
Stake, R.E. 10
Stanford, S. 1
state
as bureaucratic field 53
and neoliberalism 65–66
status hierarchy 97–99
Stets, J.E. 24, 28, 32, 33, 103, 105,
135, 136, 189
Stevenson, O. 55, 63, 64
stigma 45
Strauss, A.L. 15, 16
Stryker, S. 32, 33, 52, 105, 108, 135
Suddaby, R. 50, 66, 123, 201
theoretical codes 209
Sullivan, H.S. 32
Sumner, W.G. 163
Sykes, J. 203

systemic pride 32, 33, 51, 52
systemic shame 32, 33, 51, 52

T

Tajfel, H. 116
Tangney, J.P. 26, 34, 35, 36, 41, 43
Taylor, F.W. 54
teaching profession 66, 72
Tew, J. 163, 202
theoretical codes 209
theoretical sampling 16
theoretical sorting 16
theoretical sufficiency 16
therapy 59–61
Thoits, P.A. 23, 39, 51, 105
Thomaes, S. 36, 37
Thomas, G. 10, 18, 83
Thomas, J. 5
Thomas, T. 58
Thompson, P. 132
Thornton, P.H. 78, 79
Thrana, H.M. 203
Timms, N. 67
Ting, L. 2
Titmuss, R.M. 56, 61, 63
Todd, S. 59, 61
Tomkins, S.S. 24, 25
Torres, W.J. 37, 46
Tracy, J.L. 1, 27, 34, 35, 36, 137
Tsakalotos, E. 54
Tufts, J.H. 136
Turnell, A. 86
Turner, F.J. 61
Turner, J.H. 24, 25, 28, 29, 34, 189
Turney, D. 201

V

Van Heugten, K. 2
Vince, R. 202
Virshup, L.K. 105
Voronov, M. 202

W

Wacquant, L.J.D. 66, 125, 171, 191
Wagner, W. 206, 207
Walker, J. 8, 117
Walker, R. 45
Wallace, M. 66
Warner, J. 4, 5, 68, 69, 85, 110, 117,
    189, 191, 198, 201
Wastell, D. 70, 129, 132, 174, 196
Watkins-Hayes, C.M. 54
Webb, D. 67
Webb, S. 135
Weber, M. 54, 126, 131
welfare state 55
Wenger, E. 37
Weuste, M.B. 1

Whetten, D.A. 79, 80
White, S. 70, 146, 148, 174
Wierzbicka, A. 25, 27, 30, 34
Wiles, F. 135
Wilkinson, R. 147
Willmott, H. 104, 105, 106, 107, 111,
    116, 135, 188, 190
  theoretical codes 209
Wilson, W. 54
Winter, K. 73
Wittgenstein, L. 205
Woodroofe, K. 54, 57, 62, 117
Woolford, A. 65
Wootton, B. 62
Wurf, E. 32, 33

Y

Yelloly, M. 60, 62
Young, A.F. 54, 55, 57, 58, 60, 62
Younghusband, E. 63, 64
Yuval-Davis, N. 136

Z

Zelizer, V.A.R. 4, 57
Zellner, M.R. 25
Zwaan, R.A. 37